The Science and T

Dog Training

James O'Heare

BehaveTech Publishing

Ottawa, Canada

Title: Dog Training

Publisher: BehaveTech Publishing, Ottawa, Canada, www.BehaveTech.com

Author: James O'Heare

Cover art and book design: James O'Heare

Copy editor:

Limits of Liability and Disclaimer of Warranty:

ISBN 978-1-927744-00-0

Library and Archives Canada Cataloguing in Publication

O'Heare, James, 1971-, author   The science and technology of dog
training / James O'Heare.

Includes bibliographical references and index.ISBN 978-1-927744-00-0
(pbk.)

1. Dogs--Training. 2. Dogs--Behavior. I. Title.

SF431.O33 2014   636.7'0887   C2013-908230-1

for Roscoe 1999-2012, my best friend ever!

ACKNOWLEDGMENTS

I would like to Dr. Stephen Ledoux for a highly reinforcing educational experience and for assistance with this book.

I would also like to thank my colleagues (in no particular order) who helped me find typos and errors:

Doris Thompson

Patience Fisher

Vernessa Eadie

Michelle Hasselbach

PREFACE – READ THIS FIRST!

The Science and Technology of Dog Training is written to help novice, through to professional, dog trainers and behavior technologists expand their knowledge and skills in the natural science of behavior and technology of dog training. There are many excellent books available on dog training, but most cover only the most basic principles of behavior and training procedures. This is a suitable strategy for a broader audience, interested in the basics, without having to become familiar with technical terms, or the science behind the technology. My general objective in this book is to provide a solid foundation in the natural science of behavior, including the proper scientific terminology, and apply that science to the technology of dog training, providing guidance on basic, through to advanced, training principles, strategies, and procedures.

In the past, professional dog training was not systematically based on a natural science of behavior, but rather a more or less haphazard bag-of-tricks established by trial and error. Because it was more intuitive than systematic and principled, it was difficult to instill in new trainers. A lot has changed in the last few decades, and professional dog training is now held to a much higher standard. Professionals engaged in this trade are expected to be proficient in the technology of training, and that training should be informed by an empirically supported natural science of behavior. If one wants to formulate effective and efficient training plans to achieve specific behavioral objectives, more than a hodgepodge collection of intuitions and tricks-of-the-trade is required. This is especially the case for anything beyond the very simplest of objectives.

What I plan to provide here specifically is: 1. a solid scientific foundation in the principles of behavior from which training techniques and strategies are derived; 2. greater detail beyond the acquisition stage of training; and 3. exercises to help trainers expand their training behavior repertoire. I will assume an interest in the natural science and technology of dog training, either to provide a more solid foundation for established professionals who already train dogs regularly, or to provide a solid foundation for those just beginning to develop their training proficiencies. I will not assume prior knowledge of any science or technology; the conditioning curve might be a little steeper for those without a background in the science of behavior. The principles, techniques, and behaviors that I will address are not new, but I will address them without resorting to fads, and I will use the appropriate terminology and principles involved. No gimmicks, or '©one-true-way™' approaches; just a foundational treatment of the natural science of behavior, and technology of dog training presented from basics through to advanced techniques. I will put new terms in **_bold italicized font_** where they are introduced or discussed in detail, so they are easy to find.

This book is not intended to be a casual read. Achieving the behavioral repertoire expansion that this book promises will require careful study and reading sections more than once. The material is dense and concise. With active carful study, as opposed to a cursory reading, the reader can expect a far superior level of repertoire expansion. Ideally, it will also involve actively working with the principles, strategies, and procedures hands-on. For those who require a more basic introduction to prepare them for the material in this book, _How Dogs Learn_ by Mary Burch and Jon Bailey would be suitable.

In some cases, particularly in the planning stage, you might believe that what I propose is overkill. This may indeed be the case for those who have been conditioned through extensive experience to exhibit these planning behaviors "in their head" and/or in a truncated manner. However, the most successful strategy, in getting to this stage, is to practice the full set of planning behaviors, including preparing detailed written plans, until the process can be truncated without a loss of accuracy, efficiency and effectiveness. In other words, take the time now to engage in all of the appropriate planning processes and you will eventually be able to truncate and condense the process. Attempting to prematurely truncate the planning process will result in a deficient requisite behavior (foundation) and less proficient training skills. So, bear with me while I describe more elaborate procedures than you might believe necessary for your own skill level. Become familiar with them, and then truncate the process as appropriate without diminishing the systematic planning benefits. One might also believe that the material in chapter one, on the basic principles of behavior, is too in-depth. I would argue that it is not, and that all dog trainers should have a strong proficiency in the principles of behavior included in that chapter.

The Science and Technology of Dog Training

The Science and Technology of Dog Training is written specifically to cover all topic points at an appropriate depth for Association of Animal Behavior Professionals core areas of competence in "Principles of Behavior" and "Dog Training." Achieving the behavioral objectives established in this book will thoroughly prepare the candidate for the AABP Proficiency Exam in these two core areas of competence.

Dog training has also come a long way in terms of its use of less coercive methods. Recognizing the devastating and resilient problematic side effects of using aversive stimulation to control behavior has become apparent, and we have shifted our technology of training behaviors toward positive reinforcement-emphasized strategies. This book will emphasize the importance of utilizing these positive reinforcement-emphasized strategies to train behavior.

An appendix is included after the final chapter that will provide the reader with a set of specific exercises to complete, each one designed to help you expand your repertoire of effective and efficient dog training behaviors. These exercises can be useful and informative for both novice and professional trainers alike.

As with all my books, this book will remain a work in progress that I will update with new editions in order to shape an improved final product. I hope you find it useful for your own purposes.

The Science and Technology of Dog Training

FOREWORD BY STEPHEN F. LEDOUX

On this space rock, humans are not alone. We share the planet with many other species. For some of these species, particularly those that we describe as companion animals, we have developed an often mutually profound affinity. Cats and dogs top the list.

Many humans make a substantial time and energy commitment to the care and training of our dogs, sometimes rivaling our commitments to parenting our children. And an ever–increasing number of us are recognizing that this connection runs more than skin deep. Our concerns with managing the causes of behavior, whether the behavior of our companion animals, our children, our fellow humans, or even ourselves, remain ever present. Unfortunately, the value of science in these endeavors sometimes comes as a surprise.

Yet valuable science is to our successes, especially in the form of a sound and substantiated systematic approach, such as that found in the natural science of behavior that we call behaviorology. The openness of the researched principles and designed practices of science certainly save us from the pitfalls of chance, accidents, fads, and secret–knowledge systems that arise when we follow uninformed trial and error patterns, and handed–down tricks and intuitions.

James O'Heare's book, *The Science and Technology of Dog Training*, recognizes all that and more. It provides a thorough, albeit basic, introduction to all the aspects of behaviorology that relate to companion–animal training, especially to dog training, as the best way to understand them and train them. This enables the reader to see *why* one thing works while another fails. Rather than merely following steps in a cook–book of techniques for a simple set of prescribed animal–behavior tricks, this book enables the improving animal trainer to move on to advanced techniques capable of producing complicated behavioral outcomes, all the while emphasizing positive rather than coercive strategies which, again, is how we would treat each other, and our children, to the best effect. As such, this book benefits all levels of readers, from beginners striving to become skilled, to already established professionals.

Finally, by adhering to natural behavior science, this book helps those who love other animals glimpse the value of behaviorology for cleaning up our own human behavior acts. Humanity faces some big problems, such as pollution, overpopulation, and war. All these problems, and their solution, involve human behavior, and thus benefit by the input of behaviorology. If we fail to solve these problems, then we endanger not only ourselves but our beloved companion animals as well. By becoming more familiar with behaviorology in general, one becomes more capable not only at animal training projects but also at helping create a better world, one that can remain suitable both for us and our animal friends.

Stephen F. Ledoux, Ph.D., DLBC

Author of *Running Out of Time—Introducing Behaviorology to Help Solve Global Problems*

Canton, NY, USA

2014 February 14

TABLE OF CONTENTS

CHAPTER 1. PRINCIPLES OF BEHAVIOR

Behavioral Objectives

The objective of this chapter is to measurably expand the reader's repertoire of behaviors in relation to describing and relating the principles of behavior. Upon successfully integrating the concepts outlined in this chapter, the reader, where under contingencies to do so, will accurately:

- Define and discriminate among science and natural science

- Identify the basic assumptions of natural science

- Differentiate between behaviorology and other disciplines

- Define behavior, stimulus, and conditioning

- Identify accurately the cause of behavior at a level of analysis appropriate to training

- Distinguish accurately between operant and respondent conditioning

- Identify the terms in the 3-term operant contingency and explain their relationship to one another

- Define and relate positive and negative reinforcement, positive and negative punishment, extinction, and analyze behavior scenarios to determine which principles operate on them

- Identify the variables that affect the strength of operant conditioning

- Define the schedules of reinforcement, under what circumstances each is useful and what effect they have on conditioning

- Define operant generalization and discrimination as well as the role they play in training

- Explain how to transfer stimulus control

- Define differential reinforcement and its variants

- Define respondent conditioning and its role in the operant contingency and training

- Define habituation, potentiation, and sensitization processes as well as respondent extinction

- Graph behavior objectives, establish a baseline on the current strength of the behavior, and continue to track the behavior throughout a training project.

What follows is an introduction to natural science, and the basic laws and principles of behavior. This will provide a foundation for the rest of the material. The goal of dog training is to bring specific behaviors under stimulus control. To do this, we utilize certain strategies and tactics, which are derived from basic principles of behavior. Therefore, we will start with an introduction to these basic principles. From them, we will derive, and systematically implement, strategies and procedures to efficiently and effectively generate specific behaviors and bring them under stimulus control.

First, I will explicate science and natural science. I will discuss behaviorology as a natural science and compare behaviorology with other disciplines that seek to explain behavior.

Natural Science

Natural science is an approach to studying nature based on certain philosophical assumptions. All methods of knowing start with certain basic assumptions, and natural science is no exception; the assumptions of natural science have allowed for extremely robust and reliable products from the natural science community. The most fundamental assumption of natural science is referred to as the *naturalistic assumption*. It states that *only real events exist, that there are no nonreal events, and that all real events are theoretically measurable in terms of mass, time, distance, temperature, and/or charge* (Fraley, 2008, p.15); and that *any detectable event represents the culmination of a natural history—that is, that all things are part of a continuous sequence of causes and effects and that there can be no intrusion by non-natural events into this sequence*. In other words, nothing occurs spontaneously, all events are completely caused, and with regard to behavior, there cannot be "free-will"—behavior is no exception to the laws of nature. Some real events are challenging to measure due to our current technological capacity, but it is still theoretically measurable because it could be measured with a suitable technological apparatus. If something is not theoretically measurable, it is not real, and natural science only studies real events. The current natural science disciplines include biology, geology, physics, chemistry, and behaviorology. The label **science**, alone, would include any discipline that utilizes scientific methods but otherwise fails to adhere to the basic naturalistic assumptions of natural science.

Behaviorology

Behaviorology is the natural science, and technology of behavior (Ledoux, 2002a; Fraley, 2008, p. 36). It is founded on a philosophical framework called **radical behaviorism** devised by B.F. Skinner.[1] Radical behaviorism extends the philosophical assumption of naturalism to the study of behavior, making it a philosophy of natural science. In the 1930's, Skinner, from a natural science background, began studying behavior from a standpoint that was completely different from the standpoint from which psychology was studying it. Where psychology postulated an inner agent called the "psyche" or "mind" in order to study mental processes, Skinner proposed the study of behavior itself, for its own sake, and from a strictly natural science perspective, without reference to hypothetical constructs. Skinner's approach and topic of study are incommensurable with psychology for these reasons (Fraley & Ledoux, 2002a). Ledoux (2002a, p. 26) described the basic tenets of radical behaviorism this way:

> (a) Radical behaviorists respect behavior as a *natural* phenomenon as part of respecting the continuity of events in space and time, which, in natural sciences, accumulates as a natural history. (b) Radical behaviorists emphasize experimental control over dependent variables and the application of that control in culturally beneficial ways. (c) Radical behaviorists recognize private events, such as thinking or emotions, as covert behaviors involved in the same lawful relationships that involve overt behavior.

Natural science disciplines study the causal (or functional) relations between real variables. There are different modes of causation that form the relationship between these variables. **Mechanistic causation** is relied upon extensively in physics and chemistry and

---

[1] Note that the word radical, in this use, refers to "fundamental" and not to any kind of extremism; it is merely unfortunate terminology selected to distinguish it from some other forms of behaviorism.

deals with what comes immediately before something else and reliably triggers its occurrence. ***Selection causation*** is relied upon extensively in biology and behaviorology, and deals with selection by consequences—what comes after something, which influences the future likelihood of that thing occurring again (Fraley, 2008, p. 21).

There are three levels of analysis in the selection causation mode. One level of selection causation elucidated and elaborated by Charles Darwin in the discipline of biology involves the selection of genetically coded traits across generations via what is called ***natural selection***. Another level of selection involves the selection of the behaviors of individual organisms within their lifetime, and is called ***selection by consequences***. A third level of selection is the selection of behavior patterns (e.g., practices, traditions, rituals, norms, ethical rules etc.) among a community of individuals, and is called ***cultural selection***. Behaviorology operates under the second level of analysis, the selection of the behaviors of individuals.

Although behaviorology recognizes and utilizes mechanistic causation (as in a stimulus causes a behavior), the unique emphasis that Skinner brought to the study of behavior was the selection causation mode, and this is called the ***selection paradigm***. Just as biology had explained the perpetuation of genetically heritable traits within a population through generations (phylogeny), Skinner explained the perpetuation of behaviors exhibited by the individual organism within its lifetime (ontogeny). In biology, the evolution of populations is explained by natural selection, wherein the environment selects for and against certain genetically coded traits simply by which traits tend to result in greater reproductive rates. Similarly, in behaviorology, the environment selects for and against behaviors, simply by whether the behavior generates effective, ineffective, or aversive consequences. As mentioned, cultural selection refers to the selection of behavior patterns among a community of individuals. All three of these levels of selection are selection by consequences for the rate of genes, behavior, and cultural practices respectively (Peirce & Cheney, 2013, p. 6). Fraley and Ledoux (2002, p. 41) described selection by consequences this way:

> The consequences of the past behaviors are said to have *selected* the behaviors that now occur, and the selection paradigm takes its name from that interpretation. But in each instance of behavior, the body is assumed to behave *in the only way that it can behave* under the existing

circumstances—an assumption that respects the deterministic natural science of philosophy that informs behaviorology. No explanatory appeal is made to a redundant psychological self that would decide or choose the behavior to be exhibited by the body.

Behaviorology involves the experimental analysis of environment-behavior functional relations, and establishment and application of an efficient and effective technology for controlling behavior (Ledoux, 2002a). Because of the completely naturalistic character of behaviorology and its emphasis on environment-behavior functional relations, behaviorology is highly effective and efficient in controlling behavior (e.g., training).

Psychology

Psychology is an eclectic aggregate of disciplines, defined as the study of the "mind" and behavior (American Psychological Association, 2012). In some schools of thought, the mind is the primary emphasis of study, and in others, the activities of the mind are said to explain or elucidate more overt behavior. The mind is a hypothetical construct representing consciousness, originating in the brain and manifesting in thought, perception, emotion, will, memory, and imagination (American Heritage Dictionary of the English Language, n.d.). These manifestations of the "mind" are referred to as mental, or cognitive processes, and are the primary topic of study for psychology's most prominent school of thought: cognitive psychology. Whereas behaviorology addresses these topics, not as manifestations of a mind but rather as fully caused behaviors, psychology tends to imply that the "mind" refers to a free-willing inner agent that may spontaneously, or semi-autonomously, "choose" what behavior to perform upon consideration of the environment. This emphasis on mental processes represents the ***transformational paradigm***, prominent in psychology. Those operating under a transformational paradigm observe input (stimulation), and output (behavior), and hypothesize about how the inputs are transformed inside the organism (by the "mind"), to generate output, the emphasis of interest being placed, not on the behavior for its own sake, but rather the transformational process referred to as mental or cognitive.

E.A. Vargus (1991, cited in Fraley & Ledoux, 2002, pp. 40–41) described the transformational paradigm of psychology eloquently:

> An event occurs, described in any number of ways. The meaning of the event inheres in the action of the organism. The organism perceives, interprets, assesses, integrates, and processes its perceptions and cognitions, and then stores the results of its own actions. It then (or later) engages in performance with respect to that event—or, rather, the transformed nature of that event. In psychology's paradigm, some aspect of the world incites the organism to take action; but before that action occurs, the organism engages in a series of operations, typically called mental or cognitive, that determines the significance of the events and thus determines the nature of the action. In the transformation paradigm, the organism itself, through structures and processes inherent in it, is the agency of its action.

Where psychologists do study behavior itself, they commonly seek to explain the behavior, at least in part, by reference to mental processes. Even where mental processes are said to be completely natural, the reference to a mind as a hypothetical or unreal thing is suggestive of, and perpetuates the notion of, a free-willing agent. In any event, these mental processes are said to explain the behavioral output. This is circular reasoning—the mental processes are inferred from the behavior to be explained (Pierce & Cheney, 2013, p. 21).

In recent decades, psychology has tended to deemphasize the suggestion of a free-willed inner agent, but they have not abandoned it. A more recent trend in psychology is to equate the mind with the brain and to study the physiology of mental processes (and other behaviors) but this reduces psychology to a branch of physiology. Moreover, the physiological processes are not the cause of behavior, but rather behaviors themselves, and in the context of explaining and controlling behavior, the concomitant physiological behaviors are not nearly as informative, accessible, or useful as the environment-behavior functional relations studied in behaviorology.

Behavior Analysis

Many readers will be familiar with ***behavior analysis***.[2] Behaviorology and behavior analysis share quite a bit of ground. However, there are some important distinctions between behaviorology and behavior analysis that justify the independence and separateness of each. You will find little difference between what you read here in this book and a book on behavior analysis. One of the most fundamental differences is that behavior analysis is a branch of psychology whereas behaviorology is a completely independent and separate discipline with absolutely no influence from psychology, and is absolutely not any kind, type, or branch of psychology. This independence allows behaviorologists to work free from influence of organized psychology, and the transformational paradigm, and instead, work solidly in a natural science environment.

Ethology

Ethology is also interested in studying the behavior of nonhuman animals. Ethology is interested mostly in what they call reflexive behaviors (and what we refer to as respondent behaviors and the stimuli that elicit them), and evolutionary adaptation, or various ecological theories that describe patterns in group-structure (Fraley, 2008, p. 33). Ethology is not interested in controlling, or engineering, the behavior of individuals, but rather, in explaining evolutionary processes, describing reflexes, and general behavior patterns. While ethologists work at the level of natural selection, and cultural selection, behaviorologists work at the selection-by-consequences level of analysis, and therefore, ethology is not particularly relevant to what we, as professional behavior technologists, do.

---

[2] Actually, the ***Experimental Analysis of Behavior*** studies the laws and principles of behavior, and ***Applied Behavior Analysis*** manages practical behavior problems as a technology (Peirce & Cheney, 2013), although often the term behavior analysis is used to refer to both of these disciplines.

Medical Model Paradigm

Prior to the emergence of a behaviorological approach to controlling behavior, and professionals dedicated solely to training, veterinarians helped clients resolve problem dog behaviors. They applied a similar approach to dealing with problem behaviors as they did for disease processes—by labeling and categorizing them, and drawing on ethology and psychology to devise treatment protocols, mainly through trial and error. The labeling and categorizing of behavior patterns, and the rather haphazard approach, generated a hodgepodge of handed down treatment protocols. The behavior was left unexplained.[3] This approach is referred to as the ***medical model paradigm***. Many nonveterinarian "applied behaviorists," with a more extensive background in ethology, have adopted a largely medical model paradigm. With the emergence of a natural science of behavior, the assessment of problematic behaviors, and the training of companion animals, can now be handled systematically, and in a principled manner, based on the laws and principles of behavior.

Orientation of This Book

I will assume a behaviorology orientation in this book. I will not be speculating about what dogs may or may not understand or desire or want, or what might be occurring inside a so-called "mind" between stimulation and their behavior. I will not discuss other fictitious constructs such as "dominance," nor label problem behaviors as a supposed explanation for it (called a nominal fallacy). Instead I will focus on the actual functional relations that the behaviors of concern are a part of.

---

[3] Sometimes, the label or category was put forth as the explanation for the behavior, causing a nominal fallacy. A nominal fallacy is the mistaken assumption that naming something is to explain it.

Behavior and its Cause

Behavior

Behavior is any neurally mediated response to the environment that can be measured, be it neuromuscular or solely neural.[4] For example, walking is a behavior. Whereas the term behavior is general, such as walking, generally, a **response** is a particular instance of a behavior. So, walking in general is a behavior, and your walking on that occasion is a response. The terms are often used interchangeably, even though they have distinct meanings. The term **operant** is used to refer to a consequence-maintained behavior—a class of behaviors that may differ topographically from each other, but are evoked by the same stimulus and functions to contact the same reinforcer. For example, approaching a friend might be achieved by crawling, walking, running, driving (etc.), and these would all be the operant in that behavioral episode; we do not specify exactly what action occurs to contact the reinforcement.[5] Because behavior is a neurally mediated response, we can use the "dead-body test" to help make instances and noninstances of behavior apparent, because a dead body may "displace space through time,"—a common element of behavior (Cooper, Heron & Heward, 2007)—they cannot do so in ways that are mediated neurally. Falling due to gravity and growing hair or nails/claws are not instances of behavior, whereas jumping, walking and thinking are. Another example might involve jumping off of a cliff. The jumping is a behavior, but the falling is not. Thinking and visualizing/imagining are real behaviors, even though they are solely neural behaviors and do not involve muscular movement. Emotional responses are also real behaviors of the respondent (as opposed to operant) type. These involve the release of chemicals into the bloodstream by glands in the body.

---

[4] This definition is based on Ledoux (2014) and Fraley (2008) although I have modified the wording, Ledoux's definition for response is "EITHER any covert or overt innervated muscular movement of an organism resulting from energy transfers within the organism that other energy changes—beyond the affected body parts—evoke or elicit, OR patterns of neural activity resulting from energy transfers within the organism that other energy changes—beyond the affected body parts—evoke or elicit." Note that "solely neural" refers to consciousness related behaviors, including thinking.

[5] Some use the term operant set to refer to this kind of class of behaviors and use "operant" interchangeably with "behavior".

Stimulation

Let's consider how behaviors occur in detail, which will reveal some new, related concepts and terms. Behavior requires a transfer of energy between the environment and the body, in a way that triggers a cascade of neural firings that induce both greater energy expenditures involved in neuromuscular actions and small scale changes to the nervous system, leaving a body that behaves differently in the future (Ledoux, 2014, p. 12). Let us now consider the process of stimulation in detail. A *stimulus* is any event that affects responding, be it internal or external. In other words, the environment is not only those parts of nature outside of the skin, but is also inside the body of the behaving organism. The stream of energy from this event that impacts upon and affects behavior is called *stimulation*. When it comes to affecting behavior, stimuli can come right before the behavior, evoking it and also right after the behavior, providing the consequence for it. These are both stimuli. When we say that a stimulus impacts upon or affects an organism, we mean that the stream of energy emanating from the stimulus impinges upon the organism's sensory nervous system and this transfer of energy causes slight changes to that nervous system that then changes the way that organism responds to the environment thereafter. We call this process of behavior causing a change in the environment that is then detected by the body a *cybernetic loop* and the result, conditioning. The body's reaction to the stimulation is behavior and the thereafter-changed nervous system that results in a change in how the body reacts[6] to the environment in the future is *conditioning*. We sometimes also speak of a *stimulus class*, which refers to a number of stimuli or stimulus features that share some characteristic in common. Stimuli can evoke or elicit behavior but they do not fuel the behavior—they simply trigger it. The potential energy inside the body derived from nutrition, fuels the behavior.

---

[6] Note that when I say reaction, I mean that quite literally. There is no free-willed inner agent considering the stimulation and then deciding on behavior. Behavior is simply the body's reaction to that stimulation. No other behavior is possible. With the organism as it is structured at that time, the behavior that was evoked or elicited was the only thing that could have happened. It may seem otherwise sometimes because we exhibit thinking behaviors and awareness of its supplementary role but these thinking behaviors are also fully caused and we fail to be aware of all of the various links in the causal chain all the way back through time. Consequently, it may seem as though we are choosing when we are not.

Categories of Behavior

There are two broad types of behavior: respondent behaviors and operant behaviors. **Respondent behavior** is automatically *elicited* by an antecedent stimulus (a stimulus that comes before the behavior) and future instances are not influenced by the consequences it may generate. A body is structured in a way that makes the response inevitable when it is exposed to the stimulus, regardless of how that behavior might have been consequated in the past. It includes such behavior as blinking when a puff of air impacts the eyeball, salivating when food is placed in the mouth, and the release of various chemicals into the bloodstream (from glands) that we refer to as emotional behaviors. **Operant behavior** causes changes to the postcedent environment that provides energy feedback to the behaving body (the cybernetic loop), causing small-scale changes to it, such that the behavior is then either more or less likely to occur across subsequent occasions of the antecedent stimulus that evoked the behavior (Ledoux, 2014, p. 12). Examples of operant behaviors are sitting, walking and speaking. Rather than being elicited as respondents are, we say that operants are *evoked*.

Traits are Not Behavior; nor are they Causes of Behavior

It is important to make a distinction between traits and behavior. Laypeople may refer to stubbornness, rudeness, spitefulness, selfishness, aggression, or hostility, but these are not behaviors. In fact, sometimes people use these labels as explanations for behavior. They are so general that they fail as descriptions; they certainly fail as explanations since they involve only one variable, making them circular as explanations. A dog does not bite because they are "aggressive" or possesses some trait called "aggression" or "hostility." This fallacy (called the nominal fallacy) might persuade some people to believe that the behavior is then explained, but it fails to provide a dependent variable adequately, let alone a dependent variable and an independent variable that are said to be functionally related. It is important to ensure that actual behavior and the functional relations it is a component of are the currency of our profession and not traits, speculations or assumptions about behaviors or fictitious hypothetical constructs like "mind" or "dominance." This raises a good example of the commonness of the nominal fallacy. Some people attempt to explain certain behaviors by saying that the dog is dominant. The dog exhibits the behavior because he or she is dominant, and he or she is dominant because he or she exhibits the behavior. Notice only one variable there—the dependent variable. The word dominant is simply another word for the behavior. That is circular reasoning. Valid reasoning requires two distinct variables, the dependent variable (the behavior) and the independent variable (the thing causing it); they must be distinct events.

Accessibility of Terms in Analysis

Nor is it useful to speculate about what the dog may or may not understand or desire etc., or even what they might be thinking, albeit thinking is real behavior. It is more productive to trace private events back through the causal chain to a link that is publicly accessible, something in the environment that we can actually manipulate in order to control the behavior. In other words, we observe a behavior (dependent variable) and, instead of speculating about the thought processes or especially any mental transformations as the independent variable causing it, we trace the causal chain back to a point that we can observe, measure, and influence. For example, a mat might evoke approach and lying down behaviors, and there is no need to look for thinking behaviors that might come between the seeing of the mat (stimulation) and the approach and lying down behaviors. Instead, we identify the mat as the stimulus functionally related to the approach and lying down behavior.

Functional Relations

Nature is composed of an unbreakable continuity of completely natural events that accumulate in a natural history (Ledoux, 2002a, p. 19), a complex chain, or web, of causal relations. A *functional relation* refers to a reliable relationship between a dependent variable and an independent variable, which some would refer to as a causal relationship.[7] When we refer to a cause or functional relation, we are referring to the relationship between two things; one depends on the other for it to occur. In natural science, the thing that is being explained

---

[7] Some behaviorologists prefer not to use the word *causal* and instead use the term *functional*.

or accounted for (the thing being caused) is called the dependent variable, and the thing that causes it is called the independent variable.[8] Natural science examines the causal relationship between real dependent and independent variables. In behaviorology, the dependent variable is the behavior under consideration, and the independent variable is the environmental stimulation necessary and sufficient to produce the behavior (Vargas, 2009, p. 20).

Contingencies describe functional relations in episodes of behavior and will be a major focus of our analysis of behavior. We use the term **contingency analysis** to refer to our behavior of analyzing or describing functional relations or to the product of such behavior.

Respondent behaviors are components of a two-term antecedent–behavior contingency[9], often referred to as a stimulus–response contingency. The antecedent stimulation is a term and the behavior is the other term. Operant behaviors are components of a three-term antecedent → behavior → consequence contingency, often referred to as a stimulus-response-stimulus contingency. We will explore this below in greater detail.

With regard to respondent behaviors, the mechanistic cause is the antecedent stimulus that elicits the behavior. How does this stimulus cause the respondent behavior? The body is so structured, by natural selection, as to make certain responses inevitable, automatic and uninterruptable when the organism is exposed to certain kinds of stimuli, and also to be capable of expanding the number and kind of stimuli that can come to elicit these same responses. Behaviors that occur automatically without any previous conditioning are called **unconditioned responses**, and behaviors that occur only after conditioning are called **conditioned responses**. These are all respondent behaviors and inevitable, once elicited. To be clear, there is no free-willed agent that "chooses" to "perform" behavior or "anticipates" the unconditioned stimulus. A behavior that is elicited (or evoked in the case of operants) is completely inevitable and the organism is a passive functioning physiology that is structured in a way that it will simply exhibit the behavior when exposed to the stimulus.

---

[8] You can remember which is which with the verbal supplement that INdependent variables are the variables we INfluence and DEPENDent variables are the variables that DEPEND on the other variable.

[9] The term antecedent refers to the events occurring immediately before the behavior. This will be discussed in detail below.

The organism does not "learn" to associate stimuli or "learn to perform" behaviors. The organism merely mediates the behavior. Just because humans also exhibit awareness behaviors does not make our behavior "free-willed" and somehow different from every other occurrence in nature. It may seem as though it is free-willed because we also exhibit awareness behaviors and verbal thinking behaviors, and because our restricted capacity to apprehend all of the causes back through time is limited, but behavior is just as natural as anything else.

With regard to operant behaviors, the mechanistic cause is also the antecedent stimulus that *evokes* the behavior. And how does the antecedent stimulus come to cause the operant behavior to occur? Antecedent stimulation causes an operant behavior because of a history of consequences (specifically, reinforcement in the case of strengthening the behavior) generated by that behavior in the presence of the antecedent stimulus. That is the selection causation, the selection by consequences mechanism discussed above. Consequences involve a feedback mechanism that we have referred to as the cybernetic loop as follows. The operant behavior an organism exhibits causes a release of energy of some kind that impacts on the environment (be it inside or outside of the skin), and this release of energy causes changes to the environment. That now differently structured environment emits a stream of energy of some kind that impinges upon the sensory nervous system of the organism causing a cascade of neural firings and results in small-scale changes to the organism's nervous system and that now differently structured nervous system responds differently to the environment from that point on. In other words, the behavior operates on the environment, and seeing, hearing, feeling, or smelling (i.e., sensing) the effect of that operation causes the organism to respond differently across similar subsequent occasions. With each trial through the contingency, the structure of the organism is affected by the consequences and we call this operant conditioning. This cybernetic loop is the physics and chemistry of the selection causation process. In a given trial of a behavior that is consequated, take note that the consequence in that trial did not cause or even affect the behavior in that trial at all. For instance, it is erroneous to say that a dog sits "in order to get the treat" or, "because it pays off." These utterances seem to suggest that the consequence caused that response, but this would mean that the future caused the past. Mechanistically, the dog sat because an antecedent stimulus occurred and evoked the behavior. From a selection causation standpoint, that stimulus evoked the behavior because of a *history* of reinforcement that strengthened it. The future cannot cause the past. The consequence made small-scale changes to the organism, which made *future* sitting behavior more likely. The antecedent stimulus, rather than the consequence, evoked that occurrence of behavior.

Some people have distinguished between respondent and operant behavior, by proposing that respondent behavior is involuntary, whereas operant behavior is voluntary. This is inaccurate, because it tends to suggest that some behaviors are not fully caused by the environment and inevitable, but rather that some behaviors are reflexes and that others are free-willed. This is another fallacious influence from psychology to guard against. There are no inner agents that can spontaneously or semi-autonomously initiate behavior and no behavior is voluntary. Behavior is not "performed;" it simply, inevitably happens, naturally. Just as we do not say that a radio voluntarily performs the sounds it emits, nor do we say living things do. The radio merely mediates the sounds and living things also simply mediate behavior— we are not exceptions to the laws of nature just because many people like to think that we are.

Conditioning

Conditioning is a behavior change process whereby an organism is physically changed by energy emanating from the environment in such a way that the body responds in a measurably different way to that stimulus thereafter. Simply, conditioning is a change in behavior due to experience (Chance, 2009). Experience refers to the transmission of energy from the antecedent environment to the organism and the postcedent cybernetic loop. In other words, experience refers to trials through contingencies. With regard to respondent behaviors, the change occurs when a previously neutral stimulus comes to elicit respondent behaviors and the experience involves pairing the neutral stimulus with a stimulus that currently does elicit the respondent behavior. This pairing involves the stream of energy from each of the two stimuli impinging upon the organism at approximately the same time. With regard to operant conditioning, the change in behavior involves a change in the rate or frequency of the behavior after the consequences generated by that behavior in past occurrences of the behavior cause small-scale changes to the organism's nervous system causing that change in responsiveness. In either case, conditioning involves a transfer of energy from the environment to the organism that causes small-scale changes to the organism's nervous system, which changes how that, now different, body responds to the environment. When we talk about streams of energy, we are talking about light waves (seeing) or pressure waves entering the ear (hearing) or pressure on the body (feeling) and the like.

Training is simply arranging for conditions that will result in conditioning and bringing specific behaviors under stimulus control. The objective of a training project is to change behavior as efficiently and effectively as possible toward established objectives. We systematically identify specific behavior objectives and apply standard training strategies to condition the behavior and bring it under stimulus control. We apply the appropriate principles to formulating procedures or protocols that will achieve the objectives, and then carry them out. We achieve all of this by controlling the causes of behavior—the environment.

Operant Conditioning

Contingencies

At this point, you are familiar with a number of concepts and terms that will be applied in the sections below. This should prove useful in expanding your understanding of the principles of behavior as we introduce more terms and concepts.

You have likely been exposed to the phrase '***ABC's of behavior***'. *A* stands for antecedent, *B* stands for behavior and *C* stands for consequence. The *A* and *C* represent the environment and the *B* represents the behavior that is functionally related to *A* and *C*. Antecedent stimuli evoke, or otherwise affect, the occurrence of the behavior and the consequences strengthen or weaken the likelihood of the behavior on subsequent occasions. The ABC's of behavior can be a useful acronym for evoking the concept of the three-term contingency, which is of fundamental importance to the science of behavior. Below, I will describe each term and their relations in greater detail with more specific terminology.

Contingencies of Functional Relations

The three-term contingency is a basic formula for analyzing operant behavioral episodes. A **contingency** describes a functional relation. The three terms in the three-term contingency are the antecedent stimulus, behavior, and the postcedent stimulus (ante means before and post means after). These stimuli constitute the environmental events that affect the behavior and indeed explain it.

Antecedents

Antecedent stimuli are what occur immediately before the behavior. Unless a stimulus maintains stimulus control over a specific behavior, it is referred to as a neutral stimulus (S^N) with regard to that particular behavior. That is, the event might occur before a behavior but it is coincidental or otherwise does not control the behavior. Once we have confirmed a functional relation (that is, that the stimulus actually does evoke the behavior), we refer to the antecedent stimulus as the **evocative stimulus** (S^{Ev}).[10] There are often numerous stimuli sharing control over behavior, even though we normally simplify the analysis by identifying the stimulus that exerts the most control. After punishment or extinction, if the S^{Ev} continues to evoke the behavior, even at a diminished rate, it is still called an S^{Ev}. However, if the S^{Ev} comes to no longer evoke the behavior, it becomes an S^N again; it is a specific kind of S^N called an S-delta (S^Δ), which can be thought of as an extinction stimulus. Below, we will explore other classes of antecedent stimuli, including various kinds of function-altering stimuli.

Behavior

As discussed, **behavior** is a general term for any neurally mediated response to stimulation, that is, the body's reaction to the environment. A specific instance of a behavior is a **response**. Each response is a new response, and each new response will be topographically different even if only slightly so (Ledoux, 2014, p. 88), which makes it impossible to repeat (a onetime only thing can only happen one time). Since we cannot measure the number of times that a response occurs in a minute

---

[10] The traditional term discriminative stimulus is increasingly being replaced by the term evocative stimulus. These terms may be used interchangeably, but they do tend to emphasize a different perspective on the same phenomenon. Discriminative stimulus tends to connote the differential response to a stimulus, as opposed to other stimuli, whereas evocative stimulus tends to connote that the stimulus evokes the response.

if that precise response can only occur one single time, we use the concept of a response class.[11] A ***response class*** is a group or variety of responses that share a common effect on the environment (generate the same consequence). For instance, with operant behavior, if you verbally cue "sit" and the dog sits and you follow with a treat, each instance or trial will be a one-off response, but sitting is a response class (in this case, it could also be called an operant class or operant response class)—that is, this variety of response shares the same consequence, even though each response might be slightly different topographically. We can now talk meaningfully about that response occurring in a manner that we can measure and track quantitatively. Initially, each response might differ quite significantly. We might, at first, reinforce all of these varieties of the response to promote acquisition of the response class, but later we might reduce the variability by differentially reinforcing only certain responses within the class. In summary, sitting is an example of a behavior; a particular instance of a particular dog sitting is a response; and all of the individual responses each time the dog sits constitute a response class.

Postcedents

Postcedent stimuli comprise everything that occurs immediately after the behavior. Many things occur after a behavior, and only some of them are functionally related to the response class—that is, changing the organism in a way that affects the likelihood of that behavior occurring on subsequent occasions. A postcedent stimulus that is confirmed to change behavior, whether it was generated by the behavior or occurred coincidentally, is called a ***selector***. This stimulus selects for behavior. A selector that changes behavior coincidentally, rather than actually being generated by the behavior, is called a ***coincidental selector***, and the behaviors generated by coincidental selectors are referred to as ***superstitious behaviors***. A selector that influences behavior and is not merely coincidental, but is actually generated by the behavior is referred to as a ***consequence***. See Figure 1 below for a visual depiction of these relations and categories.

The Functional Relations in Contingencies

By determining the three-term contingency that operates in any particular behavior episode, we describe the relationship between the

---

[11] This distinction is often not made, and it is common to see the term response used in place of response class.

behavior and its environment, and therefore explain the cause of the behavior event (identifying the dependent and independent variables and their functional relation). The principles of behavior discussed below elaborate how these relations operate. Whether we are explaining a behavior event that has occurred or planning a training project, the contingency analysis is a foundation for these activities.

For now, this is a rather simplistic treatment of the topic. There can be more than three terms in a contingency and usually there are. Furthermore, with regard to a particular response class, there may be several contingencies operating simultaneously on the behavior, some reinforcing and others punishing; the response in any given trial will be the net result of these various contingencies. Furthermore, both operant and respondent contingencies are occurring simultaneously and influencing each other. These complexities are discussed in more detail below.

Before we examine contingencies further, it would be useful to discuss the symbolic notation used to depict functional relations in written contingencies. Arrows (i.e., → or its type character version –>) are used to indicate a functional relation; if there is no functional relation, no arrow will be present. If a previously operational functional relation existed but no longer does, then an arrow with a / through it will indicate this (i.e., –/–>) so as to express that the functional link has been broken. In cases where a term has not yet been identified, a question mark (?) can be used to hold its place.

Below is a general representation of the three-term contingency before any specifics have been determined or identified. Note that arrows have not yet been inserted because the specific functional relations have not yet been identified, let alone confirmed.

Antecedent – Behavior – Postcedent

Once we have determined the actual antecedent stimulus that evokes the behavior, and the postcedent stimulus that affects the future likelihood of the behavior, we depict the specific contingency in one of two ways. The first method is as follows:

"Sit" → Jake sits → Treat (+R)

31

Alternatively, you might depict it as column headings under which the specifics are included.

S^{Ev} Response   Consequence

"Sit" → Jake sits → Treat (+R)

When analyzing a situation, we start with the behavior of concern. In any given situation, there might be multiple behaviors, some operant and some respondent. The situation might even include behaviors exhibited by different subjects (e.g., the trainer and the trainee). Assuming you are analyzing an operant behavior, start with identifying the *particular* behavior you seek to explain. This clarity makes the analysis much simpler and cleaner; failing to do so is the source of much confusion when novice trainers seek to analyze a situation. Identify the behavior of concern first.

?   —   Jake sits   —   ?

Then assess antecedent events for a likely S^{Ev}. Usually, what occurs just before the behavior is what evokes it. However, if a few different events occur right before the behavior, you may have to choose one as the most likely candidate for S^{Ev}. Hypothesized functional relations can be tested and confirmed or refuted with simple experiments of trying each stimulus on its own until the one is found that evokes the behavior. At first, you may not be able to determine exactly what is evoking the behavior and you may leave a "?" in that term position, and move on to identify the consequence. You will notice the dash rather than arrow between the S^{Ev} and the response. Until the functional relation is confirmed, it is best practice to leave the dash in place.

"Sit"   —   Jake sits   —   ?

Then assess the postcedent environment for a hypothesized consequence. Usually, it will be the event occurring immediately after the behavior although as with antecedents, you might be forced to hypothesize the most likely consequence for the contingency and test it experimentally to confirm it.

"Sit"   —   Jake sits   —   Treat (+R)

If, on subsequent occasions of the word "sit" being verbalized when Jake is around and you observe that Jake does sit after the word "sit" is verbalized and that a treat is at least occasionally presented after the behavior, and no other event that is more plausible as a consequence occurs after the sitting behavior, then you have tentatively confirmed both the S^{Ev} and the consequence—in this case, positive reinforcement (+R). The confirmed contingency would look like this:

$$\text{"Sit"} \rightarrow \text{Jake sits} \rightarrow \text{Treat (+R)}$$

We can use the contingency analysis both to analyze situations for the causes of behavior we observe and to help plan a contingency we seek to create in order to train a behavior. It keeps us focused on the functional relations and the terms in a behavior episode, which improves our clarity both in explaining behavior and in planning how to change it. This clarity improves efficiency.

The three-term contingency is made up of two two-term contingencies, which together describe the entirety of functional relations between the environment and the behavior of concern in any given behavioral episode. The first two-term contingency is the $S^{Ev} \rightarrow$ behavior relation. The second two-term contingency is the behavior $\rightarrow$ consequence relation. These two contingencies are functionally and integrally related. The behavior $\rightarrow$ consequence contingency functions to strengthen or weaken the $S^{Ev} \rightarrow$ behavior relation or, put another way, to strengthen or weaken the evocative capacity of the S^{Ev} (Fraley, 2008). Notice that what is strengthened is the relation, not just a term. Again, conditioning creates changes to the structure of the body of the organism via stimulation from the environment, which changes the evocative capacity of the S^{Ev} on subsequent presentations (more accurately, it changes the organism's receptiveness to the stimuli; the S^{Ev} is not changed, the body is). Through repeated trials through the contingency, you can observe the changes in the likelihood of the S^{Ev} evoking the behavior, and you can observe the consequences selecting for or against future instances of the behavior. These processes are depicted below. Notice how the behavior $\rightarrow$ consequence contingency functions to change (strengthen or weaken) the $S^{Ev} \rightarrow$ behavior contingency on subsequent trials (Fraley, 2008). The reinforcement would continue until the behavior becomes stable and punishment would continue until the S^{Ev} suppresses the behavior and no longer evokes it. You can visualize the conditioning process as the effects of a contingency on the occurrence of the behavior on subsequent occasions and that repetition of the contingency results in a new behavior and likelihood of its occurrence on subsequent occasions. This is presented merely to highlight the relation between the two two-term contingencies. It depicts concepts (punishment versus reinforcement) that have not yet been introduced but will be below.

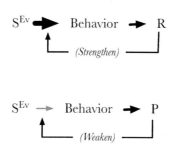

When another variable becomes important in controlling behavior, it can be advantageous and appropriate to include a fourth term in the contingency analysis. Whether we include further terms in the contingency analysis depends on how important these terms are in controlling the behavior of concern, and our interest in examining these other terms, which might provide greater explanatory power, in a given behavioral episode. The fourth, fifth or more terms can be found in the antecedent, behavior or postcedent positions of the contingency. In a section to come, we examine these complexities further.

Postcedent Principles, Processes and Procedures

Law of Effect

The *law of effect* is the perfect place to start in outlining the principles of behavior. The law of effect simply states that consequences select for or against operant behavior—some consequences will tend to strengthen behavior, while others will tend to weaken it.[12] We refer to behavior-strengthening consequences as reinforcers and the behavior-weakening consequences as punishers. Originally, the law of effect was formulated in terms of stimuli that generated a "satisfying state of affairs" and stimuli that generated an "annoying state of affairs." We no longer define laws and principles of behavior by presumptions or speculation about private experiences that we cannot verify; rather, we identify whether the consequence does, in fact, make the appropriate structural changes to the behaving body that result in an increase or decrease in the likelihood of that behavior on subsequent occasions in the presence of the S^{Ev}. The law of effect is the foundational law of behavior for operant conditioning. If an organism exhibits a behavior, it is because, in the past, that behavior has contacted a reinforcer. It is why all of us exhibit the operant behaviors we do.

We often say that consequences strengthen or weaken the behavior. This is fine when we are under contingencies to simplify the process with verbal shortcuts, but it is not as strictly accurate as saying that consequences provide the conditioning history that creates changes within the organism that increase or decrease the probability of the S^{Ev} evoking the behavior on subsequent occasions of its presentation. That is, what is strengthened or weakened is the $S^{Ev} \rightarrow$ behavior contingency, not just the behavior term. To elaborate, the consequence of a behavior does not (and cannot) affect the behavior that preceded it (a teleological fallacy), even though trainers often say that "the dog does such and such in order to get the treats" or "the consequence strengthens the behavior" or "the dog does what works." The consequence only changes the structure of the organism that then changes the future probability of the behavior happening on subsequent exposures to the S^{Ev}. It does not strengthen the behavior directly, but rather causes changes in the organism's body that thereby alter the effectiveness of the S^{Ev} on subsequent occasions—conditioning occurs physically within the organism.

We will discuss five kinds of consequences, three that weaken behavior and two that strengthen behavior. The two that strengthen behavior are referred to as reinforcement; two of the three that weaken it are

---

[12] Remember, saying that behavior is strengthened or weakened is a shortcut way of saying that the $S^{Ev} \rightarrow$ behavior contingency (the functional relation) is strengthened or weakened. Without these verbal shortcuts, our sentences would be rather cumbersome but it is important to appreciate that they are just verbal shortcuts. More on this in the next paragraph.

referred to as punishment. These four principles involve changes to the postcedent environment that change the future likelihood of that behavior occurring. They are different from the fifth kind, extinction, which involves an absence of postcedent environmental change for previously reinforced behaviors—in other words, withholding reinforcement, with a subsequent decline in responding. In reinforcement and punishment procedures, a stimulus can be added (i.e., presented), or subtracted (i.e., withdrawn). This means that you can have added reinforcement and subtracted reinforcement, and added punishment and subtracted punishment.

Historically, the terms positive and negative have been used to define the addition or subtraction of consequences. These terms have been confusing to many because positive and negative have an established connotation as good and bad, respectively. Many people have been confused by the notion of positive punishment and negative reinforcement, in particular. Positive merely means added, and negative merely means subtracted. In behaviorology, the trend is to replace positive and negative with added and subtracted, respectively because they promote clarity and reduce confusion (see Ledoux, 2002b). I will retain the traditional usage of positive and negative in this text to prevent confusion among those who are already familiar with positive and negative terminology.

Figure 1 provides a flow chart that illustrates how to analyze the postcedent stimulation of any particular operant conditioning episode and identify the principles operating on the behavior in question. This figure contains more detail than we will cover in this chapter but provides you with the detail you need to analyze at least what we do cover, while remaining comprehensive.

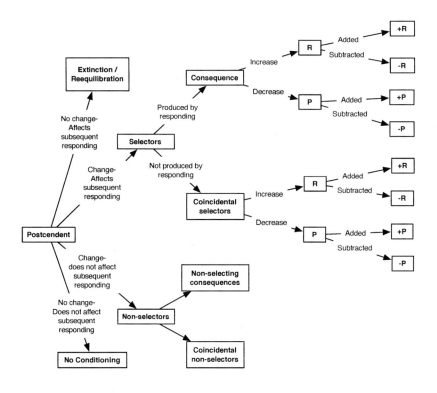

Figure 1. Flow chart depicting various operant processes and principles. Adapted and modified from Ledoux (2002b).

One of the easiest ways to conceptualize the relations among the types of operant conditioning is in the contingency diagram depicted in Figure 2, which was adapted from Fraley (2008) and Ledoux (2014). Many readers will be more familiar with a table showing the four quadrants of operant conditioning. The main problem with the traditional quadrants table is that it addresses only changes in behavior resulting from postcedent changes and ignores extinction, the fifth basic principle of operant conditioning. In other words, it is a table of consequences and ignores changes in behavior that result from a lack of previously available consequences. By eliminating the table format and using a dimensional format, Fraley has cleverly accounted for extinction along with the other basic principles diagrammatically.

Extinction is different from the other four principles. Instead of just a table of consequences, Fraley uses a diagram accounting for all of the basic principles of behavior. The other four principles occupy the four quadrants of the diagram because they involve changes to the postcedent environment (addition or subtraction of stimulation—the horizontal axis in the figure) as well as an increase or decrease in the strength of the behavior (the vertical axis). Extinction, on the other hand, involves no functional postcedent change in the environment (from the antecedent environment) for a behavior with a history of reinforcement. It therefore exists only directly on the vertical axis line; because the behavior decreases in rate, extinction is found at the bottom of the figure. Don't be confused into thinking that extinction results from punishment (which would require a left–right axis position in the figure)—it does not.

In figure 2, uppercase letters representing reinforcement and punishment (i.e., −R, +R, −P and +P) indicate unconditioned consequences, whereas lowercase letters representing reinforcement and punishment (i.e., −r, +r, −p and +p) indicate conditioned consequences. For example, a conditioned positive punisher would be depicted symbolically as +p, and an unconditioned negative reinforcer would be depicted as −R. Where the consequence is unspecified with regard to whether it is conditioned or unconditioned, the capital letter will be used as a default.

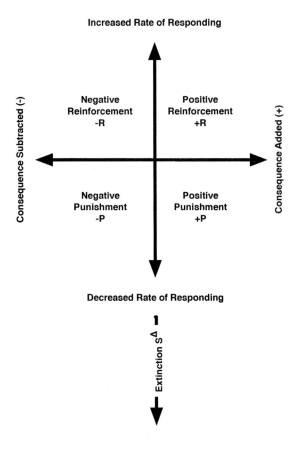

Figure 2. Diagram relating basic principles of behavior. Adapted from Fraley (2008) with additions adapted from Ledoux (2014).

Now let us consider each of the principles in turn.

Contingencies of Reinforcement

Reinforcement is a behavior change process in which a change in stimulation, during or immediately following a response, results in an increase in the likelihood of that behavior across subsequent occasions (Fraley, 2008). That is, the behavior → R relation results in a *strengthening* of the S^{Ev} → behavior relation. On subsequent occasions of its occurrence, the S^{Ev} is *more* likely to evoke the operant behavior. The consequence strengthens the relation between the behavior and whatever stimuli were present at the time.

Positive Reinforcement / Added Reinforcers

Positive reinforcement (+R) is a behavior change process in which the addition of stimulation during or immediately following a response results in an increase in the likelihood of that behavior on subsequent occasions (Fraley, 2008). That is, the behavior → +R relation results in a *strengthening* of the S^{Ev} → behavior relation. On subsequent occasions of its occurrence, the S^{Ev} is *more* likely to evoke the behavior because of that previously added consequence. A valuable way to conceptualize +R is by listing the necessary and sufficient conditions, as follows:

- **Behavior** occurs.

- Stimulus is **added** during or immediately following behavior.

- Subsequent **increase** in likelihood of behavior on subsequent occasions.

Positive (added) reinforcement can be further divided into conditioned or unconditioned reinforcement—that is, we can have a conditioned positive reinforcer or an unconditioned positive reinforcer—depending on whether or not the reinforcer was effective without previous conditioning to establish it as such before its use. We utilize both unconditioned reinforcers (aka primary reinforcers) and conditioned reinforcers (aka secondary reinforcers) in training. **Unconditioned reinforcers** are capable of reinforcing behavior without any previous conditioning to establish them as reinforcers. The body is genetically/structurally arranged as a result of evolution such that the stimulus simply is a reinforcer. These types of reinforcers commonly involve biologically significant stimuli such as food, water, or sex. However, unconditioned reinforcers such as these identified stimuli are not *always* reinforcing, and in fact, they can become aversive. If an organism is satiated with regard to the stimulus, then the body is so structured as to prevent that stimulus from acting effectively as a reinforcer, and indeed it may constitute an aversive stimulus until the satiation subsides (e.g., the last thing you want after a large meal is food and access to it certainly won't reinforce any behavior). On the other hand, if the organism is deprived with regard to the stimulus, the stimulus should act effectively as a reinforcer. Because unconditioned reinforcers can rarely be delivered with precise timing sufficient to reinforce fleeting behaviors, conditioned reinforcers are utilized in training. **Conditioned reinforcers** function to reinforce behavior but only because it has been previously paired with unconditioned reinforcers[13], something that will be discussed further below. Once a conditioned reinforcer (usually a click) is established, the conditioned reinforcer can be utilized to reinforce specific behaviors, particularly fleeting ones. The click is administered immediately following the behavior, followed itself within a second or so by the unconditioned reinforcer. This allows for reinforcement of a precise behavior and time to administer the unconditioned reinforcer.

On terminology: Laypeople commonly use the word "reward," but this is not a principle of behavior. Because it is vague, this term is best avoided altogether. A reward is something that is provided to someone else, with the intention to encourage the receiver to exhibit the behavior again, but it does not necessarily reinforce behavior (Peirce & Cheney, 2013, p. 5). Furthermore, the term reward is usually framed in terms of rewarding the individual, which is semantically meaningless. If your interest is in the behavior, rather than intentions and on whether a behavior is or is not actually reinforced, the word reward is completely inappropriate. If you are under contingencies to express something about reinforcement, it is better to use the proper terms: reinforcement or positive reinforcement. These terms are well established in everyday language, so there is no need for concern that laypeople will not recognize and comprehend their meaning.

Negative Reinforcement / Subtracted Reinforcers

Negative reinforcement (–R) is a behavior change process in which the subtraction of an ongoing stimulus, during or immediately following a response, results in an increase in the likelihood of that behavior on subsequent occasions (Fraley, 2008). That is, the behavior $\rightarrow$ –R relation results in a *strengthening* of the $S^{Ev} \rightarrow$ behavior relation. On subsequent occasions of its occurrence, the S^{Ev} is *more* likely to evoke the operant behavior, because of that previously subtracted consequence. Negative reinforcement is the strengthening of escape behavior. The necessary and sufficient conditions are as follows:

---

[13] Actually, you can pair them with already established conditioned reinforcers as well.

- **Behavior** occurs.

- Ongoing stimulus is **subtracted** during or immediately following behavior.

- Subsequent **increase** in likelihood of behavior on subsequent occasions.

Negative (subtracted) reinforcement can be further divided into conditioned or unconditioned reinforcement—that is, we can have a conditioned negative reinforcer or an unconditioned negative reinforcer—depending on whether or not the reinforcer was effective without previous conditioning to establish it as such before its use. Negative reinforcement is unique in that the consequence is a subtracted (reduced or eliminated) version of the S^{Ev} that evoked the behavior, and is ongoing, rather than added only after the behavior. In a negative reinforcement contingency, the S^{Ev} is an aversive stimulus, and the behavior functions to reduce or eliminate contact with that stimulus. Although negative reinforcement strengthens escape behavior, we commonly refer to escape from an unconditioned negative reinforcer as *escape* and escape from a conditioned negative reinforcer as *avoidance*. The unconditioned negative reinforcer is avoided, in a manner of speaking, but the contingency really involves escape from the conditioned negative reinforcer; it is escape in both instances.

Some Potentially Confusing Distinctions

All reinforcers strengthen behavior but there can be value in making certain distinctions regarding the manner in which certain reinforcers occur. There are also a few common distinctions and terms that refer to the same thing that frequently cause confusion. I will explore a few common distinctions, including some confusing ones.

In many contexts, it makes little difference whether a reinforcer occurred intrinsically or extrinsically, but under certain circumstances, it may become useful to make such a distinction. In behaviorology, an *intrinsic reinforcer* is one that is produced directly by the behavior, that is, without being mediated by another organism. An *extrinsic reinforcer* is one that is produced indirectly by the behavior, that is, being mediated by another organism. The term intrinsic is also commonly used to refer to *endogenous, automatic reinforcers*, or *endoreinforcement*—that is, reinforcers that are generated solely within the body of the subject, such as when a behavior causes the release of certain chemicals into the bloodstream. The opposite of this usage would involve extrinsic reinforcers, also known as *exogenous reinforcers or ectoreinforcement*, which refers to reinforcers that are generated outside of the subject's body, as in the cybernetic loop extending beyond the skin. To avoid confusion, I typically use the terms *trainer-mediated reinforcers* and *nontrainer-mediated reinforcers* to refer to whether the reinforcement is generated by the behavior or mediated by the trainer. Trainer-mediated reinforcement is also commonly referred to as *contrived reinforcement* and nontrainer-mediated reinforcement is commonly referred to as *"natural" reinforcement*. Since the terms intrinsic and extrinsic will sometimes be used in various sources to mean either of these two different things, these terms should evoke further exploratory behaviors to determine the intended meaning in that source.

Variables Influencing Effectiveness of Reinforcement

For reinforcement to be effective, certain conditions must be met. Although there can be many such variables, a few of them are particularly important, and these are described below.

Contingency

Contingency, as you will recall refers to a functional relation between behavior and the environment. The greater the degree of contingency (that is, the higher the correlation between behavior and reinforcer), the more effective conditioning will be (Chance, 2009, pp. 144–145). In other words, if a behavior is reinforced each time it occurs and not otherwise, conditioning will proceed quickly and efficiently. If the correlation is not as strong, conditioning will occur more slowly, with the rate depending on the degree of correlation. Contingency is particularly important in the initial acquisition stages of training.

Contiguity

Contiguity refers to the time interval between the behavior and the reinforcer. The smaller the interval, the more effective reinforcement will be (Chance, 2009, pp. 145–146; Schlinger & Blakely, 1994). Behavior is continuous; behaviors are always occurring and consequences are influencing their future likelihood. In the interval between the behavior of concern and its reinforcer, other behaviors can occur, even barely noticeable ones. The longer the interval between the behavior of concern and the reinforcer, the more likely will be the accumulation of other behaviors and the less likely will be reinforcement of the behavior of concern (Chance, 2009, pp. 145–146). Aside from the intervening behaviors, conditioning is a physiological process and pairings need to be closely related in time in order for the pairing to be physiologically effective. Schlinger and Blakely (1994) tested reinforcer delays in three subject groups: one with a delay of 0 seconds, another with a delay of 4 seconds, and another with a delay of 10 seconds. They found *dramatic* reductions in conditioning as the delay increased, with little to no conditioning taking place in the 10-second delay group. Contiguity is the most important of the variables discussed here.

Reinforcer Characteristics

Not all reinforcers are equally effective. In general, smaller, more frequently delivered reinforcers are more effective than fewer, larger reinforcers. However, in a particular trial, a larger reinforcer is generally more effective than a smaller one (Chance, 2009, pp. 148–149). "*Jackpotting*," a term common in dog training, refers to the effects of greater reinforcer magnitude on increased responding. In the jackpotting procedure, the trainer provides reinforcers of higher quality (meaning generally more effective) or higher quantity for particularly "good" responses. There is some evidence to suggest that jackpots will increase responding in the session in which they are used (Weatherly, McSweeney, & Swindell, 2004), although there is also a postreinforcement decline in responding when a high-magnitude reinforcer is used, indicating that jackpots might actually be disruptive, perhaps due to more quickly inducing satiation and/or as an emphasized post reinforcement pause schedule effect (schedule effects to be discussed further below). There is also evidence that the increase in responding itself is minimal (Bond, 2007). It may be better to simply maintain consistent reinforcement criteria.

Task Characteristics

Different species are genetically disposed such that certain behaviors will be easier to train than others. Evolution results in bodies so structured that certain behaviors readily contact highly effective reinforcement, often generated inside the subject's body. For instance, chickens will tend to begin pecking at an experimental apparatus, regardless of trainer-mediated reinforcement contingencies placed on it, although you certainly can influence the rate of the behavior by manipulating the contingencies. This concept helps explain why some behaviors are just more challenging to train than others. For instance, waiting for (rather than approaching) something reinforcing, or looking away from (rather than at) a reinforcer, or holding back (rather than pulling ahead) on leash to contact something are all examples of challenges to training due to what some might call "counterintuitive" contingencies or what might more accurately be described as contingencies with competing biologically established counter-contingencies.

Concurrent Contingencies

Concurrent contingencies are always operating in a particular situation (Fraley, 2008). That is, there are always various stimuli differentially controlling the behavior of concern or other behaviors that might displace it at any given time, although often a particular contingency is so strongly operative that it may seem as though there are no other contingencies in play. Reinforcement for a particular behavior is generally less effective if there are opposing contingencies. Furthermore, various contingencies may be operating on the specific behavior in question. Rather than contingencies promoting behaviors that would displace the target behavior, you might have some punitive as well as reinforcing consequences generated by the behavior, the net result of which might be moderate or minimal responding. In this case, elimination of punitive contingencies should increase the rate of the conditioning. Concurrent contingencies will be discussed in greater detail below.

Establishing and Abolishing Operations

Establishing and abolishing operations are kinds of function-altering stimulation and as such they change the likelihood of the S^{Ev} evoking the behavior. Establishing operations involve deprivation with regard to the reinforcer, which tends to cause an increase in responding. Abolishing operations involve satiation with regard to the reinforcer, which tends to cause a decrease in responding. A deprived body tends to exhibit behavior that contacts that reinforcer and a satiated body tends not to exhibit those behaviors (Laraway, Snycerski, Michael, & Poling, 2003).

Contingencies of Punishment

Punishment is a behavior change process in which a change in stimulation, during or immediately following a response, results in a decrease in the likelihood of that behavior on subsequent occasions (Fraley, 2008). That is, the behavior → P relation results in a *weakening* of the S^{Ev} → behavior relation. On subsequent occasions of its occurrence, the S^{Ev} is *less* likely to evoke the behavior. The consequence weakens the relation between the behavior and whatever stimuli were present at the time. Note that a punishment contingency does not make any changes to the ongoing reinforcement contingency maintaining the behavior. Because of this, we make the distinction that punishment **suppresses** behavior, whereas extinction **eliminates** it.

Positive Punishment / Added Punishers

Positive punishment (+P) is a behavior change process in which the addition of stimulation, during or immediately following a response, results in a decrease in the likelihood of that behavior on subsequent occasions (Fraley, 2008). That is, the behavior → +P relation results in a *weakening* of the S^{Ev} → behavior relation. On subsequent occasions of its occurrence, the S^{Ev} is *less* likely to evoke the operant behavior because of that previously added consequence. The necessary and sufficient conditions are as follows:

- **Behavior** occurs.

- Stimulus is **added** during or immediately following behavior.

- Subsequent **decrease** in likelihood of behavior on subsequent occasions.

Positive (added) punishment can be further divided into conditioned or unconditioned punishment—that is, we can have a conditioned positive punisher or an unconditioned positive punisher—depending on whether or not the punisher was effective without previous conditioning to establish it as such before its use. While the antecedent stimulus continues to evoke the behavior under a punishment procedure, even at a diminished rate, it continues to be an S^{Ev}. Once it no longer evokes the behavior at all, it becomes a S^N. A neutral stimulus is a stimulus that does not evoke the behavior in question.

Negative Punishment / Subtracted Punishers

Negative Punishment (–P) is a behavior change process in which the subtraction of a stimulus, during or immediately following a response, results in a decrease in the likelihood of that behavior on subsequent occasions (Fraley, 2008). That is, the behavior → –P relation results in a *weakening* of the S^{Ev} → behavior relation. On subsequent occasions of its occurrence, the S^{Ev} is *less* likely to evoke the operant behavior because of that previously added consequence. The necessary and sufficient conditions are as follows:

- **Behavior** occurs.

- Stimulus is **subtracted** during or immediately following behavior.

- Subsequent **decrease** in likelihood of behavior on subsequent occasions.

Negative (subtracted) punishment can be further divided into conditioned or unconditioned punishment—that is, we can have a conditioned negative punisher or an unconditioned negative punisher—depending on whether or not the punisher was effective without previous conditioning to establish it as such before its use. The emphasis ought to be on utilizing positive reinforcement by setting the subject up for success but if negative punishment is going to be used, a conditioned negative punisher can be utilized for the same reasons that a conditioned positive reinforcer is utilized.

Variables Influencing the Effectiveness of Punishment

For punishment to be effective, it should be abruptly intense, immediate (contiguous) and follow every instance of the behavior (contingent) (Peirce & Cheney, 2013, pp. 159–160). Establishing and abolishing operations are also important. If the dog is deprived with regard to the reinforcer that is maintaining the behavior then punishment contingencies will be *more* effective and if the dog is satiated with regard to the reinforcer maintaining the behavior, punishment contingencies will be *less* effective. In agential language, if you have already had your fill of the reinforcer, it's no big deal if your contact with it is removed for a while.

Specific to punishment, it is important to also manage the reinforcement contingency. Punishment will be less effective if the reinforcement for the behavior remains available. Of course, if one is going to address the reinforcement contingency and do so effectively, one might as well simply reinforce an alternative behavior rather than punish the problematic behavior; the punishment contingency is generally just an inefficient strategy. And, by addressing the reinforcement, we are instating extinction and so punishment should not be necessary. Furthermore, if the punishment is successful then the behavior is actually shielded from extinction, because it does not occur and therefore cannot be extinguished. Meaning, if there are no trials of the behavior failing to generate that reinforcer, then extinction does not occur, and so elimination of the behavior is replaced with mere suppression of it.

Punisher intensity also impacts upon the effectiveness of punishment. Generally, an abruptly intensely aversive punisher will be more effective in suppressing behavior than a weakly aversive stimulus, or one for which the intensity is ramped up. Notwithstanding these variables and their impact on the effectiveness of punishment, the side effects of aversive stimulation are significantly problematic.

Contingencies of Extinction

Unlike reinforcement or punishment, which involve changes in the postcedent environment, extinction (EXT) of a behavior that already has a history of reinforcement involves no postcedent change in the environment. In other words, nothing of significance is added or subtracted from the environment when the behavior occurs. In punishment and reinforcement, there is always some change in the environment, which functions to change the likelihood of the behavior occurring again; something is either added or subtracted. In extinction, the focus is on the failure of the reinforcer to occur; the behavior fails to produce a change in the environment that it used to generate. In other words, the behavior previously resulted in generating a reinforcer and now it simply does not and as a result, the behavior decreases in strength. ***Extinction***, then, is a behavior change process in which no functional postcedent environmental changes occur, and as a result, the strength of the previously reinforced behavior decreases across subsequent occasions. Unlike punishment, extinction actually changes the contingency of reinforcement that was maintaining the behavior. It therefore eliminates behavior, rather than merely suppressing it through superimposing a punitive contingency over a reinforcing contingency. The decrease in the rate of the behavior can be referred to as the extinction curve, in reference to the tracking of the rate of the behavior as a line on a graph. The necessary and sufficient conditions are as follows:

- **Behavior** occurs.

- Reinforcer maintaining the behavior is **prevented** or **withheld**.

- Subsequent **decrease** in likelihood of behavior on subsequent occasions.

Following instatement of an extinction procedure, the behavior may initially increase briefly in strength. This spike in the graphed line is called an ***extinction burst***. There may be a series of extinction bursts during the extinction process (Fraley, 2008), although they will become less and less frequent and prominent. An extinguished behavior tends to be more readily reacquired if a reinforcer is reintroduced at some point (presumably because some structures in the subject's nervous system remain susceptible to the contingency). While the stimulus continues to evoke the behavior under an extinction procedure, it continues to be an S^{Ev}. Once it no longer evokes the behavior at all, it becomes an S^{N}. Once a behavior has become extinct, the subject may occasionally, in appropriate contexts, exhibit instances of the behavior as a probe. This has been referred to as "spontaneous recovery," but of course there is nothing spontaneous about it (or anything else).

Schedules of Positive Reinforcement

A schedule of positive reinforcement sets the rule that determines which responses, among a sequence of responses, will be reinforced (Fraley,

2008, p. 557). We use different schedules of reinforcement because each schedule generates a characteristic effect on the rate of the behavior. The basic schedules of reinforcement are reviewed below.

Continuous Reinforcement

Continuous reinforcement (CRF) sets the rule that reinforcers are added after each occurrence of the behavior. A CRF schedule produces a steady reliable rate of responding with relatively little variation in form and is particularly useful in the initial, acquisition stage of conditioning. After the acquisition stage, it is best to transition to an intermittent schedule. Behaviors maintained on a CRF schedule are less resilient than those maintained on intermittent schedules, meaning that they extinguish more rapidly when reinforcement is not forthcoming. However, on certain intermittent schedules, behavior can become very persistent with minimal reinforcement delivery. There will be very little variability in the form of the behavior on CRF as well, leaving little room for shaping to fine tune the form. Furthermore, satiation can occur quickly if one is reinforcing every response. Vending machines are designed to operate on a CRF schedule. Every time money is inserted, the appropriate product is dispensed. The schedule effect discussed above can be exemplified by the likelihood of a person's money inserting behavior if the CRF schedule was switched to an EXT schedule, or even any intermittent schedule. The money inserting behavior would quickly extinguish. This would not be the case with a slot machine, which operates on an intermittent schedule to be discussed below.

Figure 3 shows the typical effect of a CRF schedule on conditioning.

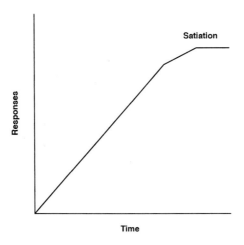

Figure 3. Typical conditioning curve associated with continuous reinforcement.

Intermittent Reinforcement

An ***intermittent reinforcement*** schedule sets the rule that positive reinforcers follow some, but not all, occurrences of the behavior. Behavior on an intermittent schedule is less susceptible to extinction and the form is more variable than under CRF. There are six basic intermittent schedules, three fixed and three variable, as discussed below.

Fixed Ratio

A ***fixed ratio*** (FR) schedule sets the rule that reinforcement will be added following the final response after a fixed (unvarying) number of responses have occurred. A number is included in the description of the schedule to identify the number of responses that generates the reinforcement. So, reinforcing after, say, four responses would be FR-4. FR schedules have a rather common set of schedule effects. On an FR schedule, the subject usually responds at a high rate, but responding wanes after each delivery of reinforcement—that is called a ***postreinforcement pause***. Because of this postreinforcement pause, FR schedules are rarely used in training. When thinning a ratio schedule (i.e., reducing the number of responses that are reinforced), only move to the next level when the current level of the behavior has stabilized. The body takes time to change structurally in response to stimulation and if you thin the schedule before the body has had a chance to adapt to the current change, the behavior may not stabilize at all and may extinguish.

Figure 4 shows the typical effect of an FR schedule on conditioning.

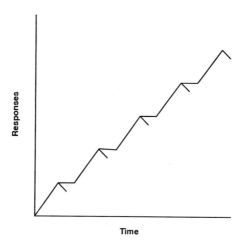

Figure 4. Typical conditioning curve associated with a fixed ratio schedule of reinforcement.

Variable Ratio

A *variable ratio* (VR) schedule sets the rule that reinforcement will be added following the final response after a specific but variable average number of responses has occurred. Variable means that reinforcement should be delivered in a seemingly random manner around the specified mean. Responding under a VR schedule is usually at a high rate and with less of a postreinforcement pause than under an FR schedule and behaviors on VR schedules are highly resistant to extinction.

The schedule effects for the VR schedule are very important for training. Slot machines are designed to operate on a VR schedule because this schedule will maintain the highest rate of responding in relation to the number of reinforced trials provided. Unlike the vending machine, the slot machine delivers its payout in a seemingly random schedule, which is in fact a VR schedule and as you would expect, subjects on VR schedules will exhibit the target behavior vast numbers of times before reinforcement is delivered (persistence), assuming the schedule is "thinned" gradually enough. **Ratio strain** can occur when a ratio schedule is thinned too quickly or the jump in the ratio is too high.

Because of these schedule effects, VR is the most useful basic schedule of reinforcement for acquired behaviors in training. As with the FR schedule, ensure that the subject's body has adjusted to the current change—evidenced by stabilization of the behavior—before thinning the schedule another step.

Figure 5 shows the typical effect of a VR schedule on conditioning.

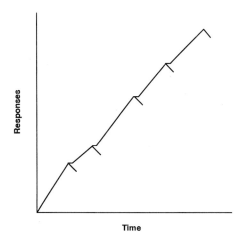

Time

Figure 5. Typical conditioning curve associated with a variable ratio schedule of reinforcement.

Fixed Interval

A *fixed interval* (FI) schedule sets the rule that reinforcement is provided immediately after the first response exhibited after a specific interval of time has passed. It is important to note the two necessary conditions for interval schedules: the specified interval must pass, and then and only then, the next response to occur is reinforced. A number and unit of measure specification are included to identify the time interval involved. For example, reinforcing for the first response after say 2 minutes would be depicted as FI-2min.

Increases in rate of responding are moderate under FI schedules[14], and the subject ceases responding after each reinforcer is delivered, in what is generally called "scalloping." Because of this scalloping schedule effect and only moderate responding, FI schedules are rarely used in training. This schedule is addressed here primarily for completeness, and because other useful schedules (discussed below) are based on the FI schedule.

Figure 6 shows the typical effect of an FI schedule on conditioning.

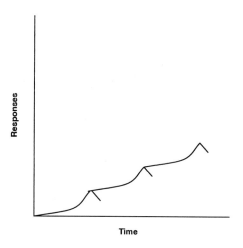

Figure 6. Typical conditioning curve associated with a fixed interval schedule of reinforcement.

Variable Interval

A *variable interval* (VI) schedule sets the rule that reinforcement is delivered on the first occurrence of the target behavior after a specific but variable interval of time has passed. As with the FI schedule, the specified interval must pass, and only after that will the next response

---

[14] Humans tend to exhibit a higher rate of responding on interval schedules because of the role of verbal behavior such as rule following (Pierce & Cheney, 2008). The schedule effect is still applicable across species; it is just that with humans, there is usually a supplementary contingency participating in the resulting responding.

be reinforced. Again, a number and unit of measure specification are included in specific instances. For example, a VI-30sec. would indicate a variable interval schedule of 30 seconds.

Increases in rate are moderate but steady under a VI schedule. It lacks the scalloping of the FI schedule, but the rate remains merely moderate compared with behavior under a ratio schedule.

Figure 7 shows the typical effect of a VI schedule on conditioning.

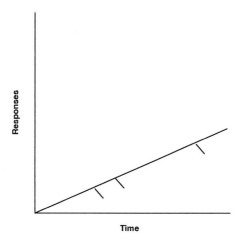

Figure 7. Typical conditioning curve associated with a variable interval schedule of reinforcement.

Fixed duration

A *fixed duration* (FD) schedule sets the rule that the behavior must be exhibited continuously or repeatedly for a specified period of time, before reinforcement is delivered. If the behavior is not exhibited within that time interval, reinforcement is then unavailable. A number and unit specification is included to identify the duration. For example, a behavior put on a fixed duration schedule of 30 seconds would be depicted as FD-30sec. Used on its own, reinforcement is provided on a CRF basis, as long as the duration criterion is met. For example, the FD-30sec. schedule would mean that each response that occurs repeatedly or continuously for 30 seconds is then reinforced.

Variable Duration

A *variable duration* (VD) schedule sets the rule that the behavior must be exhibited continuously or repeatedly for a variable amount of time around a mean average. Again, a number and unit specification is included in specific instances, such as VD-30sec. In this example, the behavior is reinforced only if it occurs repeatedly or continuously for a seemingly random duration around a mean average of 30 seconds in this case. Used on its own, reinforcement is also provided on a CRF basis, as long as the duration criterion is met for each response.

Extinction

An extinction (EXT) schedule sets the rule that no responses will be reinforced. This schedule may initially result in an increase in responding called an *extinction burst*, but responding will then gradually decline until the behavior no longer occurs at all. If the behavior was previously on a variable ratio schedule, the extinction curve may be quite lengthy; if it was on a fixed schedule, particularly CRF, extinction should occur much more quickly.

Jackpotting

The *"Jackpot"* schedule sets the rule that higher magnitude reinforcers will be provided for certain particularly "exceptional" responses and is common in animal training circles, but note the following. Higher magnitude reinforcement can promote quicker conditioning but this is not linear: with each increase, the rate of beneficial effect is decreased. Also note the phenomenon referred to as *negative incentive contrast*, in which decreased responding occurs when going back to the lower magnitude reinforcer from the higher magnitude reinforcer (Nation & Woods, 1980). Jackpotting can be disruptive for these reasons and may not be as beneficial a training practice as some believe it to be. Rather than being explicitly clear and consistent with regard to specific criteria you are working in a training project at any given time, you merely refer to some general (vague) "exceptional" occurrence and target that for higher magnitude reinforcement. By adjusting the criterion to reinforce this "exceptional" occurrence, you are deviating from the consistency of the criterion. You can reinforce that exceptional trial along with other criteria meeting responses and build it up that way. If you jackpot for significant criteria leaps, you may not be able to maintain the new criteria in successive trials and this may become disruptive to conditioning. The effectiveness of jackpotting ought not be taken for granted. More research clarifying jackpotting procedures is warranted.

One practice that is not likely disruptive but still contributes to conditioning in a similar way would be to simply ensure that exceptionally well exhibited occurrences of the criterion behavior *are* reinforced. The reinforcement is qualitatively and quantitatively the same as with other instances of its delivery but whereas in a VR schedule, these particular responses might not always end up being reinforced, so you can set the additional overriding schedule rule that regardless of the schedule, exceptional responses *are* reinforced. Some have referred to this process as ***differential reinforcement of excellent responding*** (DRE). This may be a more productive and less disruptive procedure than jackpotting.

Limited Hold

A ***limited hold*** (LH) is not a schedule per se but rather a schedule extension that may be added to schedules of reinforcement. It sets the additional rule that the reinforcer is only available for a specified period of time after the S^{Ev} occurs. In other words, once the behavior to be reinforced is cued, the behavior must then be exhibited within a specified period of time or else it does not get reinforced. For instance, if an FR-5, LH-8sec. is set, this means that every fifth response will be reinforced if it occurs within 8 seconds of the cue. Similarly if an FI-1min., LH-10sec. is set, this means that the first criterion response to occur after 1 minute is reinforced, but only if the behavior occurs within 10 seconds after the cue was delivered.[15]

Variations on Basic Intermittent Schedules

The following schedules are variations on the simple schedules of reinforcement examined above. Note that even though they are

---

[15] The duration of other responses in the sequence are usually held to the same standard. In other words, if every fifth response is scheduled for reinforcement and there is a limited hold of 8 seconds for that fifth response, trainers usually require that 8 seconds reinforcer availability for each response in order for it to be counted as a criterion meeting response. So, if 5 responses occurred in the sequence but 1 of them occurred after the 8 seconds, then that response is identified as a noncriterion response and there were only 4 criterion responses counted. The limited hold applies to the reinforced response in the sequence but it is common practice to require the limited hold criteria for all responses in the sequence.

referred to as differential reinforcement, they are better classed along with the simple schedules of reinforcement here as variations rather than as examples of the complex schedules examined below.

Differential Reinforcement of Low Rate

Differential reinforcement of low rate of responding (DRL) sets the rule that a fixed interval of time is set after which the next response is reinforced only if no responses occurred during that interval. If a response has occurred during that interval, the clock is reset on the interval. DRL is used to maintain a low rate of responding; it is generally used to reduce the rate of a behavior that is unacceptable at the current rate of responding but would be acceptable at a lower rate. The difference between FI and DRL is that, under the FI schedule, responding during the interval is permissible but simply goes unreinforced, whereas, under the DRL schedule, responding during that interval is prohibited and resets the interval clock. For example, imagine you have a stopwatch and have established a DRL-1min. schedule for a subject who vocalizes more frequently than you would prefer. You push the start button on the stopwatch and wait. If the subject vocalizes during that 1 minute, you push the reset button, and the minute starts counting from 0 again. On the other hand, if the subject did not vocalize during that interval, the very next response that occurs, you provide reinforcement.

It is common to include an LH component to DRL schedules. For example, this would involve starting the clock and, assuming you pass the interval without a response, reinforcement for a response after that interval is only available for a specified period of time. If no response occurs during that window of opportunity, the schedule has ended and the session is either over or you reset the clock to run another trial.

The DRL schedule is used for excessive but acceptable behaviors. Alternatives are an extinction procedure to eliminate the behavior altogether or an antecedent strategy to limit contact with the S^{Ev}. These options are not always appropriate for the specific objectives when it is not possible to limit contact with the S^{Ev} and the behavior is acceptable at a lower rate.

Differential Reinforcement of High Rate

Differential reinforcement of high rate of responding (DRH) sets the rule that a fixed interval of time is set after which the next response is reinforced only if a specified number of responses has already occurred during that interval. DRH is used when a behavior is occurring but not frequently enough. Unlike with DRL, in which no response is permitted during a fixed interval, DRH requires a specific minimum number of responses during the interval. In the DRH schedule, you need to set the interval and also the number of responses that must be surpassed in that interval.

Here is an example of what DRH looks like for a subject who vocalizes but not enough in the specific context under consideration. You set a DRH 10/1min (10 responses during a 1-minute interval). You push the start button on the stopwatch and then start counting responses. The trial is over after the 1-minute interval. If the subject did not exhibit a minimum of 10 vocalization responses before the 1-minute is up, you either end the session, or push the reset button and restart the 1-minute interval for a new trial. If the subject did reach at least 10 vocalization responses in the 1-minute interval, the next response after that interval is reinforced.

Differential Reinforcement of Diminishing Rates

Differential reinforcement of diminishing rates (DRD) is a schedule of reinforcement in which reinforcement is delivered at the end of a predetermined interval if the number of responses is less than a criterion that is gradually reduced across time intervals based on the behavior of the individual (Cooper, et al., 2007). This differs from DRL in that it gradually sets a lower rate as you progress through the training. Once the behavior has declined to the set criterion, the next criterion rate is set, and so on, such that the rate of behavior gradually and incrementally decreases.

Complex Schedules

There are times when multiple schedules are implemented simultaneously. The most common example is the use of a basic ratio or interval schedule along with a fixed duration schedule. For example, let's say that "sit" is on a Fixed Ratio three (FR-3) schedule and you combine that with a Fixed Duration 10 seconds schedule (FD-10sec.), this would mean that every third sit response that occurs continuously for 10 seconds would be reinforced. That would be indicated as FR-3, FD-10sec. Let's say "sit" is on a VR-6 schedule and you combine that with a FD-8sec. schedule; this would mean that every sit that occurs continuously for 8 seconds around a varying but average of every 6 responses would be reinforced. In practice, we frequently also include a limited hold extension.

Combining ratio or interval schedules with duration schedules addresses complex schedules that relate to addressing a single behavior. For instance, when you combine a ratio and a duration schedule, you are specifying criteria for reinforcement of the one behavior under consideration. There are many other complex schedules. A number of useful ones address simultaneously establishing a schedule rule for different procedures and can be thought of as complex schedules in that regard. I will address the differential reinforcement procedures/schedules in the next section.

Differential Reinforcement

Differential reinforcement is a compound procedure, in that it involves more than one principle of behavior or process in a complementary manner. It involves targeting the specified response class for reinforcement and other response classes for extinction (Ledoux, 2014). Trainers commonly think of differential reinforcement being used to target a problem behavior with extinction while simultaneously reinforcing a replacement behavior. This is indeed a powerful use of differential reinforcement, but this procedure is also used in simple training, not just when there is some specific problem behavior to eliminate. You can think of the behavior you want to train as the behavior targeted for reinforcement and any other behavior that the subject might otherwise engage in at that time as the "problem behavior." It is really about criterion behaviors versus noncriterion behaviors, be they specified or not and the rule for reinforcement delivery we assign to each.

There are several variations of differential reinforcement, each of which may be appropriate under different circumstances. The following procedures are some of the more commonly utilized differential reinforcement procedures. I include these mostly for the sake of completeness as our main focus in this book is on simple training rather than on resolving problem behaviors. In other words, our focus is on addressing behavior deficits rather than resolving behavior excesses and these procedures tend to emphasize the resolution of behavioral excesses.

Differential Reinforcement of Incompatible Behavior

Differential reinforcement of incompatible behavior (DRI) involves arranging positive reinforcement for a target response class that is mutually exclusive to the response class that would otherwise be exhibited in that context. For example, a DRI procedure is used when a dog is trained to sit to greet people rather than jumping up on them, by reinforcing sitting and failing to reinforce jumping up. If the extinction-targeted behavior cannot be exhibited at the same time as the reinforcement-targeted behavior, the procedure is DRI.

Differential Reinforcement of Alternative Behavior

Differential reinforcement of alternative behavior (DRA) involves providing positive reinforcement for a response class that, while compatible with the response class that would otherwise be exhibited in that context, is still a specific, different behavior. A DRA procedure is used when the behavior being trained is not mutually exclusive to other behaviors that are likely to compete with it.

Differential Reinforcement of Other Behavior

Differential reinforcement of other behavior (DRO) is often erroneously referred to as differential reinforcement of zero responding. This is an error because it implies reinforcement of no responding. Only behaviors can be reinforced—an absence of behavior cannot be reinforced. DRO involves reinforcing any behavior other than the target problem behavior. However, rarely does any specific behavior become reinforced adequately and the process can readily generate superstitious behaviors. The primary use for DRO schedules are in behavior change programs instated to resolve problem behaviors that are affected by strong aversive emotional behaviors such as would be referred to as fear, panic or anxiety. In these cases, the DRO procedure allows for a very high rate of reinforcement, which is thought to achieve respondent counterconditioning as a byproduct of the operant conditioning taking place. In other words, as you reinforce operant behaviors in the presence of a feared stimulus for instance, the positive reinforcers are paired with that stimulus and the problem stimulus comes to elicit responses similar to those elicited by the treats.

Managing Schedules of Reinforcement

Some of the schedules of reinforcement covered above are more useful than others in certain circumstances and at certain points during a training project. The discussion above could also give the impression that schedules are used in a rather static manner, but they are frequently used in applied settings in a more dynamic way, particularly in the thinning process.

Schedules of reinforcement are vitally important in training because the schedule effects that they generate produce the response characteristics required to achieve the training objectives and because providing continuous trainer-mediated reinforcement is usually not viable in the long run. Selecting a schedule of reinforcement in a training project depends on what effect we need from it. Under most common training situations, we begin with CRF and then quickly transition to VR, LH (with FD if needed). We then gradually thin the ratio. The ratio is reset as soon as the behavior becomes stable at the current level.[16]

We rarely use interval or even FR schedules in training, mainly because of the postreinforcement pause and adjunctive behavior that they tend to generate.

When we begin training for fluency and improving duration, distance, and distraction characteristics of the behavior, we work with these characteristics one at a time; when starting work on each, we relax the schedule of reinforcement, often back to CRF, and re-thin it. Therefore, the schedule of reinforcement typically changes throughout the project, depending on the circumstances. A duration schedule is included where appropriate and a limited hold contingency is instated to reach an acceptable *latency* (the interval of time between the cue and the initiation of the behavior).

Since noncriterion behaviors might occasionally occur during training, we usually use a compound procedure throughout. Differential reinforcement procedures establish rules for meeting reinforcement criteria and also an EXT schedule for failure to meet the reinforcement criteria. Instead of EXT, –P can be used to target noncriterion

---

[16] This progressive thinning of the ratio schedule has been referred to as a *Progressive Ratio Schedule* (Peirce and Cheney, 2013)

behaviors, although this would no longer be a differential reinforcement procedure.

Trainers rarely prepare a detailed plan for the progression of their schedules through a training project, for at least two reasons. First, the choice of schedule is based on actual responding progress during the training session. Second, training typically progresses quickly, with no time for careful planning. Furthermore, the type of progression through schedules is usually the same, as discussed above. For example, in training "sit," you might plan for CRF for the first several trials and then, once the behavior is smooth and reliable, switch to a VR-2, LH-10sec., FD-1sec. schedule. You might then quickly increase the ratio, depending on rate of responding, to ensure around 95% accuracy, and gradually reduce the LH and increase the FD, using EXT for noncriterion responses. Because increasing the ratio depends on ensuring 95% response accuracy, that component of the schedule is adjusted "on the fly," but around 95% criterion responding is a good level of precision as a general starting plan. If EXT is less successful than planned, other components of the plan should be evaluated. If raising the level of aversiveness can be justified, the EXT schedule can be changed to a −P procedure. Part of "good judgment" involves quick adjustment in schedule of reinforcement components "on the fly."

Differential Outcome Effect

The ***differential outcome effect*** is a robust behavioral phenomenon whereby discrimination (evocation) training occurs more quickly and the discrimination is more accurate when different behaviors contact different reinforcers. For example, if you are training a dog to sit, stand, and down, and you are randomly cuing each behavior, your training will be more efficient and effective if you follow each of the three behaviors with different reinforcers rather than just one. For instance, sit might generate kibble, down might generate a piece of veggie burger, and stand might generate a piece of apple. This makes the three contingencies more distinct than if the consequence were the same in all cases, and this greater distinction may be the reason for the effect. It can be particularly useful when working on intercue discrimination (evocation) training.

Activity Reinforcers (the Premack Principle)

The **Premack principle** states that the opportunity to engage in a higher probability behavior can reinforce occurrence of a lower probability behavior. That is, if an individual is more likely to exhibit one behavior than another, the opportunity to exhibit the behavior that they are most likely to exhibit can actually reinforce occurrence of the behavior that they are less likely to exhibit. For example, if you eat your broccoli, you can then eat your cake. Assuming that eating cake is a higher probability behavior than eating broccoli, you can use the opportunity to engage in cake eating as a reinforcer for broccoli eating. This has also been referred to as an **activity reinforcer**.

In dog training, the dog contacts a more effective reinforcer while exhibiting a "higher probability" behavior, and the opportunity to engage in the behavior that generates this more effective reinforcer can be used to reinforce some other, less probable behavior. A consequence of this principle in dog training is that you do not always have to use treats to reinforce behaviors. This might be done at first in the acquisition phase of training but there are many reinforcers available to dogs on a daily basis, and the opportunity to engage in behaviors that function to contact these effective reinforcers in the real world can be used to reinforce an unrelated behavior. For example, you can reinforce walking at your side on a loose leash with the opportunity to sniff a fire hydrant, reinforce sitting while the door is opened with getting to run outside. The trick is to make the opportunity to engage in the higher probability behavior contingent on exhibiting the lower probability behavior. The Premack principle helps us appreciate that we can take advantage of a wide range of things other than treats to reinforce behaviors. This is particularly important in the maintenance phase of training.[17]

---

[17] The notion of activity reinforcers is arbitrary in many, if not most or all cases. After all, we can refer to the opportunity to eat a treat as an activity reinforcer, or we can simply refer to the treat as a reinforcer. There is a way of specifying an activity in most cases that we do not consider to be activity reinforcers; the behavior the subject engages in that brings them into contact with the reinforcer is an activity. However, the Premack principle is useful in evoking attention to everyday reinforcers over more contrived trainer-mediated reinforcers.

Antecedent Processes and Procedures

The previous section mainly related to principles and processes that influence subsequent behavior by directly affecting the postcedent environment. In this section, I will explore principles, processes and procedures that influence behavior by affecting the antecedent environment. Primarily, this includes prompting, and also expanding or contracting the number of stimuli that will come to evoke the behavior. After this section, I will address more advanced topics, including some further antecedent conditions such as function-altering stimulation.

Stimulus Control: Generalization and Discrimination (Evocation) Training

Stimulus control refers to a range of phenomena relating to antecedent control of behavior (Ledoux, 2014, p. 279). Our coverage will include the two basic processes of generalization and discrimination, including the procedure for transferring stimulus control. Generalization and discrimination (evocation), which are inversely related, involve increasing or decreasing the range of stimuli that evoke the behavior.

Generalization

Generalization[18] is the process by which the range or set of evocative stimuli increases. That is, other antecedent stimuli also come to evoke the behavior in question. Reinforcement functions to strengthen not only the specific antecedent → behavior contingency it follows, but also shared features of them. In other words, when reinforcement occurs, similar stimuli (sharing common features) also become reinforced—this results in a spread (widening) of the stimuli that may evoke the behavior.

Generalization can be promoted by trainer-mediated procedures or by nontrainer-mediated events. Because stimuli with shared or similar features will tend to be evocatively strengthened by reinforcement,

---

[18] Generalization is also applicable to respondent conditioning. Where we discuss operant processes, we generally leave out the word operant; we include the word respondent when we are specifying a respondent process.

these similar stimuli will come, through repeated trials, to take on stimulus control over the behavior in question. The less similar a stimulus is—that is, the fewer shared salient features—the less likely the stimulus is to take on stimulus control. For instance, if you train a behavior to be cued by the word "sit," and the word "sip" also comes to evoke the behavior, that is an indication that generalization has occurred, but you are likely to find that the word "down" does not evoke the behavior in question. This is because "down" and "sit" do not share enough features to have been strengthened by the reinforcement of the "sit" cue and sitting behavior.

Another important generalization process involves the transfer of stimulus control from a stimulus that currently functions as the S^{Ev} for a behavior to some other stimulus that does not. Once a behavior occurs reliably immediately after a specific stimulus is presented, we say that the behavior is under ***stimulus control***. This is the process by which cues for behaviors are established. Stimuli can be categorized by what sensory system they impact upon.

To transfer stimulus control between stimuli that affect the same sensory system, one can simply take advantage of stimulus generalization and gradually make the old, established stimulus seem more and more like the new one through repeated trials. The subject will respond to the new stimulus because it shares some similar properties with the previous stimulus and through repeated trials, all of the features of that new stimulus will be strengthened until the new stimulus takes on stimulus control. This is called a ***prompt fading*** procedure. For example, when transferring stimulus control from a luring motion to a hand signal that is not similar enough to allow immediate generalization (both visual stimuli), we can gradually make the old luring motion look more and more like the new hand signal until we have achieved reliable stimulus control with the new hand signal. On each trial, you make the motion look just a little bit less like the lure motion and just a little bit more like the hand signal motion.

To transfer stimulus control between stimuli that are different sensory system categories, we cannot take advantage of this gradual generalization process. In this case, we use the following contingency sequence: new stimulus → old stimulus → behavior → reinforcement. This is called a ***prompt delay*** procedure. Through repeated trials, the new stimulus will take on stimulus control over the behavior. For example, when transferring stimulus control from a hand signal to a verbal cue (such as "sit"), we have different sensory system categories—one stimulus is visual and the other auditory. We would carry out the sequence: "sit" → hand signal → subject sits → reinforcement. In all of these cases, the range of stimuli that will evoke the behavior of concern increases and hence generalization occurs. You can test whether the procedure has been successful by delaying presentation of the old stimulus and observing whether the behavior occurs or not. You can encourage generalization by allowing reinforcement of behavior evoked by similar but not identical stimuli. Alternatively, you can discourage it through discrimination training, discussed below.

For completeness sake, ***response generalization***, another form of generalization, involves an increase in the range of operants evoked by a stimulus. Not every member of a response set is identical and in response generalization, the range of dissimilarity increases. You can promote this by allowing reinforcement of such variations in responding or you can discourage it by reinforcing only the very specific response you want and extinguishing similar variants.

Discrimination (Evocation)

Discrimination (evocation)[19] reduces the set of stimuli that will evoke the behavior rather than enlarging it (as in generalization). ***Discrimination (evocation) training*** is a procedure in which the S^{Ev} set is decreased by systematically scheduling reinforcement for responding to the precise stimulus set in question, while arranging to extinguish responding to other stimulus sets that might share some features but are not strictly members of the set targeted for reinforcement. The stimulus to be reinforced is the S^{Ev} and the stimuli to be extinguished are referred to as S-delta and symbolized S^{Δ}. Trials are arranged that include the specific stimulus to be discriminated as well as other similar stimuli. Responses upon addition of the S^{Ev} are reinforced, whereas responses upon the addition of the other stimuli (S^{Δ}) are extinguished. Through this training process, the S^{Ev} is

---

[19] The term discrimination training and discrimination are still common, just as the term discriminative stimulus is but the current trend is to refer to evocation training and evocative stimulus. Whereas discrimination refers to something the subject would do, suggestive of an inner agent and causing confusion, evocation refers to what the stimulus functions to achieve, which is more accurate and less problematic. I will retain the more traditional terminology in this text regarding discrimination training to ease the transition to newer terminology.

strengthened, and S$^{\Delta}$ that might otherwise become evocative are weakened.

For example, if you train a dog to sit when greeting you and the dog begins sitting to greet other people as well, stimulus generalization has occurred. You might reinforce this as a "general" rule and promote a greater degree of generalization, having the dog sit to greet anyone they meet. On the other hand, let's say you want the dog to sit to greet only you and no one else. In that case, you reinforce sitting to greet you, but when this occurs in response to others, you ensure it is not reinforced, thus the range of evocative stimuli is maintained narrow. Or, let's say you train a dog to wave a paw when you say "wave" and you reinforce each instance of this. You might then carry out discrimination training by saying "waze" and failing to reinforce if the dog waves. You could present other similar stimuli and do the same thing, with trials of "wave" mixed in, which you do reinforce. You will find that discrimination occurs. Instead of a wider range of stimuli evoking the behavior only that narrow stimulus-set evokes the waving behavior and other similar stimuli no longer do. To take it a step further, you might promote stimulus generalization by reinforcing when any person says "wave" at the same time as you carry out discrimination training to restrict the S^{Ev} to the exact word "wave" and not similar-sounding words. Generalization and discrimination training are used to ensure that the "right" stimuli evoke a behavior and the "wrong" stimuli do not.

Prompting

A **_prompt_** is any antecedent stimulus, other than the designated primary stimulus, that contributes to evoking the behavior of concern. The **_primary stimulus_** is the currently nonevocative or weakly evocative stimulus designated to be the cue for the behavior after conditioning. Recall that when reinforcement occurs, it reinforces all of the antecedent stimuli present and that includes any nonevocative stimuli we might seek to install as the primary cue as well as any prompts we might use and even some perhaps unintended but present stimuli. The prompt is used in order to generate the behavior in the presence of the primary stimulus so that the primary stimulus will take on stimulus control (along with other present stimuli). The evocative capacity of the prompt and the primary stimulus will be reinforced.

Once the primary stimulus takes on stimulus control over the behavior, the prompts are gradually *faded*, leaving the primary stimulus with a strong capacity to evoke the behavior on its own (Fraley, 2008, pp. 845–848). Fading the prompt as soon as practicable is important because with each trial, it too, along with the primary stimulus, takes on stimulus control of the behavior and if it becomes too well established, it will require more extensive discrimination training (including extinction trials) to eliminate. The unfaded prompt can become an established component of the S^{Ev} or act as a function-altering stimulus (to be discussed below), meaning that the behavior becomes *prompt dependent*.

Establishing and strengthening the capacity of a stimulus to evoke behavior is a major part of what training achieves. The challenge in these situations is to generate the behavior to begin with so that we can reinforce it and thereby strengthen the capacity of antecedent stimuli to evoke the behavior. In this case, we have the option to shape successive approximations of the behavior, something I will introduce further along as an advanced procedure. There are times when shaping is preferable but if all else is equal, and prompting is possible, it is the quicker means of generating the behavior. If we can utilize other stimuli or an accumulation of stimuli to, all together, evoke the behavior then we do not need to resort to shaping the behavior. Once the behavior is evoked, it may be reinforced. This reinforcement strengthens the capacity of all antecedent stimuli present at that time to evoke the behavior.

Sometimes, you will have the primary stimulus and prompt stimuli present together, both contributing to generating the behavior, and once both have been strengthened sufficiently, the prompt is gradually faded. In many cases though, your prompts will do the vast majority of the evocative work, so to speak, and you will then, once it has taken on enough stimulus control to evoke the behavior alone, transfer stimulus control to a newly introduced stimulus. So, prompts can be used along with the primary stimulus as a supplementary S^{Ev} or alone and the primary stimulus introduced once the behavior can be generated reliably. Often in this latter case, the prompt is actually evoking attending behavior or approach/contact behavior and as we manipulate the prompt stimulus, the target behavior is exhibited as the subject moves to attend, orient and approach the prompt. Some examples will help.

You might train a naïve dog to come to you by saying "here," which tends to exert weak evocative control merely because you are looking at them and vocalizing something, which often evokes approach behavior. But, it may be too weakly evocative to ensure quick and reliable approach every single time, so you prompt the behavior by supplementing the "here" with waving motions and high pitched noises that, together with the primary stimulus, generate the behavior effectively and later these prompts can be gradually faded out. This is a prime example of prompts used as supplementary evocative stimuli.

On the other hand, when training a dog to sit, you may utilize a treat in your hand to generate ***targeting*** behavior (i.e., attending, orienting and approach behaviors) and the dog follows the treat with his or her nose, which, as you move it over his or her head, he or she sits and the behavior is generated. In that case, the prompt generates the behavior pretty much alone without the primary stimulus. With each trial, the prompt takes on stimulus control of the behavior until we fade it, transferring stimulus control to either an intermediate (e.g., hand signal) or the final S^{Ev} (e.g., verbal cue), in either case, the primary stimulus.

Once the primary stimulus becomes capable of reinforcing the behavior, generalization has occurred in that there are now a greater number of stimuli that will evoke the behavior, and at that time the prompt can be gradually faded. ***Fading*** often involves presenting the prompt in a slightly less salient or prominent form with each successive trial until it is no longer being presented at all. In some very common training scenarios, the prompt is gradually transformed into what will be the S^{Ev} for the behavior, be it temporary or permanent. For example, when prompting a sit behavior with a luring prompt, the now redundant prompt is gradually made to look less and less like the luring motion and more and more like a hand signal that will then be used to evoke the behavior. This kind of fading is called prompt fading.

As mentioned, prompts are often categorized by the sensory system that they impinge upon. For instance olfactory prompts involve the transfer of energy from the stimulus to the organism through the olfactory system (smell). Tactile prompts contact the touch sensitive nerves. Visual prompts impact upon the optic nerve in the eye. Aural prompts impact upon the ear and are heard.

Sometimes physical manipulation is mistaken for prompting. A tactile prompt might involve a touch but it does not force a behavior. The so-called "physical prompt"—such as pushing on a dog's hips to generate a sit—is better called a physical manipulation. A prompt adds a contributory S^{Ev}, but physical force or manipulation is not evocative—it is just force. In fact, a physically forced behavior is not really a behavior for the subject at all (although other, often problematic, behaviors can be evoked in that scenario such as opposition or countercontrol). The fundamental problem with physical manipulation is that it is usually distracting and can disrupt training, depending on how intrusive it is. The reason it is distracting is that it can often be aversive; it also tends to introduce a separate distinct contingency into the training contingency. When one applies force to an animal, the animal may indeed eventually exhibit the behavior intended (or merely allow the movement to be forced) but it also elicits an opposition reflex, which means that the opposite muscles are activated. A physical manipulation that achieves the movement as the dog pushes against pressure may therefore promote a completely different behavior—at best. Applying the "dead body test," it is not even a behavior at all where it is just a matter of people manipulating dogs into positions; the behaviors that are exhibited in this situation are usually countercontrolling behaviors in response to the manipulation. At worst, physical manipulation imposes aversive stimulation, which also tends to disrupt conditioning.

Note that certain kinds of barricades that might be used in training—for example, practicing sit with the dog in a corner so that they cannot back up, or using a chair or leg to lure through to achieve a down—are not prompts. Prompts might also be used, but the barricade is a preclusion procedure and not a prompt procedure. It functions to prevent the possibility of certain behaviors (forms or variations) being exhibited, and can be removed later.

Advanced Operant Conditioning Processes and Procedures

In this section, I will elaborate on a few more advanced topics in the analysis of operant contingencies. I will start with introducing the idea of adding terms to contingency analyses to make contingencies with four, five, or even more terms. Next, I will elaborate on behavior episodes involving more than one contingency, including competing contingencies. Finally, I will introduce adjunctive behavior. Each of these topics will contribute to a fuller comprehension of behavior and its analysis.

Multiple-Term Contingencies

Contingencies are written with as many terms as are needed to adequately describe functional relations in behavioral episodes under consideration. Three terms are common in the simplest contingency analyses, but expanding the number of terms can provide added explanatory power, which can provide a finer-grained accounting of the behavioral episode when the terms to be added exert significant control over the behavior. Terms can be added to the antecedent, behavior, or postcedent components of the contingency. Thus far, I have explicated the basic two- and three-term contingencies. Here, I will elaborate on four and greater term contingencies. Note that adding terms does not necessarily provide a more complete accounting of the behavior episode; in some cases, it can provide needless complexity.

Added Consequating Terms

While training, we are commonly under contingencies to simply refer to a "treat," for example, as the consequence. In many cases, this is adequate, depending on what features of the episode are important, but frequently we use a conditioned reinforcer in training processes, and it can become important to include reference to this in our analysis. This contingency has the following form:

$$S^{Ev} \rightarrow \text{Behavior} \rightarrow \text{Consequence}_1 \rightarrow \text{Consequence}_2$$

The specific contingency would look like this:

$$\text{"Sit"} \rightarrow \text{Jake sits} \rightarrow \text{Click} \rightarrow \text{Contact with treat}$$

In most cases, this added term is not necessary.

Added Behavior Terms

Occasionally, a sequence of behaviors becomes important in an analysis, rather than either ignoring the extra behaviors or clumping the behaviors together in a general description of the response set. In this case, the contingency might have the following form:

$$S^{Ev} \rightarrow Behavior_1 \rightarrow Behavior_2 \rightarrow Consequence$$

The specific contingency would look like this:

"Mat $\rightarrow$ Jake walks to mat$_1$ $\rightarrow$ Jake lies down on mat$_2$ $\rightarrow$ Treat

The second behavior, which is definitely a behavior, could also be construed as a conditioned reinforcer, which helps maintain the chain of behaviors. Chaining of behaviors will be discussed in detail below.

Added Antecedent Terms (Function-Altering Stimuli)

Occasionally, a stimulus will exert control over a behavior in certain circumstances but not in other circumstances. In these situations, there is some other stimulus present besides the S^{Ev} that alters the evocative capacity of the S^{Ev}. The function-altering stimulus actually changes the organism in such a way that the organism responds differently to the S^{Ev}. The function-altering stimulus does not actually change the S^{Ev} directly as implied by the verbal short cut utilized when we say it changes the evocative capacity of the S^{Ev}. We often call these stimuli the "circumstances" or "context" of the situation. These antecedent stimuli, sometimes referred to as "distant antecedents," "setting events," "occasion setters," "sensitization," "enabling stimuli," "establishing and abolishing operations" or simply "context," can be referred to broadly as *function-altering stimuli* (S^{FA}) because they affect the likelihood of the S^{Ev} evoking the behavior (Fraley, 2008, pp. 509–533). S^{FA} are distinct from the S^{Ev} that evokes the behavior; they are stimuli that provide a context, or additional stimulation that changes the evocative capacity of the S^{Ev}. They do not evoke the behavior themselves. Specific behavioral processes such as establishing and abolishing operations, enabling stimuli, sensitization, habituation, and potentiation, etc., can act as S^{FA} in contingencies. Note that prompts are not S^{FA}. A prompt adds evocative stimuli, whereas S^{FA} only change the evocative capacity of other stimuli. Consideration of context (S^{FA}) will help us achieve a higher degree of explanatory power in our contingency analysis.

As an example of S^{FA}, suppose your job is to sit in a bunker, and insert and turn a key that launches nuclear missiles when you are authorized to do so in the form of a verbal command received through a red phone in the bunker. The mechanistic two-term contingency explaining why the behavior is exhibited would involve the key slot evoking the key-inserting and key-turning behaviors. But this accounting is inadequate because the keyhole is always present and does not always evoke key inserting and turning behaviors. To adequately analyze this contingency, we need to include another antecedent stimulus. In this case, the phone call and order act as an S^{FA} that sets the occasion to make the keyhole, previously a neutral stimulus, into an S^{Ev}. The order is the first antecedent term (an S^{FA}), the keyhole is the S^{Ev}, the behavior would be the key-inserting and key-turning behavior, and the reinforcer is as yet unspecified (likely some kind of covert verbal supplemental conditioned reinforcer).

Fraley (2008, p. 512) provides an excellent example of an S^{FA} in which the presence of a fire alarm lever will evoke lever-pulling operants, but not always. In many instances, the lever is a neutral stimulus rather than an S^{Ev}. Consideration of context (function-altering stimuli) will help us achieve a higher degree of explanatory power in our contingency analysis. The presence of flames or smoke (S^{FA}) alters the capacity of the lever (the S^{Ev}) to evoke the lever-pulling operant. Without the presence of the S^{FA}, the maintaining consequences would not occur; merely pressing a lever any time you see one would not likely be reinforced, and indeed a punitive consequence would likely suppress it (Fraley, 2008, p. 512).

Another important example might involve a situation in which a dog sits when the word "sit" is vocalized, but only if treats are obviously present (an S^{FA}). The verbal cue evokes the behavior reliably, but only if the treats are present. You can see why this fourth term becomes important in adequately explaining and predicting the behavior. The verbal cue is the S^{Ev}, and the presence of the treats is the S^{FA} because it functions to alter the capacity of the S^{Ev} to evoke the behavior. This is what can happen if food prompts are not faded; the behavior becomes prompt dependent. The verbal cue is the S^{Ev} and the treat presence would be the S^{FA} because it functions to alter the capacity of the S^{Ev} to evoke the behavior.

Notice the phrase "only if" in these examples. When you encounter a behavior episode that evokes an "only if" descriptor, you know that an S^{FA} is present.

In some cases, it can be challenging to determine which stimulus should be assigned the S^{FA} position and which the S^{Ev} position in a contingency explaining the functional relation between these two antecedent stimuli. By general convention, the independent variable is written on the left, and the dependent variable on the right (Fraley, 2008, pp. 515–516). The question remains, which is which? Catania (1998, p. 265) provides a good example with an obvious distinction. If someone says the stove is hot, that clearly alters the function of the stove. The stove may now evoke retreat or avoidance behaviors. The verbal warning is clearly the S^{FA} and the stove is clearly the S^{Ev} and not the other way around. However, many cases will not be so obvious. Does the lever evoke lever-pulling behavior only if flames are present or do flames evoke lever-pulling only if a lever is present? When the S^{FA} and the S^{Ev} coincide in time, as will be the case in dog training, the two stimuli may be separated experimentally; one of the stimuli is discriminative for the behavior and the other is not (Schlinger & Blakely, 1987). In our case, if you present flames, any number of behaviors could be exhibited and the flames themselves would not alone evoke lever-pulling behavior. The lever, on the other hand, could very well evoke lever-pulling behavior under various circumstances; the lever is discriminative. In this case, the lever is necessarily required for the behavior to occur. Furthermore, an S^{Ev} does not establish or alter discriminative relations; their control over behavior is evocative (Schlinger & Blakely, 1987). The lever, in this example, does not alter any other stimulus's capacity to evoke lever-pulling behavior but the flames do.

In the case of the treat-dependent sitting dog, the word "sit" evokes sitting behavior *only if* treats are present. The cue "sit" is evocative for sitting behavior, as opposed to any number of other behaviors. It is discriminative in this instance. The verbal cue "sit" does not alter the treats to evoke behavior. The dog does not sit, as opposed to stand, down, or anything else, because the presence of treats evokes it. Sit is the S^{Ev} and treats are the S^{FA} because "sit" is evocative for sitting in this relation. The point here is that it will not always be obvious which stimulus is the S^{Ev}, and which is the S^{FA}. When in doubt, separate the stimuli, and consider which could be evocative as opposed to altering the function of the other.

Below is a general depiction of a four-term contingency:

$$S^{FA} \to S^{Ev} \to \text{Behavior} \to \text{Consequence}$$

This can be depicted, as in the previous examples, in a way that illustrates how the contingency functions to strengthen the antecedent stimuli. Notice how we begin with a stimulus that, alone, does not evoke any behavior. This is a neutral stimulus (S^N). In this case, you can see that only when another stimulus is present does that stimulus evoke the behavior, and a reinforcing consequence functions to strengthen the capacity of the S^{Ev} to evoke the behavior *only* when the S^{FA} is present. In other words, the reinforcer strengthens both the $S^{Ev} \rightarrow$ Behavior and the $S^{FA} \rightarrow S^{Ev}$ contingencies.

$$S^N \text{ - Behavior - No Consequence}$$

Motivation is a somewhat colloquial term referring to function altering antecedent conditions that set the occasion for a behavior. One might say that their being hungry motivates eating, being warm motivates turning on a fan, or that fear motivates running away from something etc. Motivation is usually invoked when some antecedent condition exists such that an established $S^{Ev} \rightarrow$ behavior contingency resolves that condition. Laraway and colleagues (2003) proposed the term **motivating operation** to specifically refer to a condition of the body being satiated or deprived with regard to a consequence, which makes a behavior more or less likely to occur. This might be a rather narrow use of the term motivation,[20] but the operations included under this rubric can be quite useful—we will discuss them in detail now.

Motivating operations include establishing and abolishing operations and are specific kinds of S^{FA}. These are operations that result in a satiated body or a deprived body respectively. The terms establishing and abolishing operations covers the logical possibilities of making behavior more or less likely for reinforcers or punishers by manipulating how satiated or deprived the body is with regard to the

---

[20] For example, this use of the term motivation may account nicely for hunger and being warm in the examples above but does not so easily account for fear motivating escape behavior.

reinforcers maintaining the behavior of concern. ***Establishing operations*** make S^{Ev} more evocative, and ***abolishing operations*** make S^{Ev} less evocative. Our interest here is with making S^{Ev} for positively reinforced behavior more or less likely. In that context, we cause the body to be satiated with regard to the reinforcer and this makes the S^{Ev} *less* evocative (an abolishing operation) or we cause the body to be deprived with regard to the reinforcer and this makes the S^{Ev} *more* evocative (an establishing operation). Establishing operations and abolishing operations refer to the procedure we implement to establish or abolish the evocative capacity of a stimulus while satiation and deprivation refer to the state of the body in relation to the reinforcer. Deprivation is defined by a historical interval during which a body does not contact a reinforcer—the longer the interval, the more deprived the body. Conversely, a satiated body would be one that has been exposed to the reinforcer. Deprivation and satiation are inversely related. A deprived body is *more* disposed to exhibit behavior that has historically contacted that reinforcer and a satiated body is *less* disposed to exhibit behavior that has historically contacted that reinforcer. Establishing operations (a kind of S^{FA}) can be used to make behaviors we are targeting for reinforcement more likely (Fraley, 2008, pp. 844–845). Excessive deprivation is counterproductive, and indeed abusive, but a mild deprivation state—for example, hunger that commonly occurs before meals—can make training with food reinforcers more effective at that time. The satiated or deprived bodies are temporarily so structured as to affect responsiveness to stimuli.

As with prompts, S^{FA} can be faded. Once the training is well under way and the S^{Ev} is effective with a deprived body, you can gradually eliminate the condition of deprivation from your training sessions (Fraley, 2008, pp. 853–855). Although a satiated body will make training with food reinforcers less effective, the behavior will now be less under control of trainer-mediated reinforcers and more under control of nontrainer-mediated ones. This means that the food becomes less important as you proceed and the behavior becomes somewhat self-reinforcing. Professional trainers are quite familiar with the phenomenon of a dog beginning to reject treat reinforcers, apparently eager not to delay further opportunity to exhibit the behavior.

More complex multiple-term contingency analyses exist, but these three- and four-term contingencies will suffice for now. Interested readers are directed to Fraley (2008) for discussion of multiple-term contingencies and S^{FA}.

Concurrent Contingencies

Real life is dynamic and complex. Rarely is there a single contingency operating on an individual at any given moment. In fact there might never be, even in a highly controlled laboratory. In the real world, there are multiple concurrent and often competing contingencies operating on individuals vying for control over behavior. They might include reinforcers available for different behaviors and even punishers competing with reinforcers. When more than one contingency is competing for control over behavior, many unfortunately refer to this as "choice," as though the "mind" may initiatively select one of them. Although, at least with humans, much thought shares control of covert behaviors that some may refer to as "choices," these thoughts are behaviors, which are themselves evoked and controlled by environmental stimuli. So-called "choice arrangements" are better framed as *concurrent contingencies*. The reason it is useful to appreciate concurrent contingencies is that, when training, it is important to control as many of the contingencies as possible to ensure that we can get and reinforce the selected behavior instead of any number of other behaviors that might otherwise be evoked and reinforced.

A simple arrangement involves an experiment in which a pigeon may peck at one of two buttons, one of which generates reinforcement each time, and the other never generates reinforcement. Obviously, the pigeon will spend time pecking the button that generates the reinforcement and not the other button. This is a form of behavior economics: animals tend to behave efficiently with regard to maximizing reinforcers, and this is implicit in the notion of reinforcement itself. More complex arrangements involve the availability of opportunities to peck one of two buttons that generate reinforcement for every sixth response or ninth response, for example. In the initial acquisition stage, pigeons will spend time pecking both buttons, but once the responding stabilizes, the pigeon will settle on pecking at the button that generates the richest reinforcement.

In any case, dogs, like pigeons (or cats or parrots or humans) can be expected to exhibit the behavior that generates the most reinforcement relative to other behaviors. The ***matching law*** states that the distribution of behaviors will match the frequency of available reinforcers. One of our goals as trainers is to arrange the environment such that the target behavior requires less response effort than other behaviors, and generates more reinforcers or more effective reinforcers than the various other behaviors that might otherwise occur at that time. There are many ways such manipulations can be made. Highly effective reinforcers for the target behaviors and the use of mild deprivation beforehand will ensure that it is the most effective reinforcer that is being utilized. If the most effective reinforcer was previously available for some other behavior, that reinforcer can be made contingent on occurrence of the target behavior instead. The response effort (i.e., the energy expenditure required to perform the behavior) can be minimized for the target behavior, and increased, where possible, for competing behaviors. A schedule of reinforcement that competes favorably with other reinforcers available to the subject at that time can be used initially.

We are commonly under contingencies to simplify our contingency analyses by identifying only the contingency exerting the most influence over the behavior of concern. However, sometimes a finer-grained comprehension of the episode and the result makes consideration of other concurrent contingencies appropriate. You might find when you are trying to train a behavior that the rate of progress is slower than you expected. You are then under contingencies to analyze that situation more carefully, usually to identify competing contingencies that are reducing the rate of progress. In any given situation, even one that might seem simple for the most part, there may be many contingencies simultaneously exerting control over the behavior exhibited in that situation. Conflicts between concurrent contingencies might involve a conflict between two different behaviors or a conflict between the consequences generated by the same behavior; indeed, both of these kinds of conflicts can exist at the same time. There might be different S^{Ev} present, both exerting some control over evoking competing behavior. In other situations multiple sources of positive and negative reinforcement are available, and perhaps multiple sources of punishment are available. The prevailing behavior will be the net result of the accumulated reinforcement and punishment.

For instance, from a previous example, Jake lying down on his mat, the treat was the positive reinforcer of interest, and thus it was made prominent by using that contingency alone to explain the behavioral episode. Let's assume that training is not as smooth and reliable as you would like or expect, and so you are now under contingencies to analyze the situation in more depth toward the goal of controlling the behavior more effectively. Perhaps in that same situation, Jake was playing for quite some time (satiation) and relief from the physical exertion negatively reinforced lying down. You might also find competing contingencies. Perhaps Jake had been playing for only a little while (deprivation) at the time the cue was delivered and going to the mat was negatively punished by having to leave his toy. Also, in all contingencies of reinforcement, response effort is inherently punitive although the reinforcers usually outweigh the punitive aspects of expending the energy to exhibit the behavior that contacts the reinforcers.

The point is that most behavioral episodes are complex mixtures of more than one contingency, often involving competing contingencies that might present in slow progress, or vacillating behavior, or some other kind of disruption to the training process. More careful analysis can often help you identify these "reasons" for the slow progress, so that you can make adjustments to the environment to make the training more efficient. When undertaking such an analysis, write out each contingency separately, one below the other, ideally in rank order of what you believe to be the relative strength of the contingencies. This added analytical clarity could help resolve these kinds of problems.

Reequilibration (Expansion the Concept of Extinction)

Traditionally, extinction is defined as a process by which a previously positively reinforced behavior is followed by an abrupt prevention of the reinforcement and a subsequent decline in responding, as discussed above. One could logically apply extinction to both kinds of reinforcement, and to both kinds of punishment as well. In fact, the *"learned helplessness"* phenomenon is likely extinction of negatively reinforced behavior. Extinction does not need to be an abrupt process either; the postcedent environment can be made more and more like the antecedent environment gradually. The word extinction becomes troublesome when we apply it to punishment because the word extinction generally connotes a decline in something but extinction of punished behavior results in an increase instead. The term **reequilibration** is used for this broader application of extinction, as applied, abruptly, or gradually, and to reinforcement, or punishment, because the behavior returns in all cases to its previous equilibrium rate, while it was undergoing the conditioning process. I will not delve into this topic further as it is not necessary for our purposes but interested readers can refer to Fraley (2008, pp. 438–472).

Adjunctive Behavior

Adjunctive behavior is operant behavior that appears intermittently while other operant behaviors are being exhibited (Fraley, 2008, p. 601). It often appears strange or out of context since it seems unrelated to the prevailing contingencies operating at the time. Adjunctive behavior is a schedule effect. It is most common in fixed schedules, particularly fixed interval schedules and occurs during the initial part of the interval when reinforcers are not available. You might think of it as behavior that intrudes during the postreinforcement wane in responding associated with fixed schedules of reinforcement. During this interval when reinforcers are unavailable, other antecedent stimuli that exert weaker control than the stimuli that are controlling the primary behavior briefly become more evocative and can become prepotent in controlling behavior at that time. As a cyclic process occurring along with a primary behavior and its reinforcement, adjunctive behaviors can be reinforced; they can even become excessive. When you are training and observe other behaviors between cycles of reinforcement availability, you should consider the possibility that they are adjunctive behaviors. You can control these other antecedent stimuli and adjust the schedule you are using— perhaps to a variable schedule—to eliminate these adjunctive behaviors.

Adjunctive behavior is distinct from situations in which some antecedent stimulus simply becomes more strongly evocative than the antecedent stimulus that had previously prevailed. In these cases, the change in behavior is due not to a schedule effect but rather to a change in the relative evocative capacity of different stimuli, as a result of satiation, deprivation, or other variables. Changes in behavior due to a schedule effect or some S^{FA} may be seen as strange, "abnormal," or mysterious, but they are not mysterious or abnormal at all—a careful analysis of the contingencies will reveal the functional relations operating in a perfectly normal and natural law-abiding manner (Fraley, 2008, pp. 601–631).

Species-Typical Behavior (Where Phylogeny Meets Ontogeny)

Organisms do not come as blank slates. Evolution generates populations with some unconditioned behaviors. That is, genetically, individual members of species are so structured as to exhibit certain shared behavioral tendencies and responses to certain environmental stimulation because their bodies have evolved to do so. These unconditioned responses to stimuli that the species' anatomical structure generates form the basis for the biological context in which operant processes occur. The behavior relations that arise within the natural history of the *species* are genetically based and established by evolution by natural selection are referred to as ***phylogenetic***, whereas the behavior relations that arise within the natural history of the *individual*, within their own lifetime, are referred to as ***ontogenetic***.

It is important to note that respondent and operant behaviors are always occurring, including simultaneously. Contingencies involving species-typical respondent behaviors can participate or contribute in operant contingency processes (Peirce & Cheney, 2013). Unconditioned responses to certain stimuli that automatically (endogenously) function as reinforcers are instances of species-typical—phylogenetic—behavior. Most species share a number of similar unconditioned responses. For instance, food, water, and sex are effective unconditioned reinforcers for most mammalian and avian species. That is because these stimuli contribute to reproductive success in most species.

Species are also structured such that specific operant behaviors readily become prepotent. For instance, dogs bark, whereas crows caw. Dogs also dig under certain circumstances, and exhibit various social behaviors, such as the play bow and showing of teeth, growling, snarling etc. Conditioning, of course, can change these behavior relations, but the individual members of the species come genetically disposed (or "prepared") to exhibit these behavioral tendencies.

Phylogenetic selection is generally left to ethologists to study and this can inform us on the biological context in which the behavior we work with occurs. It is important to become familiar with the species-typical behavioral tendencies of species you train (in this case, dogs) because training occurs within the context of these tendencies. Moreover, these behavioral tendencies typically allow you to predict near future behavior. For example, if a dog stiffens up, flags his tail high in the air, and gives you a hard stare, this indicates a certain emotional arousal and the likely evocation of potentially harmful aggressive behaviors. If the dog maintains a relaxed stance with a gently wagging tail and gives a softer eye contact, the dog is likely receptive to training. If a dog runs toward you, bounding with a lumbering gate, this indicates something quite different than if the dog walks very slowly toward you, keeping their eyes on you at all times with a lowered head. If a dog exhibits a play bow, this indicates something quite different than if the dog is panting with a wide mouth, leaving furrows in the fur below the eyes. These species-typical social behavioral patterns indicate the occurrence of different contingencies at work, which can influence whether training should take place, and how effective training will be, or how your approach should be adjusted.

Since the principles of behavior are universal across species, appreciating species-typical behavior can sometimes be neglected, but anyone training someone else should appreciate the species-typical behavior patterns associated with that species, be they dogs, cats, or humans. Ethology and anthropology can help illuminate these behavioral tendencies. Beware irrelevant, fictitious, and redundant ethological notions such as dominance. Appreciating the likelihood of near future behavior patterns such as attacking you versus playing versus fleeing from you etc. is one thing, but speculating about group social structures, including notions of dominance is worse than useless in the context of what we do.

Respondent Conditioning

Respondent behavior is behavior that is automatically elicited by an antecedent stimulus, cannot be prevented by supplemental antecedent stimuli and is unaffected by consequences. Respondent functional relations involve a two-term contingency of the stimulus–response form, rather than an operant three-term contingency of the stimulus–

response–stimulus form. The body is structured such that when the antecedent stimulus occurs, the stream of energy causes the body to mediate the response. If the body structure that mediates the behavior is genetically based, the stimulus that elicits the response is referred to as an **unconditioned stimulus**, and the response it elicits is an **unconditioned response**. In other words, no conditioning is required for that reflex to exist. Since these relations exist as a result of survival contingencies (evolution) acting on the population over generations, they are related to biological requirements. Examples include salivating in response to food in the mouth and blinking when something touches the eyeball. Reflexes can also include the release of certain chemicals into the bloodstream when the animal is startled.

Respondent conditioning is the process whereby a **neutral stimulus** (NS), which does not elicit the response in question, comes to elicit a response after it has been paired with an unconditioned stimulus (US) (or an established conditioned stimulus). An NS is a stimulus that does not elicit the response in question. An example of an NS is the sound of a clicker before it has been conditioned. The NS becomes a **conditioned stimulus** (CS) once it elicits the conditioned response (CR).[21] The CR is usually similar to the unconditioned response (UR)[22]. When we say that the NS and the US are "paired," we mean that the streams of energy from each of the stimuli impinge upon the subject's nervous system at approximately the same time. The nervous system is then changed in such a way that the subject will mediate the response when exposed to the NS (now a CS), assuming that it is occasionally paired with the US. These processes are illustrated in Figure 8.

---

[21] Confusingly, the NS is sometimes called a CS right from the beginning of the conditioning procedure. This is not a preferred practice as it is actually incorrect.
[22] This is not always the case. Some experiments have demonstrated that a CS can come to elicit a response opposite to the UR.

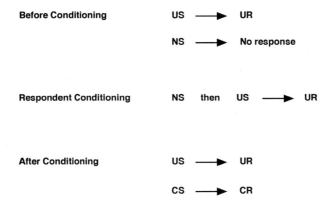

Figure 8. Diagram illustrating the process of respondent conditioning.

The two most effective respondent conditioning procedures are delayed conditioning and trace conditioning. In **delayed conditioning**, the CS is presented before the US and then ends or ceases after the US is presented. In **trace conditioning**, the CS is presented and then removed, followed shortly by the presentation of the US. Establishing a clicker as a conditioned positive reinforcer uses trace conditioning. For effective conditioning, the US should follow the CS within a few seconds to achieve satisfactory contiguity. Simultaneous conditioning, in which the CS and US are presented at the same time and backward conditioning, in which the US is actually presented before the CS, are less effective and best avoided. Figure 9 illustrates these procedures.

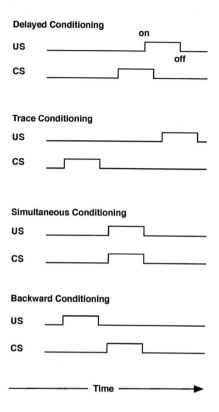

Figure 9. Respondent conditioning procedures.

A CR can be maintained if the CS is at least occasionally paired with the US. CRs can be extinguished by presenting the CS without the US repeatedly until the CS becomes an NS again.

Other processes can also affect the magnitude of respondent behaviors. Repeatedly presenting a US generates a gradual and temporary reduction in the magnitude of the UR, a process referred to as **habituation** (Pierce & Cheney, 2008). Note that, in respondent extinction, the CR is affected by repeatedly presenting the CS without the US, whereas, in habituation, the UR is affected, and merely by repeated presentation of the US. Habituation is temporary, whereas respondent extinction is much more durable, if not permanent, although less conditioning is required to reestablish the CR after extinction. If a stimulus elicits a particularly aversive response, repeated presentation may result in an increase, rather than decrease, in responding, and this process is referred to as ***potentiation*** (Fraley, 2008, p. 677; Catania 1998). Finally, startling emotional arousal can briefly increase the magnitude of responding to *other* stimuli, a process called ***sensitization*** (Catania, 1998).

Appreciating the basic respondent conditioning process is important for at least two reasons. First, respondent conditioning is how we condition and maintain conditioned reinforcers, which are important in most training projects. Second, ***emotional responses*** are respondents, involving various chemicals secreted by glands into the bloodstream. The after-effect (or neural awareness-related behaviors) of this emotional arousal is what we commonly refer to as ***feelings***. Emotional arousal can set the occasion for operants, by temporarily structuring the body so as to make certain stimuli more or less likely to evoke operants, or to make certain reinforcers and punishers more effective. Emotional arousal can render operant behaviors exhibited during that aroused state more energetic. As such, emotional arousal is part of the antecedent conditions in operant contingencies. It can even act as an automatic reinforcer itself.

Measuring Behavior

It is not always necessary to track behavior quantitatively in dog training, particularly with simple basic training project objectives. However, in some more complex projects, it may become useful and in either case, a basic familiarity with measurement of behavior can benefit trainers, even when only informally tracking behavior.

Informal versus Formal Measurement

A hallmark of a scientific approach is that it is precise, objective, verifiable and accountable. Measuring and tracking changes in behavior across time increases precision in describing the behavior and its changes, provides a finer scaled determination as to what training is achieving, increases accountability, and avoids bias or self-deception behaviors. Assigning numbers and units to specific features of the target behavior allows us to determine objectively "how much" of the behavior there is. By tracking the behavior across time, we can determine how the strength of the behavior is changing, particularly in response to our training, whether we need to adjust our plan, and eventually, whether we have achieved our specific behavior objectives or not. Most trainers exhibit a belief that their methods are successful but few can prove it. Measurement allows us to prove (or refute) just that.

Measurement related behaviors involve significant response effort, and under most basic training conditions, trainers respond effectively and sufficiently to training situations without more precise measurement. Trainers exhibit informal quantification of the features of behavior that control their training behaviors and usually do so to an adequate level in basic training. It is generally only when an unusually high degree of precision and accountability are required (such as when undertaking research, training extremely complex behaviors, or resolving complex problem behaviors) that quantification becomes sufficiently reinforcing. While behavior technologists working to resolve complex problem behaviors are commonly under contingencies to measure and track behavior quantitatively, trainers engaged in bringing relatively simple behaviors under appropriate controls usually do not require such involved formal measurement practices. Given that this book does not address the resolution of complex problem behaviors, I will keep the coverage of measuring behavior to an introductory level. This level of coverage will provide an expanded repertoire adequate to improving informal quantification and will provide a basis from which to continue studies on quantification of behavior if interest in doing so is evoked. In other words, a brief introduction to measurement will be helpful even with informal measurement estimates.

Behavior manifests with various properties or dimensions, and it is frequently useful to track a behavior independently by one or more of these specific properties. The following are the most common measures of behavior.

Measures of Behavior

Count

A *count* is the simplest quantification of behavior and simply involves counting the number of instances the behavior occurs. This alone is not usually very useful, but some computational measures based on counts can be quite useful. The rate and frequency are the two most common measures in training situations.

Rate

The **rate** is the quotient resulting from the number of times the behavior is exhibited, divided by the number of time units across which the behaviors were recorded. For instance, if you measure rate of responding for 60 minutes and the dog exhibited the behavior 30 times, the rate is 0.5 (30 divided by 60). If there are multiple timeframes, then an average rate can be determined by finding the mean average across timeframes.

Frequency

The *frequency* is the quotient resulting from the number of fulfilled opportunities to respond divided by the total number of opportunities the subject had to respond. If you measure relative frequency and provide the subject with 10 opportunities to exhibit the behavior in question and they exhibit it in three of those instances, the frequency is 0.3 (3 divided by 10) or 30% (a derivative measure that can sometimes be useful).

Duration

In some instances, the **duration** that the behavior is exhibited for is the most useful property of the behavior to measure. For example, if you measure a dog barking and they exhibit the behavior repeatedly in rapid succession, the duration of the behavior might be more useful or simply more accessibly tracked than other measures. For instance, if the dog barks when left alone, the duration might be a more useful measure of the barking behavior than the rate or frequency, although measures of the rate or frequency and the duration might be even more informative. Duration is most suitable for behaviors that are maintained in position too such as sitting, lying down, or maintaining eye contact. You may start a stopwatch when the dog commences the behavior and then stop it when they cease engaging in that behavior. Less formally (and accurately), you can usually count off seconds (but do so quietly or else the behavior might come under control of the counting). When duration is measured, often it will be a secondary measure, tracked along with rate or frequency or else it is used in small parts of the training, such as when you work the duration of the behavior specifically.

Magnitude

Alternatively, you could measure *magnitude* (or intensity of the behavior). Let's say you measure barking, for instance. You could have a decimeter to measure how loud the barking is. In most cases, this is not a realistic or informative measure.

Latency and Inter-response Time

It will not usually be your main concern but frequently, at some point within a training project, you will be under contingencies to reduce the latency or inter-response time. *Latency* refers to the amount of time between presentation of the opportunity to exhibit the behavior and the occurrence of the behavior. *Inter-response time* refers to the time between consecutive responses (Fraley, 2008, pp. 249–250).

Topography and Extensity

Less common, although sometimes useful, are measures of topography, and extensity. *Topography* refers to measuring the form of a movement. *Extensity* refers to the amount of distance over which the movement occurs, either linear or angular. There are times when these measures can be useful in tracking a target behavior.

Choosing Among Measures of Behavior

Whether you choose rate, frequency, duration, magnitude, or other properties of the behavior will depend on which is most appropriate to the behavior in question—the measure that most reflects your objective for the behavior. Here are some things to consider when deciding among these properties. What is the most appropriate/informative property of the behavior? What measure really indicates, when it changes, how well you are doing with the training—whether you are achieving or failing to achieve your objectives? If you identify exactly what you want to achieve, deciding on a measure will be easier and there will be more validity in the measure accurately reflecting what you portray it to measure.

Tracking the Target Behavior Through Time

In training simple good manners behaviors we commonly forgo quantitative tracking and instead take a much rougher, less precise approach. Whether you track behaviors through time precisely or not depends on your objectives. If you require more precision as is common in some complex training projects or to help in resolving problem behaviors then this level of precision is appropriate. But for simpler behaviors trained mainly as good manners behaviors, we usually estimate progress as we proceed without graphing the results. That said, the behavior objective should always include quantitative criteria and the behavior measured sufficiently to determine when the criteria has been met. It is also a good idea to become familiar with quantitative tracking methods for when you are called on to require more precise accountability.

Under certain circumstances, such as when you take over a training project that is already well under way (such as when you adopt a new dog or a client brings their dog to you), you may begin by establishing the **baseline** for the behavior of concern. This simply means that you present the supposed S^{Ev} through a few or several trials to determine the rate at which it is currently exhibited before training. This can help refine your behavior objective. In other cases, you will begin training with no previous conditioning and the rate of the behavior is likely to be zero. In this case, we rarely utilize a baseline phase.

Tracking the behavior quantitatively tells you the level, trend, and variance of the behavior. The **level** is the measure we have been discussing; it will tell you just "how much" the behavior is exhibited.

The **trend** is the angle the line travels on the graph—whether the behavior is generally increasing or decreasing (and by how much) or remaining stable. A horizontal or flat line on the graph represents a stable trend of the behavior. The steeper up the line is going, the higher or more quickly the behavior is trending; the steeper down the line is going, the greater the downward trend of the behavior. The **variance** refers to the "bounce" of the line, or how widely the behavior swings up and down, how jagged the line is.

A graph will have two dimensions:

- Horizontal axis

- Vertical axis

The horizontal axis will usually represent time, either continuous or the number of the session or trial. Time is usually represented in equal intervals, in units of minutes or seconds. If you use time, you might set the interval at 1 minute per unit (or 5, or 10, or whatever works best given the time frames involved). Start the intervals at 0 and continue through, past where you will be plotting.

The vertical axis will usually represent values for rate, frequency, duration, latency or magnitude. The intervals will usually be equal units and usually start at 0. Ensure that they continue high enough to allow for any measure possible or reasonably likely.

In order to record data on the graph, you place a dot inside the graph plane where the time or trial number meets the measure. So, let's say you are recording the rate of a behavior every minute. In the first minute, if the behavior occurs 3 times, place the dot over the 1-minute point on the horizontal axis and level with the 3 marking on the vertical axis. Then, in the next minute, record how many times the behavior occurred again, this time above the 2-minute mark and at the level of the number of times the behavior was exhibited.

If you measured per session instead of per minute, then in your first session your dot will be above the first point on the horizontal axis at 1, and at the level of the measure for that behavior in session 1. Then proceed to record the data through each time interval or session. Connect the dots as you write them in, to form a line from dot to dot.

See Figure 10 for a stylized graph depicting the features we have been discussing.

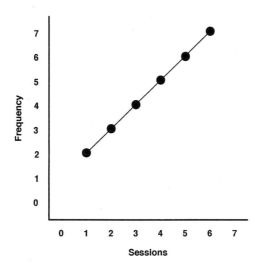

Figure 10. Stylized graph of behavior data, demonstrating the relationship between intervals of time or training sessions and the rate of the behavior.

When you end a baseline stage, make a vertical line at the time or session point where the change occurred to mark when the change was made. You will not require this line if you merely start training without a baseline. Any changes you make throughout data collection should be noted in the graph so that later you can see where the changes occurred and how the line on the graph responded to the changes. Include vertical lines with labels when you initiate any component of training that might impact upon the behavior (in other words, when you make any changes to the independent variable). This can include changing a schedule of reinforcement, increasing or decreasing criteria requirements for duration, distance or distraction etc. If the trajectory of the line changes, you will be able to ascertain what that change is likely related to. If it is in response to a change as indicated above then you can determine visually whether it is a brief adjustment blip or whether it is impacting the training in a more detrimental manner that requires changing your procedure or criteria. The line on the graph depicting the strength of the behavior represents your dependent variable and the lines you make with labels or notes represents the independent variables. The lines on the graph will provide more precise feedback (consequences) regarding your training behaviors and hence bring your training behaviors under more effective controls.

There are different approaches to indicating the various components in graphs. I will present one easy to work with method. This will provide a few important features to demonstrate graphing techniques. Each training project will require its own graph format since there will be different units of time and measures of the behavior appropriate to that project. The interested reader can see Fraley (2008), Bailey and Burch (2002) or Cooper and colleagues (2007) for more detailed treatments of depicting training graphically.

Examine the stylized graph in Figure 11 below. This graph depicts a 13 session training project. In each session, the dog is presented with 10 opportunities to exhibit the target behavior near the end of the session. The first session was used to establish a baseline and in this case, the target behavior is exhibited 0 times indicating it has not undergone any training thus far. After the baseline phase comes the training phase and in this phase, training procedures are implemented. Notice how vertical lines are also used to indicate when training began after a baseline phase, and also for when the continuous reinforcement schedule was changed to an intermittent schedule, and when distance and duration criteria were changed. As should be expected, the frequency of the behavior declines briefly in response to these changes.

The Science and Technology of Dog Training

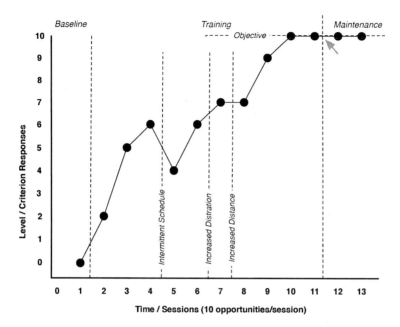

Figure 11. Stylized graph depicting a training project with 13 sessions in which the dog is provided 10 opportunities each to exhibit the criterion behavior. The graph depicts baseline, training and maintenance phases and the behavior objective. Milestone criteria changes are indicated by vertical dashed lines.

Continue the data collection process throughout the entire training project, including well into the maintenance phase, so that you can compare the baseline level (or the initial level when you started the training) and the maintenance level. This process will provide you with empirical feedback on exactly how the behavior is changing. It will indicate whether it is increasing or not and how the strength of the behavior is responding to your training (or not). This kind of objective accountability is a cornerstone of the behaviorological approach.

CHAPTER 2. AVERSIVE STIMULATION AND ITS PROBLEMATIC SIDE EFFECTS

Behavioral Objectives

The objective of this chapter is to measurably expand the reader's repertoire of behaviors in relation to describing and relating the principles of behavior. Upon successfully integrating the concepts outlined in this chapter, the reader, where under contingencies to do so, will accurately:

- Describe the problematic features of using aversive stimulation

- Explain why punishment might work in a narrow sense, but not in the long-term

- Describe general alternatives to the use of aversive stimulation in training.

Introduction

In this chapter, I will discuss the use of aversive stimulation in training, including why these procedures occur, the problematic effects associated with their occurrence and, briefly summarize alternative strategies.

Why is the Occurrence of Aversive Stimulation so Pervasive?

The use of aversive stimulation is pervasive within social relationships because it usually functions as an effective reinforcer, usually a negative reinforcer. Punishment administered with sufficient intensity, contingently (consistently), and contiguously (immediately) with a target behavior will often result in a rapid suppression of the target behavior, assuming the net punitive effect overcomes the net reinforcing effect (Ledoux, 2014, p. 359). Although aversive stimulation may result in robust and resilient long-term problems, the immediate effect is usually effective escape from the aversive stimulation that sets the occasion for the application of aversive stimulation. It is likely that many people who

97

use aversive procedures are not aware of the long-term problematic effects it will generate and do not have less problematic alternative methods within their repertoire.

Problematic Effects of Aversive stimulation

An ***aversive stimulus*** is any event that functions (a) to evoke behavior that has reduced or terminated it in the past, (b) as a punisher if presented immediately following a behavior, or (c) as a reinforcer when withdrawn immediately after a behavior (Cooper, et al., 2007). The term aversive is sometimes used synonymous with punisher (Miltenberger, 2008) or as a negative reinforcer (Vargas, 2013; Chance 2009), but these are just more narrow applications of the term. Negative reinforcement, positive punishment, and negative punishment all involve aversive stimulation. Extinction is also aversive, in the sense that the subject behaves (the extinction burst and increased behavioral variability) to contact the now absent reinforcement, escaping the frustration (aversive emotional arousal) associated with blocked access to reinforcement. Positive reinforcement is the only procedure that does not involve aversive stimulation.

Although using aversive methods may generate effective escape from aversive conditions for the person using these methods, it is also extremely risky (Ledoux, 2014, p. 358). Punitive methods tend to generate extremely robust longer-term problems. The risk of adverse side effects makes the use of aversive stimulation an unwise choice unless no better option is available (Fraley, 2008, pp. 909–921). It is important to note that expert application of aversive procedures can minimize the intensity of some of the problematic side effects, but side effects are not just an indication of improper application—they are an inherent result of salient aversive stimulation, and are common, even when specifically controlled for. It is also important to note that some procedures are more aversive than others. Extinction and even negative punishment, for instance, are not as likely to generate as serious side effects as positive punishment and negative reinforcement. Furthermore, some negative reinforcers and positive punishers are more aversive than others. An irritating *"Psssst!"* sound is likely to be less aversive than a shock to the neck (although some milder aversers are simply distraction).

Below is a brief overview of some of the problematic side effects that commonly occur when strongly aversive stimulation is applied. The problematic effects can be divided into respondent effects and operant effects, although these categories interact integrally.

Problematic Emotional Arousal and Conditioning

Aversive stimulation can elicit emotional behaviors that are detected in ways we would refer to as fear, anxiety, or panic. These aversive emotional behaviors function physiologically to energize and exaggerate escape behaviors (operants), which are discussed in the next section. The stimuli present at the same time as the specific aversive stimulus will tend to become conditioned aversive stimuli, which elicit the same problematic emotional behaviors as the unconditioned aversive stimulus. Furthermore, these can generalize—a wider range of stimuli come to elicit the emotional behavior. This can quickly become a robust and resilient growing problem. The incipient preparation behavior associated with the initial conditioning can also come to elicit the problematic emotional behaviors. That is, the subject automatically self-punishes the behavior.

Part of the problem with emotional behaviors is that they are robust and resistant to change. Eliminating problematic emotional behaviors is a very long and involved process. A few moments of punishment can generate extremely aversive emotional behaviors that can take years to resolve, if they are ever resolved. An excellent source on this topic is Fraley (2008, pp. 909–921).

Escape Behavior

Escape behavior is any behavior that functions to reduce or eliminate ongoing aversive stimulation. The term *escape* is used in reference to unconditioned punishers, whereas the term *avoidance* is used to refer to escape from conditioned punishers, and delay or prevention of unconditioned aversive stimuli (Ledoux, 2014, p. 361). This category covers a lot of ground. The escape behavior generated by the application of aversive stimulation will often be problematic itself, quite aside from the problematic behaviors that led to the initial punitive technique. The escape behavior might be aggressive in nature, or result in attempts to increase distance between the subject and the aversive stimulus or anything associated with it. As mentioned above, aversive stimulation will generate problematic emotional arousal that may generalize and also come to be elicited by other stimuli that are present. These emotional behaviors can energize and exaggerate escape behavior.

Escape behavior might also involve significant adjunctive behavior and so-called "submissive" behavior problems, such as urinating when exposed to the aversive stimulus. In fact, escape often involves self-mutilation and other self-destructive behaviors. All of these behaviors function to minimize or eliminate the aversive stimulation. A strong history of research has demonstrated that subjects exposed to aversive stimulation may countercoerce and/or attack those inflicting the punishment or others.

Aversive stimulation may also result in a reduction in creativity, resilience, and industriousness, as well as in general response depression, particularly if the aversive stimulation is inescapable and/or unpredictable.

Clarifying Punishment and its Role in Changing Behavior

This section will provide clarity on common misunderstandings regarding the punishment of behavior.

Punishment, as a postcedent intervention on its own, superimposes another contingency (an aversive one) onto the original problematic contingency, which is maintained by reinforcement. The punishment procedure does not, on its own, change the existing reinforcement contingency that was prevailing on that behavior—that would be extinction. In that regard, punishment must be considered less efficient than extinction. Procedures involving punishment often result in postpunishment over-recovery of the problematic behavior (a brief increase in the strength of the behavior) (Fraley, 2008). At other times, punishment seems to suppress the behavior for an extended period of time after the punishment contingency is discontinued, but this is not usually a result of punishment alone. Below, some relevant points of distinction between these results will be explored.

If a behavior is exhibited, it has a reinforcement history; that contingency is in effect (assuming extinction has not been instated). When a punishment contingency is superimposed on the behavior, we merely add that contingency to the existing reinforcement contingency. If the reinforcer is stronger than the punisher, the behavior will continue to occur, although perhaps at a reduced strength. If the punishment is stronger than the reinforcer, the behavior will be suppressed to some extent, depending on just how much stronger the averser is. Indeed, the behavior may be suppressed to a rate of zero. But as soon as the punishment contingency is discontinued, the existing reinforcement contingency prevails again, and the behavior would be expected to reequilibrate (restabilize) to prepunishment strength (Fraley, 2008).

If the behavior is reduced dramatically, perhaps to a rate of zero, after the punishment contingency is discontinued, it is usually (if not always) a result of concurrent processes and not punishment alone. Whereas punishment suppresses behavior, extinction eliminates it, and often an extinction procedure is inadvertently instated along with a punishment procedure; elimination of the behavior would then be a result of the extinction procedure and not punishment. However, if the punishment procedure is very effective in suppressing the behavior, extinction cannot occur. In fact, an effective punishment procedure will protect the behavior against extinction because there is no opportunity for the behavior to occur and the usual reinforcement to be withheld. In his classic work, Estes (1944) elaborates on this point:

> Probably the most important practical implication of the present study is the demonstration that a response cannot be eliminated from the animal's repertoire more rapidly with the aid of punishment than without it. In fact, severe punishment may have precisely the opposite effect. A response can be permanently weakened only by a sufficient number of unreinforced elicitations and this process of extinction cannot proceed while a response is suppressed as a result of punishment. The punished response continues to

exist in the animal's repertoire with most of its original latent strength. While it is suppressed, the response is not only protected from extinction, but it may become a source of conflict. An emotional state, such as "anxiety" or "dread", which has become conditioned to the incipient movements of making the response, will be aroused by any stimuli which formerly acted as occasions for the occurrence of the response.

In other cases, punishment may have created a behavioral void filled with some other behaviors, and it is the occurrence of these other behaviors that displaces the punished behavior. Of course, this just means that if punishment is to be used, other procedures need to be implemented in conjunction with it in order to achieve a lasting result. However, the problematic side effects associated with use of aversive procedures can rarely be justified. "Not only does extinction yield a more lasting method of behavior reduction than temporary suppression under punishment, an extinction procedure is also less likely than punishment to produce troublesome aversive emotional side-effects" (Fraley, 2008, p. 397). This is particularly true where extinction is used as part of a differential reinforcement procedure rather than alone.

Another way in which a punishment procedure might result in elimination of a behavior is if the emotional arousal generated by the stimulation is strongly aversive and becomes associated with the stimuli involved in controlling the problematic behavior; these stimuli then come to elicit the aversive emotional arousal, which makes the behavior less likely. Furthermore, incipient actions toward this behavior are likely to come to self-punish the behavior. Stimuli present before the behavior is exhibited, often associated with the S^{Ev} that sets the occasion for the behavior, or incipient behaviors leading to the behavior of concern become associated with the aversive stimulation and act as conditioned punishers. This is often referred to as avoidance, but it is really escape from the conditioned punisher.

The research shows that the use of aversive stimulation does not work any better than positive reinforcement–emphasized methods and, in fact, is fraught with problematic secondary effects (see Sidman's classic work, 2001). In that sense, it is difficult to convincingly argue that aversive stimulation "works" in the real world in a long-term, putative sense.

Punishment results in a decline in the rate of a specific behavior but it does not, in itself, address the reinforcement contingency that the targeted behavior functioned to access. Punishment and reinforcement work in opposite directions (Azrin, 1956). If a particular behavior is punished and the reinforcer that was contacted is not made accessible by other behaviors, the subject may simply experiment with other behavior in order to regain access to the reinforcer. If one behavior is punished, others will emerge as long as the stimulus maintains its reinforcing capacity. This **countercontrol** is often interpreted as the subject being "manipulative" or "dominant." While it is true that in some cases these other behaviors might be acceptable, often any operant that functions to contact the reinforcer in question is a problem.

In a particularly interesting study, Balaban, Rhodes, and Neuringer (1990) hypothesized that "as aversiveness (usually, intensity) of a punisher increases, its hedonic consequences generate a DR [defensive response], which competes with the OR [orienting response] and consequently diminishes the subject's ability to process the informational value of the punishment contingency." Orienting responses are respondent reactions to attend to a stimulus, which increase sensitivity to external stimulation. A defensive reaction, on the other hand, stimulates the so called "fight-or-flight response," which reduces receptivity and limits the effects of external stimulation. Balaban and his colleagues hypothesize that the DR competes and interferes with the OR, and hence should negatively affect conditioning. To examine this, they assigned human subjects to two groups: the informational punishment (IP) group and the aversive punishment (AP) group. All subjects were given moderately challenging tests, which would ensure errors. When members of the IP group made an error, it was immediately followed by a brief tone sound. When the AP group members made an error, they were exposed to the same tone, but 20% of the time the tone was followed by a mild electrical shock. The researchers compared the two groups in terms of skin conductance responses, interbeat heart rate intervals, state-trait anxiety levels, skin temperature, and task exhibition. Surprisingly, they did not find a statistically significant difference between the two groups in global sympathetic arousal. What they did find was that the IP group did significantly better in their tests than the AP group! The tone in the IP group was found to elicit an OR. For the AP group, the tone became a conditioned stimulus eliciting a DR. The AP group did show higher skin conductance and cardiac acceleration than the IP group. Not only did the IP group perform more effectively, but as the test continued, they continued to improve. These findings are consistent with the notion that the DR interferes with the OR, and the result is less effective conditioning. The activation of the fight-or-flight mechanism creates an internal environment that is not conducive to conditioning.

Many studies have shown that harsh aversive stimulation suppresses behavior (see Lerman & Vorndran, 2002). However, many of these studies considered the temporary suppression of a simple behavior, rather than the total effects of the procedure on the subject in the short term and, particularly, in the long-term. This failure to consider other variables beyond the rate of the discrete behavior in question may lead to an inappropriate picture of the advisability of punitive methods.

A study carried out by Hiby, Rooney, and Bradshaw (2004), comparing the behavior of dogs trained with punishment-based methods, on the one hand, and positive reinforcement–emphasized methods and miscellaneous methods (i.e., not obviously either punishment- or reinforcement-emphasized), on the other hand, found that dogs reported to be trained with positive reinforcement–emphasized methods scored highest on obedience scores. Those who were trained using punishment ranked lowest, and those who were trained using both ranked in the middle. In none of the obedience tasks were punishment–emphasized techniques most effective. Dogs reported to be trained with positive reinforcement–emphasized methods were also found to have the fewest current behavior problems, whereas dogs reported to be trained with punishment, or punishment together with positive reinforcement, were found to have the most current behavior problems. While this was a correlational study rather than an experimental one, and no causal relationship can be assumed nor confirmed, the results are consistent with many other studies on the topic, adding to replication in the field and increasing confidence in the results. What is also interesting about this study is its high degree of ecological validity—these were dogs living and being trained in the real, dynamic, and complex world, rather than in a laboratory, and the dependent variables were also real-world concerns.

Alternatives to Aversive Control of Behavior

This book should provide a decent treatment of alternatives to punitive methods, so I will present a brief preview of the material to follow. If the behavior objective calls for establishing a new behavior (resolving a behavioral deficit), the most powerful strategy for achieving it is to prompt it (where possible) or shape it (if necessary). Arrange the antecedent environment to make the behavior as likely as possible, and then positively reinforce it and bring it under the appropriate controls. If the behavior objective calls for reducing a behavioral excess, arrange the antecedent environment to make the behavior less likely and some replacement behavior more likely, reinforce the replacement behavior, and, if necessary, extinguish the problematic behavior. A major benefit of using positive reinforcement–emphasized methods to resolve problematic behaviors—in particular, ones maintained by negative reinforcement—is that beneficial respondent conditioning occurs as a byproduct.

CHAPTER 3. DOCTRINE OF LEAST INTRUSIVE EFFECTIVE BEHAVIOR INTERVENTION FOR TRAINING

Behavioral Objectives

The objective of this chapter is to measurably expand the reader's repertoire of behaviors in relation to describing and relating the principles of behavior. Upon successfully integrating the concepts outlined in this chapter, the reader, where under contingencies to do so, will accurately:

- Explain why ethics are important, particularly with regard to decisions regarding the use of aversive stimulation

- Identify ways of efficiently and effectively training without resorting to aversive stimulation

- Determine when increased levels of aversiveness are justified.

Introduction

Very little published in the animal behavior consulting literature directly addresses the topic of how professional trainers and technologists should decide whether or not to use aversive stimulation, and under what circumstances a particular level of aversiveness is justified. This is surprising, considering how important the topic is, and how much it is discussed and debated among professionals. Here, I will propose a best-practices model, including a decision-making algorithm and a levels of intrusiveness table, regarding the use of aversive stimulation. I will discuss in detail how to work through the decision-making process. This process will be referred to as the Least Intrusive Effective Behavior Intervention (LIEBI) model.

Opinions on this topic differ widely. While recognizing that there may be instances when aversive stimulation is called for, this algorithm emphasizes how to implement the least intrusive but still effective intervention possible and, when a more intrusive intervention is required, how to ensure that the decision and implementation are carried out with due professional diligence. It also establishes a "red zone," which identifies practices that involve an extremely high degree of invasiveness and should be avoided except under the most dire and extreme of circumstances—so extreme that most technologists should never have a case that would justify these practices. The point of this model is to help professionals avoid getting to the red zone.

The version here focuses on training new behaviors alone rather than objectives involving the elimination of problem behaviors. The full LIEBI Model can be found in its most recent version online through the Association of Animal Behavior Professionals, linked to throughout the Professional Practices Guidelines.[23]

Preliminary Concepts

It is important to avoid dogmatic positions when discussing what level of intrusiveness in behavior change programming is justified under what circumstances. An argument regarding whether to use aversive stimuli should recognize some initial assumptions, which I will discuss here to help us avoid an excessively simplistic treatment of the topic. Questions such as whether to use aversive stimulation, under what conditions, and how to choose what form it will take in a behavior change program are always about weighing the likely benefits and the likely risks of the intervention in question, in the context in which it resides. This decision requires recognizing that intrusiveness can be thought of as a continuum from mildly intense and unlikely to result in harm to highly intense and much more likely to result in harm. In the weighing process, it is important to remember that, because we are committed to "do no harm," and are ethically obliged to ensure that we choose the options that are the least intrusive possible.

An aversive stimulus is any event that functions (a) antecedently to evoke behavior that has reduced or terminated it in the past, (b) consequentially as a punisher if presented immediately following a behavior, or (c) consequentially as a reinforcer when withdrawn immediately after a behavior (Cooper, et al., 2007). The term is sometimes used synonymously with punisher (Miltenberger, 2008) or with negative reinforcer (Chance 2009; Vargas, 2013), but these are just

---

[23] www.associationofanimalbehaviorprofessionals.com/guidelines.html

more narrow uses of the comprehensive, verifiable, and unambiguous definition above. We cannot be sure ahead of time what will function as an aversive stimulus, but it can usually be predicted fairly well, just as we can predict what is likely to be a punisher or a reinforcer; this can be verified after the stimulus has occurred. As Vargas (2013, p. 341) puts it, "the only way to be sure about the effect of a stimulus in a particular situation is to make it contingent on behavior. If behavior is strengthened when it is removed, you have an aversive stimulus." In summary, if a stimulus evokes escape behavior, its withdrawal reinforces a behavior, or its presentation punishes a behavior, it is an aversive stimulus. Whether stimulation is aversive or not is an all-or-none phenomenon and can be readily verified.

Whereas aversiveness refers to the subject's response to stimulation, intrusiveness is another perspective on this same functional relation that emphasizes the technologist's intervention process and how aversive it is expected to be, or turns out to be. Intrusiveness of an intervention corresponds to the intensity or magnitude of the procedure. We are often compelled by contingencies to refer to the *level of aversiveness* of a stimulus. This can usually quite simply be determined by measuring the magnitude of the stimulation. For instance, a shock may be measured by the voltage applied, and a leash check or striking by the force applied. Alternatively, just as we can experimentally determine whether a stimulus is aversive, we can experimentally determine whether one stimulus is more or less aversive than another by how the rates of behavior are changed in their presence. For example, simple titration design experiments can determine the relative evocative strength of two antecedent stimuli, and aversive contingencies can be compared and ranked in this context. Predicting how aversive a procedure will be ahead of time without such experimentation is not always precise because the aversiveness of the procedure relies not only on the procedure itself but also the subject's response to it at any given time. This challenge will not stop us from recognizing the obvious fact that some procedures are clearly more aversive than others. For instance, turning your car's steering wheel on a curve on the highway, you are barely aware of the aversive stimulation that evokes your wheel-turning behavior. On the other hand, if someone puts a shock collar around your neck and activates it, eliciting various extremely unpleasant emotional responses, and evoking escape behavior and problematic respondent associations with the collar and the person activating it, you are quite aware of that event.

In theory, aversiveness could be measured physiologically by determining levels of certain chemicals in the bloodstream (i.e., emotional behaviors). A more accessible measurement is to identify how strong the functional relations are and the relative changes in responding. These will all be estimates or approximations of aversiveness.

Intrusiveness might also be defined by the degree to which a procedure affects a subject detrimentally in one way or another. Generally, the more problematic the side effects an intervention is likely to generate (e.g., injury, generalized problematic emotional behavior, increased aggressive behaviors, apathy or generalized behavioral suppression, countercontrol), the more intrusive the intervention would be considered.

The LIEBI model is open to any of several measures of harm or intrusiveness. I will leave further exploration of this topic for elsewhere. For now, it is plainly obvious that some interventions are more or less intrusive than others, and how we objectively measure just how aversive something is should not stand in our way of providing ethical guidance on the use of various strategies that are clearly of varying degrees of intrusiveness.

The term Least Intrusive Effective Behavior Intervention may be new, but the principle is not. It has been known for 40 years (Bailey & Burch, 2005) by a few names, including the "Least Intrusive Behavior Intervention" (LIBI) and the "Least Restrictive Environment" (LRE) in behavior analysis or behaviorology. The term is not as important as the principle involved.

The Ethics of Effectiveness and Minimal Intrusion: Why We Consider This Issue

Interventions are judged not only by how effective they are narrowly, in terms of the impact of the intervention on the target behavior, but also in a broader ethical context of the impact on the individual as a whole and, to a lesser extent, on the guardian, the professional, and the field as a whole. Effectiveness is an important feature of an intervention, but if we make effectiveness the only criterion by which we determine the appropriateness of an intervention, we risk failing to consider some other ethical objectives.

Friedman (2009) makes the very important observation that effectiveness of an intervention is insufficient as a criterion for the use of aversive stimulation. It is widely agreed among those from a wide variety of philosophical orientations that treating others in an invasive or highly intrusive manner, where it is unnecessary to do so, is morally problematic. We recognize ethically that the autonomy and dignity of others deserves respect. A cornerstone ethical principle in the helping professions is that we implement the least intrusive intervention available. We are ethically obliged to construct interventions that are not only effective but also minimally intrusive. It is better to explicitly acknowledge and ground our discussion in ethics rather than ignore the reason we explore this topic to begin with.

The companion animals we deal with in our profession are vulnerable parties in the professional relationship we establish with them and their guardian, much like young children are in counseling relationships between a psychologist, a child, and the child's parents. Companion animals cannot provide informed consent regarding the interventions that we choose to implement for them. Therefore, the responsible technologist must ensure that the interests of the companion animal are carefully considered and that the animal is accorded respect for their basic moral rights, by intervening in a minimally intrusive manner (Association of Animal Behavior Professionals, 2008, principle 2.02; Behavior Analyst Certification Board, 2010, guideline 4.10). An effective behavior change program that helps the companion animal build their repertoire of adaptive behaviors is in the animal's interest, but effectiveness is not enough.

Aversive stimulation produces well-known side effects (see Sidman, 2001, for a general overview) that can cause serious secondary problems that may not be considered if one looks at the level and trend of the target behavior alone. Any question about the effectiveness of aversive stimulation must also look at the broader effects on the individual. In this regard, I have argued that harsh punitive interventions do not "work" in this broader context (O'Heare, 2007, pp. 261–265).

Why Implement the LIEBI Model?

The LIEBI model is proposed as a "best practice," because of its careful attention to ethical responsibility. What reinforcers are available to maintain behavior that comports with the LIEBI model? After all, it clearly requires a higher response effort and may indeed limit access to certain other reinforcers. Delaying an immediate impulsive payoff in favor of a much higher long-term payoff is sometimes called wisdom (Chance, 2009). Considerately working through the process of finding the least intrusive effective intervention is a wise choice, partly because it avoids excess side effects associated with highly intrusive methods, which affect both the target behavior and the general behavioral wellbeing of the subject as a whole. If you avoid the side effects associated with aversive stimulation, these side effects will not be able to interfere with your goals. Bringing behavior under the controls of practices described in the LIEBI model tends to generate pride related feelings. Benefits accrue to the subject, guardian, individual trainer, and field itself as a whole when professional behavior comports with the LIEBI model. The subject benefits from the standard by experiencing a higher degree of comfort and behavioral wellbeing, being conditioned to exhibit acceptable adaptive behaviors that ultimately promote a more adaptive social relationship within the family. The guardian benefits from the standard by avoiding having to deal with the well-known side effects that commonly occur with the use of highly intrusive methods, and they will achieve their goals in an orderly manner. The individual trainer benefits with stronger success rates, reduced risk of injury and liability exposure, and the respect and trust of colleagues and allied professionals. The field as a whole benefits from the standard with market growth and increased respect from the public and allied professionals. Notice that these are the same reinforcers available for adopting all best practices and high-standard ethical guidelines. Adopting a high standard of ethical behavior, including a dedication to implementing the LIEBI or similar model, benefits us more in the long run than failure to adopt such a practice.

Key Features of the LIEBI Model

The most prominent discussion of this topic I am familiar with outside of my own (O'Heare, 2007, pp. 307–311) is in the Delta Society's (2001) booklet, *Professional Standards for Dog Trainers: Effective, Humane*

Principles, which outlines an algorithm to help dog trainers decide when to use aversive training methods. The model presented here has some similarities with the Delta Society algorithm but is unique in that its focus is behaviorological. As well, it more strongly emphasizes avoiding implementation of highly intrusive interventions by diligently attempting to find less intrusive solutions and, when needed, ensuring that the decision-making process is carried out responsibly. It emphasizes tracking the target behavior quantitatively—"success" will involve meeting objective, quantified goals with minimal harm from side effects. Failure to achieve the goals leads first to careful reevaluation of the goals, the contingency analysis, application-related variables, the choice of procedure, and the objectives. Only upon careful reevaluation and consideration of other, less intrusive options is consideration of a more intrusive approach justified. Furthermore, rather than treating intrusiveness as just an all-or-none phenomenon, the LIEBI model recognizes a continuum of intrusiveness, even if we can only present this as a general approximation. A proficient technologist should be able to work their way through cases in this manner, avoiding almost all use of highly intrusive interventions in their behavior change programs.

The flow chart in Figure 12 depicts this process.

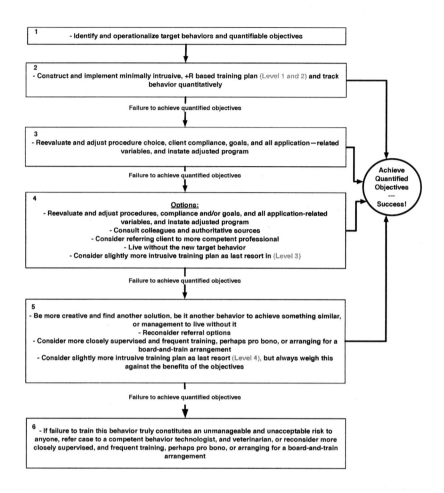

Figure 12. Algorithm for protocols in determining when to implement intrusive behavior interventions.

Box 1. The first step in the decision tree is to identify and operationalize specific target behaviors and quantifiable behavior objectives. Without clarity, specificity, and objective accountability, success will be less likely. The target behavior must be operationalized (i.e., described in a manner that is directly observable and quantifiable/measurable), not vague or speculative. Reference to "dominance," for instance, is unacceptable unless it is operationalized appropriately (in which case, the term "dominance" is no longer useful at all, and indeed is usually counterproductive and inflammatory). Training is an evidence-based endeavor, where scientific research methods are applied to describing, explaining and changing specific behaviors. As in all scientific approaches, reliable quantification of the dependent and independent variables is necessary.

Box 2. In this phase of the project, the training plan is constructed. The plan includes the basic strategy and procedures to be implemented, the objectives for the program are established, plans for how to achieve acquisition of the new behavior, fluency, and maintenance. The training plan is not a hodge-podge of anecdotally supported intuitions and "hit or miss" "tricks of the trade," but rather an evidence-based application of strategies and procedures well supported in the scientific literature. Utilizing a science-based approach makes it far less likely that one will meet with failure and hence a supposed need to formulate a more intrusive approach. Competence or proficiency is our best defense against increasing intrusiveness. Once the systematically constructed training plan is implemented, the target behavior is tracked in all but the simplest of cases. At this stage, interventions are positive reinforcement emphasized.

Box 3. A well-constructed and well-implemented training plan meant to achieve realistic goals ought to be successful, but even well designed plans can sometimes fail to achieve success. If the goal is not achieved, it is time to critically examine all of the components of the training plan and its application. Much behavior-environment interaction is complex, and there are many variables involved in effectively changing behaviors. This reevaluation process is not to be a cursory "technicality" in which you recognize only obvious mistakes. If everything is accurate and reasonable, then you should be achieving success (perhaps not at an acceptable rate). If you are not meeting your goals, there is a problem with what has been done so far. This is your opportunity to identify that problem and fix it rather than resort to more aversive methods and tools.

Consider the possibility that the plan makes false assumptions. Even in a simple training plan, you may have misidentified the effectiveness of reinforcers involved in the target behavior or other potential behaviors that might be exhibited in that environment. Consider any other contingencies that might be operating on the subject in these training session environments. The following are some further ideas for reevaluation (but this is not an exhaustive list):

- Are the objectives realistic?

- Are the procedures chosen to address the target behavior appropriate in the situation?

- Have you addressed antecedent conditions adequately? Many trainers focus on consequences and fail to appreciate the importance of antecedent conditions.

- Are the clients applying the procedures correctly and responding to variations appropriately or are they sabotaging the training with unintended training at other times?

Application-related variables include many things. This is where you are looking at all the nitty-gritty details, including examination of:

- deliverability of reinforcer

- contingency and contiguity of delivery of reinforcer

- size of approximations

- fluency of prerequisite skills

- response effort and competing reinforcers

- schedule of reinforcement and pace at which they are changed.

Remember, competing reinforcers are always available. Your goal is to ensure that you are controlling the reinforcers available for each behavior, and that the relative effectiveness of each reinforcer is such that the subject will exhibit the target behavior rather than other behaviors.

Many variables affect the strength of conditioning and what is actually being conditioned. Identify the variables that can affect the conditioning you are working on and any other conditions that may not have been taken into account. Training can be complex in the real world, largely because of the dynamic nature of the environment and the variables influencing conditioning. When a well-constructed plan fails, this is largely where it does so. Identifying the application-related problems that are resulting in failures can be challenging. If you have achieved some success, analyze why that has succeeded and other components have not for clues as to which criteria are not being adequately met. Often, video-recording the training in its environment can help you better critique the problem and your approach. Consulting a colleague can be helpful for a fresh perspective.

Box 4. If the intervention has not been sufficiently effective to this point, reconsider how diligent you were with previous steps. If you have not been sufficiently effective in your intervention and reevaluation of it, it would be tempting to increase the intrusiveness of the intervention at this stage. However, instead of resorting to this option right away, it is better to refer to authoritative sources or consult a colleague with specific proficiencies that may help you avoid having to increase the intrusiveness of your program. Often, a fresh perspective is called for to identify problem areas and ways around them. Another option is to seek supervision on the case, which has the added benefit of helping you develop your own formal proficiencies. This is an excellent way to meet your objectives with this intervention, and promote your professional development, as well as broaden your skill sets. If you have been making some progress but it is slow, consider accepting the fact that it will simply take longer to achieve your goals.

If these options are unavailable or you are otherwise still not able to identify the problem, you should consider referring the case to a professional with specific proficiencies related to the issues involved in the case. The Association of Animal Behavior Professionals[24] is a useful resource, since certified members are behaviorologically oriented and specifically dedicated to noncoercive methods. Certified members of the International Association of Animal Behavior Consultants[25] are another option. It is not a moral failing to lack proficiency in certain skill sets; recognizing and acknowledging a lacking in specific proficiencies is laudable.

The further along the algorithm we go, the more prominent becomes the necessity to carefully weigh likely risks and benefits of intrusive interventions. If you have diligently reevaluated the case, reevaluated it again and researched authoritative sources; if consultation, supervision, or referral are ineffective or not viable options; and the plan is still not sufficiently effective, you should consider being more creative to find a different solution be it a different behavior or else simply living without this particular behavior. As always, the intrusiveness of specific interventions considered must be compared, and the least intrusive effective ones will be preferable.

---

[24] www.associationofanimalbehaviorprofessionals.com
[25] www.iaabc.org

Note that level 1 procedures should be effective unless there are extenuating circumstances such as a strong history of conditioning for an alternative behavior in that situation or emotional arousal interfering with conditioning. If level 1 training is not achieving effective results, a more exigent and effective strategy would be to analyze the contingencies and identify the problems rather than moving to level 2 strategies.

If reevaluation and consultation or supervision options are unsuccessful at this stage, consider constructing a slightly more intrusive plan as a last resort at this level of escalation. For instance, if a level 1 intervention was unsuccessful, perhaps a level 2 intervention could be considered (see Table 1, below). This approach is still minimally intrusive for most dogs.

Box 5. Re-re-reevaluate and be more creative. If you have reached the stage where you cannot achieve your goals, after careful reevaluation of every component of the case, colleagues and authoritative sources have not been able to help sufficiently, and you cannot refer the client to a competent professional with specific proficiencies that would make success more likely, you need to consider just how important the goal is before proceeding to construct a more intrusive plan. As mentioned above, this whole process is a continuous weighing of the likely benefits and risks of any given training plan component in any given context.

If the behavior is vital to the subject's quality of life consider supervising the client's training behaviors more closely, perhaps being present for all training sessions and consider increasing the frequency of supervised training. This will help ensure that the client is not sabotaging training with their lack of experience and it helps ensure the subject gets trained and the client is well coached. You might consider offering a discount or make this option more affordable in general, or providing this extra time *pro bono*. You might also consider establishing a board-and-train arrangement so that a professional can train the subject, and once the subject is trained, the guardian can be coached on how to maintain the training. These options are more or less onerous for various reasons but worth considering if you have legitimately reached box 5.

It should be extremely rare that any professional trainer would ever need to get to Box 5, let alone have to move to box 6.

Box 6. Box 6 is provided for sake of completeness, but I am unaware of any legitimate training project that required a box 6 consideration. In fact, I have never seen a training project that legitimately required a box 5 consideration either. The question at this stage is: Does failure to train this behavior constitute an unmanageable and unacceptable problem? By unacceptable, we mean: is the situation likely to cause significant harm to anyone at all, including the subject? The more likely the harm and the greater the degree of harm that is likely, the easier a "yes" answer will be. If absence of this behavior is particularly risky in this regard and also unmanageable, then the problem is direr. Unmanageable refers to the inability to find an acceptable means other than the behavior in question of avoiding a high-risk situation. Usually, one can adjust routines, practices, or physical elements of the environment that will prevent or mitigate the behavior or resulting harm. For example, tools such as muzzles can be used. At this stage, it should become evident that the professional trainer has mistaken the case as simply requiring training when in fact there is a serious problem behavior involved requiring the specialized skills of a qualified behavior technologist. Refer the case to a qualified professional!

Table one below provides the options available in escalating the intrusiveness of training plans. The first level is positive reinforcement-emphasized with careful antecedent control to minimize or even eliminate extinction trials. Level two introduces the slightly aversive training principle of negative punishment used for noncriterion behaviors, but the focus should remain on minimizing negative punishment trials as much as possible. Level three increases the level of aversiveness of negative punishment by utilizing deprivation with regard to the reinforcer and increasing the negative punishment interval. No allowances are made for more aversive strategies that might include negative reinforcement of criterion behaviors or positive punishment for noncriterion behaviors because these methods can never be justified in simple training projects.

Table 1. Levels of intrusiveness in dog training plans

Level 1

Antecedent control and graded differential reinforcement

Antecedent control procedures. Set the subject and yourself up for success by manipulating the antecedent environment to ensure minimal distraction, distance, and duration; to ensure appropriate satiation is planned for; any subject sensitivities are accounted for; and that prompting is minimally intrusive, if it is necessary. Set the subject up for success, get the behavior every time, and apply positive reinforcers. Target noncriterion behavior for extinction, but minimize extinction trials as much as possible with effective antecedent control.

Level 2

Graded positive reinforcement and negative punishment

Utilize all of the measures in level 1 but utilize conditioned negative punishers and loss of opportunity to contact reinforcement for several seconds contingent on noncriterion behaviors.

Level 3

Graded positive reinforcement and negative punishment with increased aversiveness

Utilize all of the measures in level 1 and level 2. To increase the aversiveness, instate establishing operations. This level of aversiveness is best avoided where possible and using it must be weighed against the unpleasantness it generates for the subject as well as increased risk of problematic side effects.

CHAPTER 4. EQUIPMENT

Behavioral Objectives

The objective of this chapter is to measurably expand the reader's repertoire of behaviors in relation to describing and relating the principles of behavior. Upon successfully integrating the concepts outlined in this chapter, the reader, where under contingencies to do so, will accurately:

- Select appropriate equipment to aid in training

- Identify equipment that operates on principles of behavior that involve aversive stimulation versus equipment that does not.

Clicker and Treat Pouch

You will need a clicker. These are the training devices that mark exactly when the criterion behavior is exhibited and will act as your conditioned reinforcer, "bridging the gap" so to speak, between occurrence of the behavior and delivery of the primary reinforcer. There are several kinds available, including the simple small box with a hole in which a metal plate is found. These work well, and can be found at any pet shop. These days, most clickers have a protruding button instead of just the hole, which is easier to use for most people. The i-Click Jewel[26] is particularly comfortable, and if you plan on doing a lot of training, you should invest in a good clicker.

You can usually get stretchy wristbands to go with your clicker so that you can let go of it when necessary and it will stay put. You should also get a treat pouch. They look like the pouches used by rock climbers to hold their chalk. A good treat pouch holds itself open, easily facilitating quick treat retrieval, and they usually clip onto a belt or waistband. Many have edging to help prevent treats from bouncing out.

---

[26] www.clickertraining.com

Distance Training Device

For longer distance training, such as training the dog to go to a specific spot like their mat, or working distance into certain other behaviors, a remote treat dispenser is often useful. Developed by Dr. Sophia Yin, the MannersMinder® is perfect for this and can be found through Premier.[27]

Restraints

A drawback of the standard neck collar, if you attach a leash to it, is that when the leash goes tight, it may harm the dog under some circumstances, and it will elicit the dog's opposition reflex, so the dog will pull away from the leash. It may also elicit problem emotional arousal (i.e., stress). Furthermore, some dogs, such as greyhounds, with small heads can slip out of even a tight collar.

A standard body harness can resolve the slipping problem, and also prevent the opposition reflex and reduce stress. This is not to be confused with harnesses that tighten to punish pulling on leash or negative reinforces walking closer to you. The leash attaches at the top in most versions. Moving to a standard body harness can often resolve pulling problems. It is also much easier on the neck. Again, it must not be too tight, as excessive tightness can injure the dog or prevent breathing, but should not be so loose that they can wiggle out of it or pull out of it if they move backwards away from the trainer. Some harnesses are quite well padded, while others are not. If the dog has very short fur, consider a padded brand.

There are harnesses designed to apply pressure, sometimes under the armpits, when the dog pulls, but generally, I would avoid any tool that applies aversive stimulation; instead, focus on equipment that simply limits movement and carry out the relevant training. There are several kinds of anti-pull harnesses operating on a number of different principles. Not all of them tighten to create pressure. Some simply attach at the front of the dog's chest rather than on their back so that

---

[27] www.premier.com

the dog is easier to guide. These and perhaps some others are not as prominently aversive.

Use a standard 6-foot nylon leash.

Head halters are contraptions that attach around the dog's head rather than their neck or body. A band typically goes around the back of the head and one goes over the muzzle. Commonly, the leash attaches under the chin although some attach at the back of the head pulling the muzzle downward when tightened. They are commonly used to direct the orientation of the head, and therefore the direction the dog moves. Head halters are aversive for most dogs, in my experience, and while some dogs may become accustomed to them, it is generally advisable to avoid equipment that requires desensitization—it will disrupt your training. Most dogs do not become sufficiently comfortable with the head halters and continue to fight them. Under no circumstances should a head halter be used with an extendible leash. The risk of the dog hitting the end too quickly and injuring the neck is too great.

What Not to Use

Choke chains should *not* be used on dogs. *Period.* These are chains that form a noose and tighten around the dog's neck if they pull or if the handler yanks on the leash. These are used as positive punishers for behavior they follow and as negative reinforcers for behaviors if loosened contingent on their occurrence. Similar is the prong collar that has prongs or spikes that pinch or dig into the dog's neck. Again, do *not* use these devices, because they are based on aversive principles of behavior, and will cause more harm than good, as is common with all aversive methods and tools. There is no excuse for such inhumane tools. Nor should you use collars that either shock or spray noxious substances into the dog's face when triggered by barking, moving outside of a specific range, or by a button controlled by the handler. These devices exist, but there are no humane uses for them.

CHAPTER 5. TRAINING STRATEGY AND PROJECT PLANNING

Behavioral Objectives

The objective of this chapter is to measurably expand the reader's repertoire of behaviors in relation to describing and relating the principles of behavior. Upon successfully integrating the concepts outlined in this chapter, the reader, where under contingencies to do so, will accurately:

- Describe an efficient and effective general strategy for training animals based on nonaversive methods including how to establish specific quantifiable behavior objectives

- Describe how to plan a training project prior to training in order to make training the most effective and efficient it can be

- Describe how to arrange the environment to make the target behavior more likely, and how to administer reinforcement for the behavior to promote acquisition of the behavior

- Describe how to transition a training project from acquisition to training for fluency, undertaking generalization and discrimination training, bring the behavior under stimulus control, and beginning to thin the schedule of reinforcement, as well as proofing behaviors against increasing distraction, duration, and distance

- Describe how to transition fluent behaviors to maintenance, transitioning to nontrainer-mediated reinforcers, finding a suitable long-term schedule of reinforcement and refreshing training when required

- Systematically prepare a training plan, ensuring it includes all necessary information to proceed with implementation.

General Systematic Training Process

Training involves bringing specific behaviors under specific controls. That involves manipulating the antecedent environment in order to generate the target behavior, and manipulating the postcedent environment in order to reinforce the target behavior to the exclusion of other behaviors. More specifically, the target behavior is manufactured in the presence of an antecedent stimulus, and followed by a reinforcer. Through repetition of this experience, the antecedent stimulus takes on stimulus control over the behavior; it becomes more likely to evoke the target behavior. Each new experience with the contingency increases the capacity of the antecedent stimulus to evoke that behavior and any prompts are faded. Discrimination (evocation) and stimulus generalization training fine-tunes exactly what stimulus will evoke the behavior, and setting generalization training ensures the behavior is reliable in appropriate settings.

Different general strategies and principles of behavior can be used to achieve training. We could, for example, simply punish any behavior other than the one we want, until the subject reliably exhibits the target behavior. That's one strategy. We could also arrange for aversive stimulation to be present until a target behavior is exhibited, and cease the aversive stimulation contingent upon exhibition of the desired behavior, thereby negatively reinforcing it.[28] That's another strategy. These strategies are wrought with problems, both in relation to effectiveness and efficiency, as well as ethically.

A more efficient and effective strategy is to encourage occurrence of the target behavior, and provide positive reinforcement contingent upon it, arranging the difficulty of the task in a gradual and incremental manner, ensuring success for the subject and trainer. One might use other, more eliminative principles of behavior, such as punishment, or extinction to discourage alternative behaviors, but these are best avoided where possible, in favor of the graded approach. A **graded approach** involves breaking tasks or goals down into smaller components, or working on specific dimensions of a task, to ensure a greater likelihood of success and gradually integrating the components or combining dimensions. For example, if we want to train a dog to sit under high levels of distraction, we would arrange a hierarchy of intensity of distraction and start by training under the least distracting circumstances. Once that was reliable, we would move to the next most distracting circumstances, and on like that, until the dog exhibits the behavior reliably under highly distracting circumstances. This would not likely have been successful if we had tried to train the behavior immediately in a highly distracting environment. If you see the word graded before the name of a procedure, this instructs that the procedure should be applied in this graded manner.

---

[28] Unfortunately, this is not a joke and used to be a common method of training. It is still common in certain circles.

The Science and Technology of Dog Training

I will focus on positive reinforcement-emphasized methods, favoring a graded approach, and utilizing a systematic series of steps common to most, or all, training projects. Becoming familiar with this general process will promote the ability to design and implement training projects for novel behaviors. Training should not be haphazard and mysterious. The approach here is intended to make the process principle-based, empirically supported, and systematic. Dog training should not be restricted to those who just seem to "get it." Training is composed of behaviors, and as such, it can be analyzed and conditioned.

Training new behaviors involves the following general steps:

Phase 1. Preliminaries

- Planning and Preparation

    o Identifying and defining the target behavior

    o Assessing the dog's current proficiency

    o Preparing a formal behavior objective

    o Identifying reinforcers and establishing the conditioned reinforcer

Phase 2. Acquisition

- Determine and implement antecedent tactics

- Determine and implement postcedent tactics

Phase 3. Fluency

- Begin fading prompts

- Begin thinning schedule of reinforcement

- Refine form, latency, and speed parameters

- Bring behavior under stimulus control

- Proof against three D-parameters (distance, duration, distraction)

- Discrimination training

- Introduce release cue

Phase 4. Maintenance

- Work toward maintenance of fluency

Each step is discussed below, including some training tips.

Phase 1. Preliminaries

Planning and Preparation

Every training project should begin with a training plan—a formal written presentation of the key elements that will go into identifying and achieving the objectives that the training requires. How elaborate the plan is will depend largely on the complexity of the project and the experience level of the trainer. A very simple training project, such as for example, to train a dog to give a paw, might include only a statement of the behavioral objective and perhaps a statement indicating the procedure that will be utilized. If the project involves some complex procedures, a more elaborate written plan is called for. If you are training someone else's dog, for or with them, you will likely want a more elaborate plan as well, in order to increase accountability and confidence in the training, more than you might need if you were training your own dog alone. I will elaborate on all of the vital aspects of a formal training plan that might be called for in the most complex of plans—the planning process can be truncated for very simple training projects. I will wrap up the section with a sample training plan.

Identifying and Defining the Target Behavior

An effective training project begins with identification of a **target behavior**, also known as the **behavior of concern**. The definition of the target behavior should describe a single behavior in operational terms. Your *plan* might include more than one behavior, but where it does so, it should have a definition for each distinct behavior involved (however, see the following section on preparing a formal behavior objective). Your plan should not involve interpretations of the behavior, or assumptions or speculation about what it implies experientially etc. although it should contain all the necessary and sufficient conditions that will validly allow for accurate identification of when the behavior has, and has not, occurred. Vague definitions are sloppy, even for simple behaviors, and do not instill confidence by those with a vested interest in the project, such as guardians, shelter managers, or certification boards looking at case studies, for example. An operational definition will convincingly demonstrate, to all concerned, what the strength of the behavior is before, during, and after the project.

There are generally two kinds of target behavior definitions: function-based definitions and topography-based definitions. A **function-based definition** designates the operant class based on the common effect on the environment (Cooper, et al., 2007, p. 65), though it still describes actual behavior. For example, one might define going to a mat as any responses that result in the dog going to, and arriving at, the mat. There might be a number of specific responses that differ topographically, but all achieve the function the trainer seeks to establish. In the example above, the dog may run, walk, crawl, or otherwise get to the mat any number of ways, and they may get there from various different places, but the common element in all of these related responses is getting to the mat. It is also common to specify a limited hold in order to ensure that the dog exhibits the behavior within a reasonable period of time. A **topography-based definition** identifies the form of the behavior (Cooper, et al., 2007, pp. 66–67)— the actual and specific movement of body parts. For example, giving a paw might be defined as lifting the left paw off of the ground and placing it on a person's hand.

Whether you use a function-based or topography-based definition depends on the specific requirements you have for the behavior. The function for the behavior may be more important in a given case than the specific topography. Likewise, your objective may require a very specific topography, and that becomes the most important feature of your definition. Most definitions will involve some function-based components even when the topography is the most important feature. For example, you might want to train a dog to give a paw, and have very specific requirements for how it is to look. This might include them sitting when they do so and lifting the left paw only slightly above the human's held out hand before resting the paw right in the middle of the hand. This behavior might be best defined topographically in this case. On the other hand, if you want to train the dog to sit, generally, and this might occur from standing, or lying down, or any other potential position, a function-based definition would be more useful.

Whether one generates a more function-based or topography-based definition, the definition should be operational in the sense that it refers to specific, measurable behaviors, and is not vague or ambiguous. For example, if you use a function-based definition for sitting as in the example above, you still define the sitting behavior parameters. The definition should be complete and concise, including any, and all, necessary criteria or conditions to determine reliably whether the behavior did, or did not, occur in any given instance. It should include any boundary identifiers, such as for example, whether it must be exhibited within a specific amount of time, ruling out noninstances of the behavior. As a test of its reliability, you should be able to produce a written definition for your target behavior, and without further coaching or input, other independent observers would all produce the same measures with regard to when that behavior was, and was not, exhibited.

Clients commonly define the behavior of concern poorly. They often refer to the dog "going crazy" or being "dominant" or "stubborn" or that they want the dog to "be polite." Trainers need to operationalize these descriptions, as none of them are actual behaviors, and they violate all of the requirements described above.

A good target behavior definition will often contain criteria for antecedent and postcedent conditions as well. By identifying the specific antecedent conditions and the specific reinforcers to be achieved right in the behavior definition, trainers can more effectively plan for them. This usually includes requiring specific forms of distraction in which the behavior is expected to occur, and the less contrived reinforcers with which the behavior will be maintained. This allows the trainer to explicitly plan for certain discrimination training, fading, and gradually thinning schedules of reinforcement, allowing the behavior to become automatically reinforcing rather than relying on treats indefinitely.

Assessing the Dog's Current Proficiency

Once you have defined your target behavior (or target behaviors if a behavior chain is involved) with appropriate criteria, you should assess the dog's current proficiency with the behavior or behaviors. Can the dog currently exhibit the behavior in its final form? If they do not, what approximation of it does the dog exhibit? If they do exhibit the behavior, is it within the criterion latency. What other criteria does the behavior currently meet and not meet? The behavior might not currently be cued by the S^{Ev} you plan for it, but if it is not, what does cue or prompt it? Appreciating the current proficiency of the dog to exhibit the behavior, and which criteria are currently met and not met, will inform your behavior objectives, particularly in terms of what time-frame it might require to train the behavior to criteria. This will also inform what procedures you might require, or where in the process you will need to begin. Prepare a statement identifying the proficiency of the dog in exhibiting the target behavior as part of the training plan.

Preparing a Formal Behavior Objective

The **behavior objective** is your statement of exactly what you want to achieve from your training project. A formal behavior objective should include 1. the S^{Ev}, 2. the behavior it is to evoke, in operational terms (including a suitable measure for it, and other criteria), and 3. a tentative time point at which you plan to achieve the stated functional relation at the stated measure.

Your formal behavior objective will be written out although it will commonly be included in the graph that you use to track the behavior as well. Revisit Figure 11. A dotted line labeled "Objective" indicates the level of the behavior objective. Where the beginning of the maintenance phase (time), and the objective level lines intersect (see grey arrow in Figure 11), you find the specific behavior objective point. The trend of the line during the training phase can be used to prompt continuing the training as is, or adjusting it in order to meet the objectives (or, if the trend cannot be maintained, reevaluating the feasibility of the objectives). In this case, you can see that the behavior objective was achieved before the 12th session.

To clearly establish your behavior objective, you should identify a time point at which you expect to achieve the behavior at the specified strength. You will not always be under contingencies to identify a precise quantification and time point, especially with simpler behaviors, but it is a good idea to at least have a tentative idea of precisely what strength of the behavior you want, by what point in time, as this will help you determine whether you are on track, or not, and whether you might need to make adjustments to your objectives, strategy, or procedures.

Below is an example of a formal behavior objective that contains all the required information. As you can see, this includes the S^{Ev}, the behavior, and the time point. The graph will help reveal you if you are on track toward achieving this objective.

Behavior Objective

S^{Ev}: Verbal "sit."

> **Behavior**: The dog will contact their rear end to the ground (or as close as is physically possible) with front legs straight at as close to an 80 - 90 degree angle to the ground (back at around a 45 degree angle) and with front paws on ground.

> **Criteria**: Latency—2sec.; duration—until released or cued otherwise, min. 1min.; frequency—100% through 10 trials; distance—min. 6 meters; distraction—various; time-point—3 sessions at ~5min. each.

Training new behaviors is all about bringing a target behavior under stimulus control. This formal behavior objective presents a definition for the target behavior that is likely to be highly reliable, and it provides adequate information to ensure criterion, and noncriterion, responses are accurately identified, but it is also concise. The boundaries and the measures are clear; the frequency is established, and a time point goal is established. This allows you to devise a manner of tracking the frequency of the behavior if you are under contingencies to track the progress quantitatively. This might be done in this instance with a simple chart or graph. The take-home message here is that if you include all of the necessary information concisely in a single place, you are well prepared to settle on a strategy and plan for how you will achieve that objective, and to track progress so that your training is accountable and precise.

Although, as recommended above, a behavior objective should involve a single behavior, there are times when a single project will involve a closely related set of behaviors and it becomes excessively complex to address each behavior completely separately (Fraley, 2008, p. 788). This might include a series of behaviors chained together and exhibited in rapid succession, always the same behaviors and always in the same order, or a series of approximation behaviors geared toward shaping a single terminal behavior. In these cases, include a list of behavior approximations in your single training plan or your task analysis for a behavior chain.

Identify Reinforcers and Establish the Conditioned Reinforcer

Identify the most effective **unconditioned reinforcers**. An informal approach of merely observing and noting what the subject currently expends significant energy contacting (ideally, in the specific context in which you want the target behavior exhibited in) is sufficient, and guardians are usually quite familiar with what works most effectively as well. You will probably want to rely on **generalized reinforcers** later in the process—that is, using more than one unconditioned reinforcer and including fewer trainer-mediated reinforcers. Initially, however, an easily implemented unconditioned reinforcer is necessary. In most cases, a pea-sized treat works best; in other cases, praise, and play, or contact with a specific toy will effectively strengthen behavior.

Identify what kind of **conditioned reinforcer** you will use as well. I recommend a clicker, because it is a sharp, distinct, and salient sound that will not be rendered ineffective by daily nontraining exposure. For sensitive subjects, a retracting pen, or a Snapple® or similar bottle lid can be used, since the click is softer (however, you can also use a standard clicker in your pocket, or wrapped in material, to dampen the sound).

Some trainers find it challenging to master the physical skills necessary to operate a clicker along with treats and leashes. In these cases, the word *"Yes!"* can do instead, however, if your ambitions involve training at more advanced levels, you should consider expanding your clicker multitasking repertoire.

Establishing a conditioned reinforcer is straightforward, and one of the first things you do with the subject, training wise, if you have not done so previously. In order to establish the conditioned reinforcer, you simply repeat the sequence *Click!* → *Treat* several times. Follow the click with the treat within a second or two. Repeat this sequence several times with several seconds between each trial. Perform several trials of this sequence, and ensure you do so in different locations to ensure that a single location does not become paired with the click. Avoid clicking without following up with the treat, as a general rule, to ensure a high degree of contingency, and a strong conditioned response.

Phase 2. Acquisition Stage Training

Once you have decided on a target behavior, have assessed the subject's current proficiency with it, and established a formal behavior objective, you will begin training. There are several decisions to be made regarding how you will carry out the training. Although the whole contingency must be considered, and is integrally related, it is useful to consider antecedent and postcedent tactics separately for planning purposes. They will all come together as a unified strategy.

Antecedent Tactics

Behavior must occur in order to be reinforced and brought under stimulus control. Sometimes you can simply allow an uncontrived or unaugmented environment to evoke the behavior, and merely take the opportunity to reinforce it. More often, trainers must contrive circumstances to get the behavior to occur in its final form—this usually involves prompts. We then fade the prompts once the behavior has been strengthened. There are other operations that can contribute to generating behavior, quite distinct from prompting, including establishing and abolishing operations that create a deprived or satiated body, which is more or less likely to exhibit the behavior when exposed to S^{Ev}. Alternatively, the current environment or stimuli might be too weak to evoke the behavior in its final form, or they simply have no evocative capacity in that regard, but they might evoke an approximation of that behavior, and in which case, you can simply reinforce that approximation and shape the final form, an advanced procedure to be discussed below.

Prompting

Prompting was discussed in the section on antecedent tactics in Chapter 1. Where a behavior cannot readily be evoked, prompts can be used to help generate the behavior so that it can be reinforced and other antecedent stimuli can be strengthened, the prompt faded afterward, leaving only the now strengthened S^{Ev}. The less intrusive the prompt the better, as minimally intrusive prompts will be easier to fade. Often, all that is required is to provide the opportunity for the behavior to occur and minimizing distraction from concurrent competing contingencies. This is an example of a minimally intrusive prompting procedure. However, this is not always sufficient to generate the behavior. As required, contrived trainer-mediated prompts can be used to generate behavior. This might include pointing, luring, or making sounds, or even touching the subject, although generally, the less physical contact the better (as physical contact can be distracting and disruptive).

Motivating (Establishing and Abolishing) Operations

Motivating operations (i.e., satiation and deprivation) were discussed in the section on antecedent tactics in Chapter 1. Establishing and abolishing operations act as function-altering stimuli and change the function of existing antecedent stimuli. It is always useful to be aware of the current condition of the subject's body, with regard to satiation and deprivation of the reinforcers in question, and where necessary, you may train during times of deprivation rather than satiation.

Postcedent Tactics

Identify the Required Procedure

Although flexibility is important, and the subject's progress should inform adjustments to the plan as appropriate, it is still important to plan your postcedent strategies for reinforcing the behavior.

Is the target behavior a series of discrete behaviors that you will want exhibited with a single S^{Ev} at the beginning of the sequence?[29] If so, identify ***behavior chaining*** as the procedure you will use. The current proficiency of the subject should also inform the procedures you will use. If the behavior is readily prompted in its final form, a simple graded positive reinforcement procedure, or graded differential reinforcement, is best. If the target behavior cannot be readily prompted in its final form, you will use a ***shaping*** procedure. Prepare a statement identifying the procedure, or procedures, that you will use to train the behaviors.

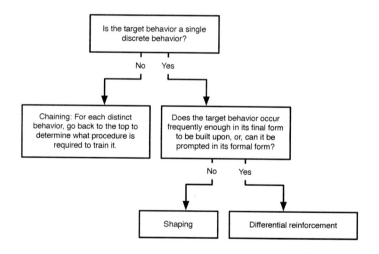

Figure 13. Flow chart for determining which procedure to use in training new behaviors.

---

[29] You will see reference to 'discrete behaviors,' particularly when it comes to discussing behavior chaining. Please note that behavior is continuous, and the notion of discrete behaviors is a little misleading and arbitrary in that regard. Our use of the concept of discrete behaviors is mainly just to distinguish between components in a chain of behaviors.

How to Handle Noncriterion Responses

What should the trainer do if a noncriterion behavior is exhibited during training, that is any behavior that is not the target behavior, including doing anything at all? The need to respond to a failed trial, or noncriterion behavior, indicates a failure to manage the environment well enough to ensure the behavior of concern is exhibited—if the controls were present, the behavior would have occurred. This might mean there may have been a failure to condition requisite behaviors, moving too quickly to the next level of challenge, or allowing for excess distraction, for example.

Behavior reduction procedures are best avoided in favor of a graded approach that improves the likelihood of setting the subject and trainer up for success, but occasionally noncriterion behaviors occur, even with careful attention to setting the subject up for success. When this happens, you have two tasks. First, avoid reinforcing the behavior. That means extinction, and where appropriate, negative punishment if there is an ongoing reinforcer present. Second, try to identify the source of the failure; what did you do or fail to do that resulted in inadequate environmental controls to generate the target behavior? If you are carrying out the first task, ensure that you give careful attention to this second task as well. Resolving the cause of the failure is more important than simply extinguishing or punishing a single trial in a training project, even though many trainers are excessively focused just on first task as though it was the "dog's fault."

As always, it is important to minimize the aversiveness of training, and also to maintain the smooth pace of the training. Positive punishment is unjustified, as it is far too risky. Minimal use of extinction, or negative punishment, can help contrast effective and ineffective responding, allowing you to get training back on track, but again, the occasion to consider these aversive procedures indicates your failure to manage the training project, and not the subject's failure, so at best, consider these ways to get back on track, and they should always be accompanied by a review of your training behaviors.

Which of the two principles of behavior reduction you use, to prevent reinforcement of noncriterion behaviors, depends on whether the reinforcer involved is ongoing or not. Recall that, procedurally, extinction involves the failure of a reinforcer maintaining a behavior to follow that behavior, and that negative punishment involves the subtraction of an ongoing stimulus following a behavior. The distinction, in practice, will not always be obvious. If you are training using treats, and cue a sit but the dog lies down instead or looks over at a squirrel nearby, you would administer extinction, and withhold the treat that has been maintaining the sit behavior. In some cases, your ongoing social contact is just as reinforcing as the treats, and in later stages, it can sometimes become even more prominent as a reinforcer. This is an ongoing reinforcer, and if you briefly subtract social attention contingent on exhibition of a noncriterion behavior, this would be an example of negative punishment (assuming that noncriterion behavior is reduced as a result). In that case, you are really exhibiting both extinction and negative punishment, since you withhold the treat and subtract the ongoing social reinforcer. The basic distinction is preventing the reinforcer that maintains the behavior versus subtracting an ongoing positive reinforcer. Another way of framing the distinction is that extinction withholds the reinforcer maintaining the behavior, while negative punishment subtracts some *other* source(s) of reinforcement (Fraley, 2008, p. 161).

In any event, extinction is preferable, where available because it manipulates the actual reinforcer that maintains the behavior. Where necessary, negative punishment may be used alone, or simultaneously, with extinction. A ***conditioned extinction stimulus*** such as saying *"Oops!"* can be used for the same reason that conditioned reinforcers are used—it marks the specific noncriterion behavior to clarify the extinction contingency in place for that trial. If you incorporate negative punishment, you might manifest it in a procedure called "time-out" at that point as well. To perform a time-out, withdraw social attention, or some other source of reinforcement, turning away for a few seconds. Then, turn back, and cue the behavior again. During those few seconds, reinforcement is not available, even if the criterion behavior is exhibited.

However, before we leave it at that, take note of the examples provided above. If the dog exhibits a different behavior in response to the cue, obviously intercue discrimination (to be discussed later) has not been effectively carried out yet. If the dog exhibits a behavior in response to some other aspect of the environment, like looking at a squirrel, distraction levels have been increased too quickly. In either of these cases, and in all others, this is not a "fault" of the dog; the dog simply responds to the stimulation present and the history of conditioning in place. The "fault," if we shall call it that, is in the planning and/or execution of the training project. Avoid or minimize extinction and negative punishment trials, by utilizing a graded approach—put the dog in a position to succeed!

Phase 3. Fluency Stage Training

Training for fluency generally includes these practices in the order presented:

1. Begin fading prompts

2. Begin thinning schedule of reinforcement

3. Refine form, latency, and speed parameters

4. Bring behavior under stimulus control

5. Proof against three D-parameters (distraction, distance, duration)

6. Discrimination training

7. Introduce release cue.

Planning Fluency Stage Tactics

Once you have trained the behavior through the acquisition stage in a minimally distracting environment, at a minimal distance, and requiring minimal duration, you are ready to begin transitioning to training for fluency of the behavior. **Fluency** is a characteristic of operant behavior featuring stability and reliability, that is, that the contingency is strong, and the behavior is exhibited smoothly, and without hesitation (Fraley, 2008, p. 796).

Broadly, you will be fading prompts, thinning the schedule, refining the behavior features, proofing against the three D-parameters, establishing the S^{Ev}, and working on generalization and discrimination. It also involves introducing a release word to replace the conditioned reinforcer. All of the refinement procedures are geared toward bringing the project to a point of simply maintaining that training indefinitely.

Training to achieve fluency involves quite a bit of work refining the form, latency, and speed of the behavior, and then three D-parameters, which trainers are so familiar with, as well as carrying out generalization and discrimination training, and thinning the schedule of reinforcement. We usually refer to working through the three D-parameter processes as ***proofing*** in the training field, and that is largely composed of stimulus control strengthening, and generalization processes. Generalization training is carried out to ensure that the behavior is evoked in an appropriate range of settings, and by suitable variation in the chosen S^{Ev}. Discrimination training is carried out to ensure that the chosen S^{Ev} reliably evokes the behavior, while other stimuli do not. Schedules of reinforcement are manipulated to make the behavior reliable and resilient against extinction, and to allow for variable responding, so that we can fine-tune the form of the behavior. Some of these processes are conducted simultaneously, but I will discuss each general process in turn.

Through the training process, you will be working on a number of specific features of the behavior of concern. Some of these you can work together while many should be worked separately. When you introduce new D-parameter variables to the training, increases in distraction (i.e., concurrent contingencies), distance between you and the subject, duration of the behavior being held or repeated etc., briefly go back to CRF, and then re-thin the schedule. Thin the schedule gradually and seemingly randomly, but avoid thinning the schedule so quickly that ratio strain occurs, and the strength of the behavior decreases. Settle at a schedule that is as sparse as possible, while maintaining the behavior at an appropriate level.

The following sections will not be broken into separate antecedent and postcedent sections because a chronological treatment is more effective here.

Begin Fading Prompts

Once you have the behavior occurring relatively smoothly with minimal distance, duration, and distraction, you can begin fading prompts, in particular, treats used as lures. If the prompt has been used as an unconditioned reinforcer (as with treat luring), fading should begin right away. Establish the S^{Ev} that you wish to use indefinitely, ideally after the behavior is exhibited reliably in its final form, and all criteria have been established. In some cases, you might be able to begin using the S^{Ev} right from the beginning. This would be the case for simple behaviors that you are at least 95% sure that your subject will exhibit when prompted, and that will occur to criteria right from the beginning (for example, this is often the case with sit and down). In other cases, you may need to shape the behavior in order to ensure its form meets criteria before you can start using the cue. Fading prompts that include the unconditioned reinforcer (treats in hand) is usually the first thing you do in the fluency stage. This often starts as soon as you have a few good solid trials prompted and reinforced.

A prompt that is used both antecedently as a prompt and postcedently as the unconditioned reinforcer is unique. With other kinds of prompts, the prompt and the S^{Ev} both take on stimulus control, and once the S^{Ev} becomes strong enough on its own, the prompt can be faded, usually quite easily. Fading prompts that also function as the unconditioned reinforcer quickly is important, because these prompts are particularly salient—they quickly take on stimulus control over the behavior and will be more challenging to fade. Since the prompt is not the stimulus we want to act as the S^{Ev} for the behavior, it is best to fade it before this occurs. This usually works well though, because the first part of the fading procedure involves completing the same luring motion without the food in your hands. By the time you complete this part of the fading procedure, the S^{Ev} has become even stronger, and then you are left in the position of fading the luring motion (now, without the added distraction of food in your hands).

One of the most common amateur mistakes is failure to fade prompts that include the presence of the unconditioned reinforcer. The prompt ends up becoming a S^{FA} for the behavior. This has led to the inaccurate criticism of using unconditioned reinforcers in prompting (treats as prompts), and even in training with food altogether; although it is a specious argument, it results in people abandoning positive reinforcement-emphasized training. The problem is simply a failure to fade this particular kind of prompt.

To fade prompts that involve using the unconditioned reinforcer to lure a behavior, take advantage of behavioral momentum. Lure two or three responses in rapid succession, and then lure again, but this time without the treat in your hand (your hand will still smell like treats, and this prompt is partly olfactory). The dog will almost certainly exhibit the behavior again—reinforce this. In most cases, you can simply continue luring without the treat in your hands from that point forward. If this is ineffective, lure with treats in hand, and out of hand, seemingly randomly, but continue to increase the percentage of prompts without treats in hand until you are switched over completely.

Once you have the treats out of your hand during luring, begin fading the luring motion prompt by transitioning from a lure motion to a hand signal. We can use this hand signal as the cue while we fine-tune the form and latency of the behavior, putting the permanent cue on nearer to the end result. The two kinds of fading procedures were covered in Chapter 1, however I will briefly summarize the process here. Gradually make the lure motion seem more and more like the hand signal. In fading the prompt, you can take advantage of generalization, which will promote exhibition of the behavior in these similar stimulus conditions. If the subject responded to the lure motion, they should respond to something very similar to it, and then once they respond to that, they should again respond to something very similar, and on until your lure motion is actually the hand signal. This is the **prompt fading** procedure.

Begin Thinning the Schedule of Reinforcement

In the acquisition stage of training, CRF is used in order to achieve a steady and rapid increase in the rate of the behavior. As soon as the behavior is being exhibited reliably, you enter the training for fluency stage, and it is time to start **thinning** the schedule of reinforcement. This is important because CRF is challenging to maintain in the long run, and variable intermittent schedules produce behavior that is much more resistant to extinction. The thinning process is a kind of roller coaster ride through the training project. You may begin thinning it, but each time you begin working on a new level of distraction, distance, or duration, you will return to CRF and begin thinning the schedule again. Any time you increase the level of challenge, increase the density of reinforcement, and begin thinning it again. This will promote high levels of responding and effective conditioning. The thinning will promote resilience.

Refine Form, Latency and Speed

Once you have achieved the hand signal, this will be your working cue while you fine-tune the form, latency, and speed. As usual, work these criteria separately. If you need to change the **form** of the behavior, that is, the way the body parts move, be it in a wider arch, or tighter etc., identify the exact change you need first, and set that as your current criterion. You may be able to use a prompt to get that variation. If that is not viable, you likely need to shape the present form of the behavior toward the terminal form you want.

If you want to reduce the time between when you deliver the cue and the subject begins exhibiting the behavior, you are said to be reducing the **latency**. To reduce the latency, identify the current average latency and set a new shorter latency criterion that will ensure that most trials will meet the criterion. Reinforce only responses that occur in that interval. If the interval expires and the response has not been exhibited, administer extinction or negative punishment, and try again. Once responding within that interval criterion is stable, set a new one a little shorter, and repeat the process until you have reached the final target latency criterion.

The **speed** refers to how quickly the behavior is exhibited—the amount of time it takes to complete the behavior once it has begun. This, too, is conditioned gradually by resetting the criterion in successive trials to ensure most will be reinforced at the new criterion, and building on that speed.

Work through each of the above criteria one at a time. Once you have good form, latency, or speed, you should maintain those criterion levels. In other words, when you make progress on form, latency, or speed, you do not backtrack or relax that progress. When working one of these criteria, you should bring the schedule of reinforcement back to CRF and thin it again (it will go much quicker on subsequent runs through thinning), and it would be a good idea to relax the three D-parameters as needed (to be discussed below). However, to repeat, once you have established a form, latency, or speed, you should continue to maintain those without backtracking (as you would with the three D-parameters and schedule of reinforcement).

To illustrate a problem of timing when training a new behavior, let's assume, for example, that you have a behavior that generally seems to take too long to complete. This can mean at least one of two things in practice: the behavior might be deficient if the subject begins exhibiting the behavior too long after you deliver the cue, even if the behavior itself is exhibited in a quick motion once it begins (poor latency); or, the dog might begin moving right away but exhibit the behavior itself quite slowly. Whether sub-criterion latency or sub-criterion speed, it is one component of the target behavior objective that is deficient, and you should work on it with a graded approach. Let's say the latency is deficient, and the body part currently begins moving only after three seconds, on average, after you deliver the cue. In that case, keep the distance, duration, and distraction levels relaxed/minimal, and return to CRF. Set the latency at ≤3 seconds, and begin running through trials until you get say four reinforced trials in a row. That might happen right away, since we set the criteria at a point where the dog is already usually exhibiting. Now set the criteria at ≤2.5 seconds. Reinforce only responses that occur within that interval, and extinguish noncriterion responses. Once you have around four criterion responses in a row, reset the criterion to ≤1.5 second and work it the same way. With this approach, gradually decrease the latency criterion until the dog is exhibiting the behavior to that criterion. If the behavior was simply being exhibited too slowly, you would set a time unit for beginning to end of the behavior, and gradually, as described above, reduce it until the behavior will meet target criteria. Once you have achieved your goal for that criterion, put the behavior back on a thinning intermittent schedule for a few trials, and then work on another one, at first relaxing the distraction, distance, and duration criteria a little.

Training is a constant balancing act between maintaining progress on the one hand and not pushing too hard on the other. If you set the criteria too low, very little progress will be made, and the subject will become bored and easily distracted. If you set the criteria too high, on the other hand, there will be too many extinction or negative reinforcement trials, and the subject will become frustrated. One result of such frustration is the subject becoming apprehensive, behaving excruciatingly slowly—the more intensely one demands a behavior, the slower it seems the subject moves. Finding just the right balance in the pace of training for the particular individual requires careful judgment. Keep training fun, upbeat, and reasonably achievable, yet challenging, but not overwhelmingly challenging. Indications of boredom and distraction or frustration are indications of a problem with the pace of your training. With experience, trainers become conditioned to manage this pace effectively, on the fly.

Bring Behavior Under Stimulus Control

At this point, the behavior is actually under stimulus control but usually only by the temporary cue used through training. In most cases, this is the hand signal. At this stage, it is time to bring the behavior under stimulus control of the cue that you seek to establish as the permanent cue for the behavior, usually a verbal cue.

Once the behavior is being exhibited in the appropriate form and with an appropriate latency (that is, you have the behavior just the way you want it), you can transfer stimulus control from the hand signal to a verbal S^{Ev} that you seek to use for this behavior with a ***prompt delayed*** procedure. To do this, present the new stimulus (the verbal S^{Ev}), followed immediately by the current stimulus (the hand signal), which will evoke the behavior and generate the reinforcement. Repeat this sequence (i.e., contingency) several times. The new stimulus should take on stimulus control and come to evoke the behavior without the previous stimulus being used, and you can then drop the previous stimulus from the sequence. Continue to reinforce the behavior throughout the process.

Proof Against the Three D-Parameters (Distraction, Distance, & Duration)

The ***three D-Parameters (or The Three D's)*** of training are distraction, distance, and duration (Donaldson, 2005, p. 144). I will discuss each in turn. These parameters are all kept minimal during the acquisition stage of training, thus sets you and the subject up for success. Once you begin the fluency stage of training, you will begin increasing these parameters of the contingency. To begin this process, it is vitally important to success that you work only one of these parameters at a time. Once you have worked more than one of the parameters through, you can begin working those together. For example, if you are working distraction in the early fluency stage of training, relax duration and distance. In other words, even if you have worked one or more of these other parameters before distraction, take those back to minimal while you work through distraction. Once you have worked multiple parameters, you can begin gradually working them together. When you work through a parameter, do so gradually, and ideally, variably. In other words, increase the parameter in small enough steps that you will not destabilize the behavior. Avoid doing so in precise increments. Make some extra small, others larger, and even work in a couple below where you are in the process. This variability will help make the responding resilient.

Plan to proof behaviors against the three D-parameters to a higher criteria level than you expect to require in maintenance. Consider what can be expected as usual for the behavior and even unusual levels, and proof the behavior against even higher levels to ensure that in maintenance, the behavior is less likely to deteriorate.

When working on a new D-parameter, reinstate CRF and re-thin it—do this any time you introduce a new level of a D-parameter and each time you introduce a new D-parameter. This rule of working one D-parameter at a time, and when starting a new level or D-parameter, relaxing the other D-parameters as well as the schedule of reinforcement is restricted to these criteria. We work in a similar manner on improving form, latency, and speed, but note that you should not backtrack or relax them as we do with the three D-parameters. In both cases though, relax the schedule of reinforcement and re-thin it.

Distraction

Distraction refers to the imposition of competing contingencies into your training environment. In the acquisition stage, it is important to keep distraction minimal. However, in order to train a behavior to be reliable in everyday situations, gradually introduce distraction throughout the fluency stage, to ensure that you can reliably cue the behavior, even when alternative competing contingencies are vying for control over the subject's behavior. When attempting to identify distractors, look for reinforcers. Is there something else in the environment that the subject attends to or behaves to contact (or even escape)? The presence of other people or other animals can distract the subject from the contingency you are training. What these others are doing can contribute to the magnitude of the distraction. If the other person is sitting, faced away from the subject, and not engaging the subject in any way, this will be far less distracting than if the person is calling the subject or holding a toy or treat etc. These will be the kinds of variables you will manipulate as you incrementally increase distraction levels during your training sessions. In many cases, you can use access to the distractors as the reinforcer for exhibiting the behavior you are training. Always consider what other contingencies exist in the training environment, how much and what kinds of distraction you can have present and still achieve the training you need to achieve, and how you can increase the intensity of the distraction by very small increments to ensure you are successful. Throughout proofing against distraction, you will always be attempting to cover as many bases as you can and working the intensity of exposure successfully.

Distance

Distance refers to the distance between yourself and the subject during training. In the acquisition stage of training, distance is kept minimal and is increased later in the fluency training stage. In many instances, you will eventually want to be able to deliver a cue for a behavior from further away than you did in your initial acquisition training. This is achieved gradually. Often, subjects cued from a greater distance, without any specific distance training, will come to you in order to then exhibit the behavior right next to you. This is especially common with "sit," and it can be very useful to work distance into this behavior. For example, if there happens to be traffic between you and your dog, you need a way to ensure the dog will not come to you, but rather sit right where they are when cued and remain there until cued otherwise. In fact, you may wish to establish an alternative cue that is visual rather than auditory for such occasions as extreme distance or noise will prevent you from cuing the behavior effectively; many trainers use raising your right hand high into the air to cue this "emergency sit."

Duration

Duration relates to how long the behavior is held in position, or for how long the behavior is continuously or repeatedly exhibited, before you release the subject and deliver the reinforcer. As with the other parameters, maintain duration at a minimum in the acquisition stage, and increase it gradually in the fluency training stage. You will recall the duration schedule from Chapter 1. This feature relates to thinning that schedule in order to increase the duration of the behavior. Not all behaviors will call for increasing duration but some will. "Sit" and "down" are good examples of behaviors you should train the subject to continue holding beyond the point when they actually achieve the position.

Discrimination Training

The introduction and fading of prompts is a form of discrimination and generalization training in the sense that they increase and decrease the number of stimuli that will evoke the target behavior. Further discrimination and generalization training is required though. One of the tasks at this stage involves intercue discrimination. Once you have at least three behaviors trained to this level, you will be able to deliver them in random order, so that you can extinguish merely changing position rather than exhibiting the behavior cued. Deliver cues for different behaviors in a random order, reinforce criterion responses, and extinguish noncriterion responses.

You should also narrow the S^{Ev} by extinguishing responding to similar yet unacceptable stimuli. Present the specific S^{Ev}, interspersed with similar stimuli. Differentially reinforce responses to the S^{Ev} and not to these other stimuli, thereby reducing the range of stimuli that will evoke the behavior. Use CRF when working on discrimination.

Although some generalization will have occurred prior to this stage, there will be further generalization training to achieve here. This usually involves delivering the S^{Ev} in different ways, in different places, or having other people deliver the cue. Ensure that the behavior is exhibited in various locations and under various conditions. For example, a good challenge in a group class that will drive this point home is to ask for the guardians to cue a sit, which they will achieve with no problem. Then ask them to face completely away from the dog, or to lie down on their back, and deliver the cue. Many of the dogs will fail to respond or be slow to respond. This demonstrates how behaviors need to be generalized.[30]

Together, discrimination and generalization training will promote occurrence of the behavior in the appropriate circumstances and not in others.

Introduce Release Cue

The behavior is fluent at this point, and it is time to discontinue using a clicker. The clicker is only used for training new features. In order to transition from using the clicker to a release cue, simply begin using a release word such as "Okay," instead of the click. Follow this with reinforcement if the dog breaks position. If the dog does not break position when released, prompt it and reinforce it. You can use the release cue now to end a behavior, or you can simply administer a new cue for some other behavior. The release cue will become a conditioned reinforcer, especially if you follow-up with treats or other unconditioned reinforcers at least occasionally, effectively replacing the clicker.

Phase 4. Maintenance

Working Toward Maintenance of Fluency

Once the behavior is fluent, we transition from active intensive training to daily *maintenance* of the conditioning. That is, once the S^{Ev}, under an adequate range of conditions, reliably evokes the behavior in its final form, speed, and latency, even when distractions are present, and the schedule of reinforcement has been thinned appropriately, you are ready to settle into simply maintaining what you have achieved so that it does not deteriorate.

---

[30] The novelty in such an arrangement may evoke approach and investigative behaviors, which would be distraction as well. This kind of training will address both, distraction in this way, as well as generalization.

Another component of maintenance training is transitioning from contrived trainer-mediated reinforcers to less contrived nontrainer-mediated reinforcers. This will help maintain a behavior on a very thin schedule. When positive reinforcement is used to train a behavior, the occurrence of the behavior comes to elicit emotional responses that can help maintain the behavior. This intrinsic or automatic reinforcement contributes to maintaining the behavior, even when the trainer-mediated reinforcers are sparse. The behavior itself generates satisfactory reinforcement within the dog's body, and occasional trainer-mediated reinforcement helps maintain that contingency. Professional trainers are all familiar with the phenomenon of dogs rejecting treats, seemingly in order to get back to the training more quickly. This happens when occurrence of the behavior, and the changes that it generates in the environment, reinforce the behavior more effectively than treats.

The primary task in this phase is to settle on a schedule of positive reinforcement that will maintain the behavior adequately and is realistically achievable in the long run. If the behavior ever deteriorates, refresh the training. Also, ensure you refresh the training in different environments from time to time.

Constructing a Systematic Training Plan: Putting it All Together

We have addressed the components of a systematic training plan. Recall also that we discussed whether you would generate an elaborate plan or a short and simple one, as dictated by how extensive and elaborate the training project is. You may settle for simply identifying the target behavior objective and a few comments regarding how you will generate the behavior and reinforce it. This would be suitable for training simple behaviors, commonly with your own dog. Where you will need more detailed instructions for a client, to increase confidence and accountability, or where the training will be complex, as in shaping or chaining projects, you should include more elaborate detail in the written plan. In this section, I will bring together what we have covered to illustrate what a more elaborate training plan might be composed of. I will use a simple behavior for illustration purposes, but I will include more elaborate detail to present all of the features discussed above.

The Science and Technology of Dog Training

Every training plan should contain the following information:

- Subject's name and breed

- Client's name

- Client contact information

- Target behavior objective

- Assessment of proficiency

- Contingencies

- Conditioned and unconditioned reinforcers

- Acquisition tactics

  o Antecedent tactics

  o Postcedent tactics

- Fluency tactics

The first three items are simply to help keep track of the case, and this is only necessary if you are working with a client.

Provide a statement regarding the target behavior in the case of a simple training project, the target behaviors in the case of a chaining project, or the target terminal behavior and approximation behaviors in the case of a shaping project. These topics will be discussed in greater detail below. Provide a full definition, including any measures that will be required, and where necessary, prepare any charts or graphs that will help you track the behavior through time.

Provide a statement regarding your assessment of the dogs' current proficiency in exhibiting the target behaviors or components of it.

Diagram the contingency you will create. For instance:

$$\text{"Paw"} \rightarrow \text{Dog gives paw} \rightarrow \text{Treat (+R)}$$

The S^{Ev} should be the final cue you want to control the behavior. The behavior should be concise, and where appropriate, refer to the full target behavior definition provided separately. The reinforcer should identify the unconditioned reinforcer you will use during the training process, through the acquisition and fluency stages. You may include the conditioned reinforcer as another term, or include it along with the single consequence term—most trainers simply forgo the conditioned reinforcer altogether. If there are any other significant contingencies, particularly competitive ones, which will exist concurrently with the target behavior, include those, and label them as competing or concurrent contingencies. These competing contingencies may become obstacles to overcome, and having a record of them will be useful. Although a punitive response effort contingency always exists when a behavior is exhibited, it is not usually included unless the response effort is particularly high and perhaps the dog is satiated.

Present a statement identifying any antecedent tactics you will use to generate the behavior.

Present a statement identifying the postcedent tactics that you will use, including whether you will require positive reinforcement only, graded differential reinforcement, shaping, or behavior chaining. Include details on each behavior in a behavior chain and approximation details for a shaping project.

Present a statement regarding what schedules you will utilize in the fluency stage and how you plan to proof against distraction, distance, and duration. Identify those variables and how you will manipulate them to incrementally increase their intensity.

This does not usually need to be a very long, nor detailed document, in the case of simpler behaviors, but it is a good idea for training projects to evoke preparation behaviors, even with simpler projects. The practice will become handy when you face a more complex training project, that will require shaping approximations, or chaining techniques. The more extensive plans are most useful when you will be providing clients with training responsibilities that you cannot supervise. The clarity of a plan can be very helpful for them to refer to.[31]

Below is a sample training plan for 'give-a-paw,' since that is the example we used in previous sections. I will include information in all relevant sections, but I will use a simple behavior for illustration purposes. You will require much more elaborate information for more complex training projects, and for simple projects, you might elect to omit a few sections, particularly with extensive experience training the behavior in question.

Training Plan

Subject's name, breed, age: Taz, Doberman Pinscher, 8 months

Target behavior objective

Behavior Objective

S^{FA}: Presenting hand, palm up, in front of subject

S^{Ev}: Verbal "give a paw."

Behavior: Taz will raise his left paw off of the ground and place it on the person's palm

Criteria: Latency—5sec.; duration—minimum. 1sec.; frequency—100% through 10 trials; distraction—various*.

* Distractions to include various people around, engaged in various activities including handling toys and talking, as well as with other dogs around, playing. Same thing but outside of house as well.

Assessment of proficiency

Taz currently lifts a paw slightly when people are near, and will usually place paw on hand if the hand is presented right beside his paw, at a

---

[31] When having clients work on training on their own, ensure that you demonstrate the procedure, discuss how they are to progress, and provide them written instructions for their reference. Have clients demonstrate the procedure, and remediate any deficiencies before leaving them to train unsupervised.

frequency of 80%. Not under stimulus control of a verbal cue, and hand needs to be lower to ground and closer to paw than required.

Contingencies

$$S^{FA} \rightarrow S^{Ev} \rightarrow \text{Behavior} \rightarrow \text{Consequence (+R)}$$

Present hand $\rightarrow$ "give a paw" $\rightarrow$ Dog gives paw $\rightarrow$ Veggie burger bits

Conditioned and unconditioned reinforcers

Clicker as conditioned reinforcer and veggie burger bits as unconditioned reinforcer.

Acquisition tactics

Prompt with hand presented near paw, light touch to ankle if necessary. If unsuccessful, plan for shaping project. Fade later by gradually having hand further up and away from Taz.

Establishing operations: Train before meals and utilize most effective reinforcers only for training.

Postcedent tactics

Graded differential reinforcement. Negative punishment only if necessary. Shaping if necessary.

Fluency tactics

Fade food prompt right away.

Utilize CRF for the first several responses, and once stable, an intermittent variable ratio schedule, gradually thinned based on progress.

Work duration first up to one second, then work distraction gradually, including other people present, then other dogs, then outside of the home in yard, and then away from home. With each change, return to CRF and re-thin.

10 Laws of Training

1. Plan your training ahead of time, including a target behavior objective, the strategy you plan to take and procedures you will need to utilize. This will prepare you well to respond quickly and efficiently to challenges throughout the project.

2. Keep training sessions short, so that participation remains reinforcing and the subject does not satiate with regard to the unconditioned reinforcers used or with regard to social contact.

3. End sessions with successfully reinforced trials, even if you have to relax distraction, distance, and/or duration in order to generate a series of successful responses, and ensure the last few trials generate reinforcement.

4. At the beginning of each new session, review some of the progress made in the previous session—this will ensure smoother transitions in new sessions.

5. Deliver the cue only once. If the behavior does not occur, troubleshoot for a solution, but do not repeat the cue for that trial. Repeating the cue will train the dog to wait for some specific number of cues before responding.

6. Participation in training should always remain highly reinforcing. Use tone of voice, energy level, pace of training, direction of attention, prevention of failure etc., to keep the training reinforcing. Manipulating these variables can make or break a training project.

7. Start with minimal distraction (competing contingencies). Arrange the environment to make occurrence of the target behavior, rather than other behaviors, most likely so that you

set the dog and yourself up for success. You can gradually introduce greater distraction at a later stage in the project.

8. Before moving to a new phase in a training procedure or raising a criterion parameter, ensure the behavior rate has stabilized at the current phase or step to ensure the subject's nervous system—the thing being conditioned—can keep up with the pace.

9. When you begin working a new D-parameter, relax other D-parameters and the schedule of reinforcement. (For instance, if you are going to begin training through gradually increasing duration of a behavior, relax the distraction and/or distance criteria, as well as the schedule of reinforcement, while you build duration up.) They can be combined when each has been worked separately.

10. Transition to training in less contrived trainer-mediated environments without specific dedicated sessions. Starting with training in specific sessions sets the occasion for the training and increases the likelihood that the behavior will occur. Once the behavior is occurring, begin also training during everyday life with no specific sessions per se.

CHAPTER 6. ADVANCED TRAINING TECHNIQUES

Behavioral Objectives

The objective of this chapter is to measurably expand the reader's repertoire of behaviors in relation to describing and relating the principles of behavior. Upon successfully integrating the concepts outlined in this chapter, the reader, where under contingencies to do so, will accurately:

- Define shaping and describe under what circumstances this procedure, as opposed to others, would be most appropriate

- Determine when prompting would be most appropriate

- Describe a systematic series of steps necessary in planning a shaping project

- Prepare a list of behavior approximations

- Define chaining, differentiate this from sequencing and describe under what circumstances this procedure, as opposed to others, would be most appropriate

- Differentiate between forward chaining and backward chaining, and determine which is most suitable for particular behavior objectives

- Conduct a task analysis to determine which behaviors will constitute the chain.

Introduction

Sometimes, the behavior we seek to train does not occur in the subject's repertoire at all in its final form and cannot readily be prompted. Other times, the goal calls for a series of behaviors, exhibited in sequence, with only one cue at the beginning. These are examples of situations in which more advanced training procedures are called for. In this chapter, we will explore the three most powerful advanced training procedures used for such situations: shaping, behavior chaining, and sequencing.

Shaping

Definition and Appropriate Uses

Shaping involves the differential reinforcement of **successive approximations** of a target behavior. Shaping is a special type of differential reinforcement. All differential reinforcement procedures other than shaping change the rate of a target behavior. Shaping changes the *form* of the behavior, making it a unique kind of differential reinforcement. Another way to conceptualize shaping is that it involves a series of standard differential reinforcement procedures carried out in succession. The rate of an approximation to the terminal behavior is increased through differential reinforcement, and then the same thing is done to another, closer, approximation to the terminal behavior. This is repeated until the terminal behavior is exhibited. The rate of each approximation is increased and overall, the terminal behavior is achieved one small step at a time.

Behavior is variable. That is, not every response in a response set is the exact same. This variability in different features of a behavior from one occurrence to another allows for selection and reinforcement of some variations over others. The initial approximation is set such that it will occur frequently enough to be reinforced or that it can be readily prompted. Once that behavior has a history of reinforcement, it will occur more frequently. Then, that behavior is put on extinction and a common byproduct of extinction is increased behavioral variability. We ensure that the second approximation is set such that it will fall within the range of variants caused by the extinction process. In other words, the next approximation can't be too much different from the one you just finished establishing. That approximation is then targeted for reinforcement and its rate is increased. This process of reinforcing, extinguishing, and selecting to reinforce a closer approximation to the terminal behavior from the variants exhibited is what shaping entails. The shaping process continues until the terminal behavior is exhibited fluently.

Shaping is an appropriate procedure for single discrete behaviors that do not occur frequently, or where the behavior cannot be readily prompted in its final form. If the behavior can be readily prompted in its final form, then a simple differential reinforcement procedure is best used. If the behavior is actually a complex series of discrete behaviors that you want exhibited sequentially with a single cue at the beginning of the sequence, behavior chaining is the most suitable procedure, although each discrete behavior in the chain must be trained and may involve shaping. Shaping is also used in many training projects using simple differential reinforcement in order to fine-tune the form of the behavior.

Shaping is a postcedent procedure because it manipulates what comes after the behavior. That is, shaping involves manipulating consequences in order to change the likelihood of the behavior on subsequent occasions. Shaping itself does not specify any antecedent conditions; it does not specify whether the behavior is evoked by a trainer-mediated stimulus or not. The somewhat colloquial term "*free-shaping*" indicates a shaping program in which prompting is avoided. There can be value in avoiding prompts in shaping projects, where possible, particularly when attempting to reinforce creativity[32] and persistence in general as well as the specific behavior in question.

There are some limitations to shaping that trainers should consider. Cooper and colleagues (2007, p. 425) point out that shaping can be time consuming, progression through approximations is often erratic rather than linear and smooth, the trainer must be extremely attentive for indications of a need to change criteria, and shaping can be misapplied and promote problem behaviors. I would also add that it requires extensive experience and proficiency in a number of trainer behaviors to be exhibited well, and if it is not executed well, the subject (and the trainer) can become frustrated, which can cause significant disruption to training and indeed other aspects of the dog's life.

Planning Behavior Objectives and Lists of Behavior Approximations

Preparing for a shaping project generally requires more planning than for most other procedures. As in any training project, one must establish a behavior objective. First, define the S^{Ev} and an operational definition of the terminal behavior to be exhibited, including a suitable measure for it (e.g., specific rate, frequency, magnitude, or duration).

---

[32] Creativity refers to novel and productive responding.

Finally, set a time point at which you expect or need to achieve the terminal behavior. This time point should be tentative and flexible, but it is good practice to set a time point nonetheless. This might be after a specific number of trials, sessions, opportunities to exhibit the behavior, or number of minutes, hours, or days. Once the terminal behavior is defined, the list of behavior approximations can be prepared.

Determining the list of behavior approximations requires careful judgment and flexibility. The best way to start is with observation of subjects exhibiting the behavior proficiently. Find a subject who already exhibits the behavior, and either observe them exhibit the behavior, or better yet, video-record it and watch it repeatedly, perhaps in slow motion. You might be able to find such a video already prepared and posted on YouTube or other public video sharing web sites. This will allow you to prepare a more accurate list of approximations. If this is not possible, visualize the behavior occurring, and prepare your list based on this. With experience, you will become familiar with the approximations to use for some of the more common behaviors.

The first approximation must occur frequently enough to provide adequate opportunity to strengthen the behavior. You need to be able to easily prompt it, or otherwise have it occur, so that you can reinforce it. Each approximation needs to make the next approximation likely to occur frequently enough to strengthen it also, whether it occurs within the normal range of variability when behaving the approximation before it or it is prompted. If you are not able to quickly make the next approximation occur, it will likely be frustrating for both the trainer and the subject, and training will progress slowly. Remember, a high rate of reinforcement is required to maintain pace and high levels of responding, and to prevent frustration. The approximations should be large enough that the subject is not rapidly skipping multiple listed approximations at a time, but small enough that progress remains smooth and efficient. Err on the side of smaller approximations because frustration is particularly disruptive to training. The approximations should be designed to be as gradual as possible so that training may move smoothly from approximation to approximation. Ensure that each approximation describes specific body part movements.

Next, for each approximation, it is good practice to break it down into two or three small sub-approximations, in case you need to quickly utilize them to prevent frustration. You can write them indented so that you can ignore them unless they are needed.

Next, look at each approximation. For the particular behavior identified, is there an acceptable alternative response set that still progresses toward the terminal behavior? In other words, prepare yourself now for any step along the way where you might not immediately get the specific approximation you listed, but it is possible you might get another variation or operant that is still acceptable because it still functions as a suitable approximation toward the terminal behavior. This may not be possible for all terminal behaviors and is usually more applicable to more complex terminal behaviors. If you need to continue a new branch of approximations from there to your terminal behavior, do so. Perhaps you can put these alternative operants in a column to the right. This step is one that experienced professionals can usually achieve on the fly. It is good practice to start planning ahead on these issues before you attempt to truncate the process.

Do not confuse a list of behavior approximations for a set of training steps you plan to use in training the behavior. This is not what the list of behavior approximations is. The list of behavior approximations is a list of the subject's behavior approximations toward the terminal behavior that needs to be trained. This starts with the first approximation and lists each one in order. This list tells you what to reinforce, and then once it is exhibited reliably, what is targeted for extinction, and then what is expected as the next approximation toward your subject's terminal behavior. The behavior approximation list will describe only the *subject's* behavior and never the trainer's behavior. For instance, in training a dog to spin in a circle, you might set 'moving head to left' as the first approximation and 'stepping to left' as a second approximation and on through what is required to get to a full turn. A list that starts with something like "charging the clicker," or "I prompt..." cannot be behavior approximations.

Implementation of the Shaping Plan

Implementing a shaping plan is a complex skill requiring quick and effective judgment, usually based on significant experience. It is an advanced training skill to carry out effectively and efficiently.

Remember, a poorly executed shaping program can be frustrating for the subject as well as the trainer.

Managing the smooth progression through the approximations involves several fluent trainer behaviors, including proficiency in making quick adjustments to both the plan and the techniques used at a given moment. For example, if you need to break a step into smaller steps, or you need to add a prompt, this needs to be exhibited effectively and quickly.

The list of approximations will be your guide to training, but remain flexible and prepared for off-list behaviors, be they acceptable ones or unacceptable ones. If the training is going smoothly and you are experiencing very few extinction trials, there are no long periods of time that go responseless, and the subject is focused, you are likely right on track. If, on the other hand, the subject is losing interest, exhibiting very few and/or noncriterion behaviors, or is exhibiting noncriterion behaviors, you are likely moving at an inappropriate pace. If you move too slowly, you risk the subject losing interest and participating in competing contingencies in the environment. If you move too quickly, you may begin to get more extinction trials and greater frustration. When beginning an approximation, there will necessarily be some extinction trials, but if you set the approximation appropriately, there should be very few. You should quickly progress to 95-100% reinforced trials.

If you reach a challenging part and the subject becomes frustrated, it can be useful to take a break. Toss a treat to change the focus temporarily away from the contingency at hand, and identify what variables are causing the problem so you can fix them. Perhaps call the dog to you, request a sit, and provide an enthusiastic reinforcement package (treats, praise and energy). If need be, take a small break to do something different, be it fun or relaxing before proceeding again.[33] Occasionally it just seems as though a frustration loop develops and has the potential to deteriorate the training; taking a very brief break can be immensely helpful in this regard. A dog that responds to training with aversive emotional arousal bodes very poorly for effective training. If

---

[33] Always be on the lookout for negatively reinforced behaviors that will be disruptive to training. If a noncriterion behavior results in an end to a session that is aversive then you can expect that behavior to increase, which will be a behavior disruptive to training. The goal is for training to be reinforcing. If it is not, this should be your area of focus in solving this problem.

162

that occurs, you will need to take it very slowly, ensure success at first and ensure it is fun. My book *Empowerment Training* is written specifically for rehabilitating these kinds of situations.

It is important to remain at any particular approximation long enough to establish stability in responding, but not longer—mastery and maintenance are reserved for the terminal behavior. Moving to the next approximation before the behavior stabilizes will result in a greater number of extinction trials in approximations to follow, and frustration will result. Remaining at an approximation too long will result in too strong a conditioning history and require more extinction of that approximation in preparation for the next approximation. A good rule of thumb is that the training in any given approximation should be progressing smoothly. Where it is not, adjustments need to be made. Are you expecting too much or not enough? Are you moving too quickly or too slowly? Boredom and distraction are indicative of going too slowly, and frustration is indicative of moving too quickly.

If, when you move to the next approximation, that behavior is not exhibited quickly, you need to be prepared. There is something to be said for allowing the subject to "figure it out" on their own—that is how they become conditioned to exhibit persistence and creativity. However, if it goes on too long, they can become frustrated, and this will definitely disrupt training. If the subject does not exhibit the behavior quickly, you can go back to the previous approximation, work through several trials of it and then insert an intermediate approximation or two or three (these should already be planned for in your list of approximations). That step might have been too much, and in that case, you can insert an easier approximation, so that you will be likely to get the target approximation, and you can continue moving forward. Having a plan will make it easier for you to quickly come up with intermediate approximations when needed. A well-placed prompt can also get you over the hump and back on track.

Chaining

Definition and Elements

Cooper and colleagues (2007, p. 690) provide a detailed definition of **behavior chain** as follows: "A sequence of responses in which each response produces a stimulus change that functions as a conditioned reinforcement for that response and as an S^{Ev} for the next response in the chain; reinforcement for the last response in a chain maintains the reinforcing effectiveness of the stimulus changes produced by all previous responses in the chain." A behavior chain will have these features:

1. Occurrence of a specific series of discrete responses in close temporal succession;

2. Occurrence of each response in the sequence changes the environment such that it generates conditioned reinforcement for the previous behavior, and it evokes the next response (Cooper et al. 2007, p. 436).

Notice that completion of each behavior serves a dual function; it functions as a conditioned reinforcer for the behavior the subject just exhibited, and it acts as the S^{Ev} for the next behavior in the chain. The opportunity to exhibit the next behavior in the chain reinforces the behavior, and this occurs for each link in the chain until the final behavior, which produces the trainer-mediated unconditioned reinforcer. This final reinforcement maintains the chain and the conditioned reinforcers that make it up. In other words a behavior chain is a sequence of behaviors with one trainer-provided cue at the beginning, and only after the last behavior in the chain does the trainer provide the unconditioned reinforcer—you cue a sequence of behaviors.

To train a complex behavior (chain), we break it down into component behaviors (links) and train them separately, linking them together later (that linking process is chaining). For example, training a subject to retrieve involves training the subject to run to a thrown object, and then grab the object, and then return with it, and then drop it into your hand or at your feet. This complex sequence of behaviors becomes quite easy to train if you train each component behavior and then chain them together. Often we use simple differential reinforcement for training each component, but we may also need to shape component behaviors also. Training each discrete behavior can involve a separate training project, requiring the use of procedures appropriate to that particular behavior. Behavior chaining is really about how to bring the whole sequence of behaviors, as a set, under discrete stimulus control.

There are no interjected cues by the trainer (the cues between each behavior are created directly by completion of the behavior before it). Interject verbal or physical cues in the sequence of behaviors is distinct from chaining. The section on sequencing below will elaborate this distinction. I raise the issue here so that you may proceed without any misunderstandings. Prompts are not to be confused with interjected cues. Prompts may be used initially in training the component behaviors, or in linking them together, but they are faded as soon as possible. Interjected cues are not faded; they are maintained as a component of the final sequence product.

Behavior chaining projects involve three steps once you determine that chaining is the most suitable procedure for the behavior in question:

1. Constructing and validating a task analysis

2. Assessing level of proficiency of requisite behaviors

3. Chaining behaviors.

Constructing and Validating a Task Analysis

The first undertaking in the planning stage of a chaining project is to construct and validate a *task analysis*. Constructing a task analysis involves breaking a complex behavior event into a sequential set of discrete component behaviors. The most useful way to construct and validate a task analysis is to observe a proficiently exhibited behavior chain. It is a good idea to observe multiple proficient occurrences of the sequence of behaviors to identify any useful variations that can inform the task analysis. Observing video is helpful because the same behavioral episode can be viewed multiple times. The task analysis can be constructed from simple visualization of the sequence of behaviors, but this method carries less validity than planning based on actual occurrence of the sequence. In other words, if you wing it, you are more likely to run into unforeseen problems during the training. The trainer can also construct a tentative task analysis and run a quick pilot session, working through the sequence in order to refine the task analysis (Cooper, et al., 2007, pp. 435–438). From this careful observation, the trainer can prepare a diagram that identifies each discrete behavior, including the S^{Ev} generated by each. The example below, involving a retrieve related sequence of behaviors, illustrates the product to be generated:

Given that a ball is thrown and the trainer says "git yer ball," the subject will:

- Run to ball

- Take ball in mouth

- Run back to thrower with ball

- Drop ball at feet.

Below I will provide a more detailed elaboration of the sequence of behaviors that illustrates the actual changes to the environment that each response generates and acts as the conditioned reinforcer for the behavior it follows, and the S^{Ev} for the behavior to follow it:

- S^{FA} (throw ball) → S^{Ev}_1 ("git yer ball") → Behavior$_1$ (run to ball)

- S^{Ev}_2 (arrive at ball) → Behavior$_2$ (take ball in mouth)

- S^{Ev}_3 (getting ball in mouth) → Behavior$_3$ (run back to thrower with ball)

- S^{Ev}_4 (arriving at thrower with ball in mouth) → Behavior$_4$ (drop ball at feet)

- S^{Ev}_5 (dropping ball at thrower's feet) → Behavior$_5$ (sit) → Reinforcer

Assessing Level of Proficiency of Requisite Behaviors

Once you have constructed and validated a task analysis, your next undertaking is to determine which component behaviors the subject already exhibits and with what level of proficiency. There are a few ways to assess the subject's current proficiency level. First, identify which, if any, of the component behaviors the subject can exhibit on cue. Second, determine if the subject can be cued to accurately exhibit a segment of the behavior chain (i.e., more than one of the behaviors exhibited in the proper sequence without interjecting cues or prompts). A third approach, that can be taken in some cases, is the ***multiple-opportunity method*** wherein the trainer cues the behavior chain and provides minimal prompts as needed to achieve exhibition of the entire behavior chain or as close to it as can be achieved (Cooper, et al., 2007, pp. 438–441). Physical manipulation should be avoided. Identifying where prompts are required and how salient/invasive the prompts need to be will inform the trainer regarding proficiency level.

Behavior Chaining Methods

Once component behaviors are trained, there are at least two ways to attach the links of the chain—carry out chaining a sequence of behaviors:

- Forward chaining

- Backward chaining

In ***forward chaining***, the behaviors are trained in the order they are to be exhibited once complete. There are at least a couple of approaches to forward chaining.

For very simple and short chains, you may prompt or cue each behavior in the sequence, reinforcing only at the end of the sequence. Prompt or cue the first behavior, and then prompt or cue the second behavior, and on, until you have worked through the entire sequence. Repeat this sequence several times, and you should then be able to begin fading the prompts and interjected cues. Present the first cue, and then continue as before, but then either (a) gradually fade the prompts, or (b) delay the next cue for a second or two to determine if the dog will exhibit the next behavior. If the subject exhibits the next behavior, reinforce this. See how far you can get through the sequence, and reinforce for successful exhibition of the smaller sub-chains. You may then need to work on adding more behaviors to the end of that chain in order to get all of the behaviors chained together. If you cannot get far, you can try (a) several more trials, perhaps through a few sessions, or (b) fading the volume of the cues, or (c) the method described next.

In the retrieve example above, you would start by cuing the subject to run to the ball when you throw it, and deliver the verbal cue. Then you would evoke the picking up of the ball behavior. You can then fade the prompt you interject, and when that is achieved, you cue bring the ball back to you, and then fade the interjected prompt for that linkage as well. Now you have all three behaviors linked in a chain.

For slightly longer or more involved chains, or if the other method is not progressing well, you can reinforce after each component behavior, and thin the reinforcers gradually. The first method described above is a short cut that is often successful in simpler chaining projects, but in many cases, this more involved procedure should be used. Begin by cuing the first behavior, reinforcing that, and then cueing the second behavior and reinforcing that. Thin the schedule of reinforcement on the first behavior, and maintain the second behavior on CRF. Once the first behavior is not being reinforced, and the chain is maintained adequately with the CRF for the second behavior, begin cueing the third behavior after the second behavior. Maintain the third behavior on CRF, and begin thinning the second behavior as you did with the first behavior. Progress through the entire chain in this way, that is, adding new behaviors to the end and thinning the schedule of reinforcement on the behavior before it.

Forward chaining is used for relatively simple behavior chains, or where the first few behaviors are particularly easy to generate. The more proficient each component behavior is, the more likely forward chaining will be effective.

In **backward chaining**, you train the sequence in backward order. Evoke the final behavior in the chain and reinforce it, and once that is reliably evoked, prompt or evoke the second to last behavior of the chain, and then evoke the last behavior right away and reinforce. Fade the interjected prompt or cue, and once this chain is exhibited reliably, start prompting or evoking the third to last behavior, followed by the previous chain, and then fade the interjected prompt so that all three behaviors are exhibited when cued and reinforcement is provided only after the final behavior. Continue this process until the entire chain is trained.

Backward chaining is often chosen when the final behavior is critical in the sequence. In the retrieve example, you would start by evoking dropping the ball at your feet, and once that was reliable, you would evoke bringing the ball to you before dropping the ball at your feet, fading the prompts as you go, and on until you have worked through the entire chain.

Behavior chains can be trained to include a limited hold extension as well. In a behavior chain with limited hold, the subject must exhibit the behavior within a specified interval of time in order to contact the final reinforcer. This can be useful in instances where quick exhibition is important (Cooper, et al., 2007, p. 436). You can use the limited hold extension near the end of training in order to tighten up the speed.

Behavior chains do not always need to be trained in exactly this manner. Some trainers train the new component behaviors as they go rather than training the individual links beforehand, and then attaching them with a fading procedure.

You must be concerned with the quality of the chain. Particularly in relatively long chains, the subject may skip component behaviors, or behave sloppily in the initial part of the chain. This effect resembles scalloping evident in certain fixed schedules of reinforcement. The subject responds poorly at first, and only responds adequately in the final steps of the chain because reinforcement is provided only at the end of the sequence. It is important to ensure each component behavior is well trained, that the reinforcers used are highly effective, and that only full criterion occurrences of the behavior chain are reinforced. Do not reinforce subpar chains. It can be tempting to reinforce any completion of the behavior chain, but what you reinforce is what you get. Extinction and negative punishment can be helpful here.

Sequencing

Sequencing involves training a subject to exhibit a number of discrete behaviors and/or chains, and interjecting cues after component behaviors or chains to initiate the next behavior or chain of behaviors. The entire behavioral episode is referred to as a sequence (Alexander, 2003) and the cues used between component parts are referred to as interjected cues.

Sequencing can be extremely useful where a higher level of flexibility is required than a static behavior chain can provide. The example sometimes used involves a particularly long and complex agility run, in which the particular obstacles are arranged differently in each competition, and while each obstacle involves a chain of component behaviors that remain stable, the trainer must deliver cues in order to get the dog to initiate the next appropriate behavior or chain of behaviors.

If your goal is to train a series of behaviors that will remain the same each time, and you will utilize a single cue to initiate that process, you will be training a behavior chain. If you simply cue a number of behaviors sequentially (each with its own cue), this is not a behavior chain. If the task requires flexibility (such as in an agility run), you may need to utilize sequencing. The process will involve training a number of behaviors and/or behavior chains, and using verbal or physical cues "on the fly" to cue the next behavior or chain.

CHAPTER 7. TRAINING PROJECTS

Behavioral Objectives

The objective of this chapter is to measurably expand the reader's repertoire of behaviors in relation to describing and relating the principles of behavior. Upon successfully integrating the concepts outlined in this chapter, the reader, where under contingencies to do so, will accurately:

- Implement a training plan for common good manners related behaviors, applying the systematic strategies previously discussed based on a systematic plan previously discussed.

The behaviors discussed below are common behaviors trained in basic good manners classes. These are the everyday behaviors that help guardians manage their dog, so that everyone can remain safe, and so the dog can easily fit in to human society. Training each is basically the application of the systematic strategy outlined above. Think of the basic strategy outlined above as the formula and the information below as the specific details and extended examples. This chapter will build on the previous two chapters by providing more application related details to the more general information provided in previous chapters.

Pay particular attention to sit. This will include many details that I will avoid repeating in the behaviors that follow it. These details are important, but it would just be too tedious to read through the exact same material for every single behavior.

You might notice there is no stay behavior. Staying in the position cued is simply the duration parameter of that behavior being maintained, and is therefore, controlled by the cue that evoked that behavior. For instance, the cue to sit means to sit and remain in that position until cued otherwise, rather than sit and then you are immediately free to do anything else you want, except if you are cued to stay. Stay is redundant; it is simpler to treat it as the duration parameter of the behavior cued. Where a dog is already in the position you wish them to remain in for some duration, wait is used. It is similar to what one might refer to as stay, except that the behavior is already being exhibited and was not initially cued. If the dog is already in a position you want them to remain in, cue them to wait until released, but if you cue a behavior that involves duration, maintaining the position until released is simply the duration parameter of the behavior that was cued.

Name

A dog's name is nothing more than another S^{Ev}. In this case, the dog's name cues attending to the person saying it, usually in preparation for another cue to be delivered. It should not be used as a recall cue, as it is important to have a cue that simply and immediately evokes increased attention to you without any other specific behaviors. Nor should the name be used to express disappointment or to cue off as is common. This can be particularly useful in a multi-dog household, where you may want to cue a behavior from an individual and not from any other dogs that are present. In that case, the name evokes attending behavior from the dog named and no other dog.

Behavior Objective

S^{Ev}: Verbal "Name."

Behavior: Orient to look at the vocalizer (without approaching).

Criteria: Latency—1sec.; frequency—100% through 10 trials; distance—minimum 6 meters; distraction—various; time point—3 sessions at ~5min. each.

Stand close to the dog. Say the dog's name, and chances are the dog will look at you—simply attending to the novelty of the vocalization. Click and treat. It is important to stand close to the dog, so that they do not approach you. The criterion for this behavior is simply to look at you. If the dog does not look at you right away, make a noise (prompt) that will ensure you get the dog's attention, and then click and treat when you get it. Repeat a few more times, transitioning to an intermittent schedule of reinforcement and praise. Begin moving gradually further from the dog, at very small increments. If the dog moves toward you (other than to orient the body to better attend to you, administer a conditioned negative punishment, such as "Oops," turn away, and remain unresponsive for several seconds. Then turn back, go to the dog and try again, this time perhaps closer, so that the dog cannot move toward you, or with something between you, thus blocking their access to you. This will rule out accidental reinforcement and maintain look to you alone as the behavior being reinforced. Try to avoid these punitive trials though as this is one of those "counter-intuitive" (remember 'task characteristics' from chapter 1) contingencies that can be challenging to train, particularly if the name has previously been used as a recall cue. It is ideal to move at such a gradual pace that this does not happen, but in my experience even a very slow graded approach does not prevent occasional approach behaviors. Next, simply begin using the dog's name before cuing other behaviors, and avoid using it to as a synonym for here or off or any other specific behavior aside from attending. It will take on greater stimulus control as you use it in training.

Sit

Phase 1. Preliminaries

Behavior Objective

S^{Ev}: Verbal "Sit."

Behavior: Contact their rear end to the ground (or as close as is physically possible) with front legs straight at as close to an 80 - 90 degree angle to the ground (back at around a 45 degree angle) and with front paws on ground.

Criteria: Latency—2sec.; duration—until released or cued otherwise, minimum 1min.; frequency—100% through 10 trials; distance— minimum 6 meters; distraction— various; Time point—3 sessions at ~5min. each.

Notice that this is a function-based definition because there are at least two topographical response sets involved in this operant class (sitting from a down position and sitting from a standing position, and there could be others such as sitting right from a walking gate). Even though we have provided a function-based definition, it is important to address these two common topographies in training. You can train them both at the same time simply by ensuring that you include both behaviors into your training sessions.

Some breeds cannot actually place their rear ends on the ground, but a *sit* for them will be for them to put it as close as they are capable of (their upper rear thigh or rump area will touch their hocks as the joint articulates as far as it is capable). Eventually you will include the criteria that they exhibit the behavior within say two seconds of being cued, and they will remain in the position until cued otherwise, say a minute or two. As per a graded approach, begin with these criteria relaxed and build those up gradually.

The distraction criteria are vague in our behavior objective. That is partly because this is general, rather than specific, to an individual and also for conciseness purposes. If you allow a vague reference to distraction (or any other criterion) in your behavior objective, it is usually a good idea to include an addendum or footnote with some specific details. You might need the dog to sit close to traffic, in a crowded mall, with a bunch of other dogs or children running around, or when greeting all sorts of people. Identify the specific requirements, and prepare a list of those.

Identify the conditioned reinforcer and unconditioned reinforcer you will use. Use a clicker and small pea sized treats.

Phase 2. Acquisition

Increase rate of responding by conducting training when the dog is not satiated with regard to either your social presence or food. Train at a time when the dog is not too tired, but also not hyperactive to ensure concentration. These establishing operations prevent other contingencies from taking control over the behavior. Ensure that you begin training in a low distraction environment—this means there are few competing contingencies that would control the dog's behavior. You can allow for increased distraction later in the process—for now, set yourself and the dog up for success with a graded approach.

In the case of sit, prompting is usually a quick and easy antecedent strategy for getting the behavior to occur. To prompt a *sit*, place a small treat between your thumb and fingers. Ensure you have a good grip on it so that the dog cannot grab onto it before you let go of it. With palm up, allow the dog to sniff the treat. Move it around to ensure the dog is "targeting" it, that is, the nose goes where the treat goes. Once they are targeting the treat, move the treat slowly over their head so that they crane their neck to continue targeting it. If they jump up to target the treat, this likely means you are holding the treat too far above their head. In that case, quickly withdraw the treat and try again, this time with the treat held a bit closer to their head. If they back up while you lift the treat over their head, withdraw the treat quickly and try again. If they do this again, you might want to perform the targeting with the dog's rear end close to a wall or corner so that they are unable or back up. As they crane their neck to target the treat, they should sit. You now have a reinforceable trial. Once the dog has exhibited the target behavior, immediately click the clicker, and deliver the treat to the dog right away. The click ends the trial so if the dog gets up after the click is sounded, that is not a problem. Carry out a few more trials in succession. You should notice that you are able to perform the luring motion more quickly and effortlessly in each successive trial as the prompt and other stimuli take on stronger control over the behavior.

Phase 3. Fluency

Begin Fading Prompts

After the first few trials, begin fading the food component of the prompt. Whenever you use the unconditioned reinforcer as a component of the prompt, you should fade this part of the prompt quickly so that it does not become an establishing component of the S^{Ev} for the behavior (or a S^{FA}). This is the first thing you will do in the fluency phase of training. Start with a few rapid trials of the sequence with the treat in your hand. Then in the next trial, leave the treat in your treat pouch, and perform the prompt motion just as before. The momentum, the similarity of the trials, and remaining odor of the treat in your hand will promote evocation of the behavior. Once exhibited, click and treat (i.e., reinforce). Through the next several trials, continue to reinforce on a CRF schedule. In most cases, you can simply fade the treat-in-hand stimulus permanently this way.

If the dog seemed "apprehensive" with this change, you can fade the prompt more gradually. In that case, carry out that first trial without the treat in your hand as above and reinforce. Then carry out another trial, this time with the food in your hand. Through the next several trials, ping pong back and forth between having the treat in your hand and not, in a seemingly random manner, gradually increasing the ratio of food-out-of-hand until you can run through several trials without the treat in your hand, and the dog exhibits the behavior smoothly.

This might be a good time to end the session on a good note. If you believe that the dog is becoming satiated with regard to the reinforcer (i.e., bored), restless, or otherwise that the training may soon begin slowing down in terms of progress, end the session there. If you believe the dog can continue without deterioration of the training, then continue, but always strive to end sessions before deterioration of any component begins.

To start your next session, briefly review the training from the previous session, to ensure a reliable start to training. There are a few new protocols to execute at this stage of training. You should now be delivering the prompt without food in your hands at all. The luring motion should be taking on stimulus control of the behavior at this point. Before this becomes too well established, begin fading the prompt, transferring stimulus control from the lure motion to a hand signal. The hand signal for sit is a palm up motion from a straight arm to a bent arm while you stand straight up. This resembles the lure motion, and so transferring stimulus control is a fairly easy process. Taking advantage of stimulus generalization, on each successive trial through several trials, make the current stimulus (i.e., the lure motion) seem (in this case look) more and more like the new stimulus (i.e., the hand signal). Do this incrementally and gradually, and the dog should continue to exhibit the behavior reliably through each trial. If not, this likely means you are moving too quickly through this process. You should now be able to evoke the behavior with the hand signal alone every time. Use this S^{Ev} until the behavior is fully formed the way you want it.

Begin Thinning the Schedule of Reinforcement

Until this point, the behavior has been on a continuous schedule of positive reinforcement. You can now move to an intermittent schedule of reinforcement and begin thinning that schedule. The schedule of choice for sit and similar behaviors is a variable ratio schedule. The goal here is to gradually thin the schedule of reinforcement in a minimally discernable pattern (re-thinning it each time you introduce a new D-parameter or level of one of them). Start by failing to reinforce a response, but quickly carry out another trial and reinforce that one. The "disappointment" (i.e., emotional arousal elicited by extinction) will not have lasted long and you will begin conditioning resilience. Now, gradually increase the number of unreinforced trials to reinforced trials around a gradually increasing average. Ping pong it around to avoid discernable patterns. Go from a VR-2 toward, say, a VR-6 or VR-8. Move at a pace that continues to maintain the stability of the behavior. Beware of ***ratio strain***, wherein the schedule is thinned too quickly, the dog becomes frustrated, and the behavior becomes unreliable or unstable. Move at the dog's pace.

Refine Form, Latency and Speed

Utilizing a graded approach, begin working form, latency, and speed, one at a time, gradually and as needed until each satisfies the behavior objective requirements. Assess the features you need to change based on current proficiencies and the target criteria. This might include decreasing the latency or training a quicker motion from beginning to sit to being seated—speed. Work through one feature at a time. Refining form gradually means shaping. If any components of the form are inadequate, identify exactly what movement(s) need to change and what they will look like when satisfactory. You may need a list of approximations if there is a significant difference between the current motion and terminal motion, but often, this kind of refinement simply requires slight shifts in form that can be achieved with one or two levels of approximations.

Bring Behavior Under Stimulus Control

Once you have the behavior's form and latency to criteria, you should establish the permanent verbal cue. To transfer stimulus control from the hand signal to the verbal cue, simply repeat the sequence of new cue (verbal "sit"), followed by the old cue (hand signal), followed by occurrence of the behavior, followed by reinforcement. Achieve several trials through the contingency, and the new stimulus ought to take on stimulus control of the behavior. Pause after saying sit, and wait for the sitting behavior. It might take an extra second or two, as the subject waits for the hand signal, but they will likely exhibit the behavior. If not, repeat several more trials, and try again until the new verbal cue evokes the behavior on its own.

Proof Against the Three D-Parameters

You now have the target behavior under stimulus control, and it is time to begin "proofing" the behavior against dynamic real world challenges. This would be the three D-parameters. Remember to work only one at a time.

Let's start with distraction. Start by introducing small distractions such as another person nearby, but not really doing anything in particular. Take the schedule briefly back to CRF and thin it gradually with the new D-parameter in place. Introduce more and more distractions, but again, do this at a pace that maintains the stability of the behavior. Once you are able to cue the behavior under rather distracting circumstances, you might introduce another kind of distraction— evoking the behavior in other locations. For instance, instead of training in your living room, try several trials in the kitchen, remember to relax other D-parameters briefly and re-thin the schedule. This can usually be done quickly, but always manage the level of frustration and stress, keeping these minimal and training fun. Then you could attempt trials in a boring backyard (perhaps after already being out for a while to promote satiation with regard to the other reinforcers in the yard). Then you could run through the training with other distractors added in. Then you could run through the process away from the yard, on a sidewalk. Have you ever noticed a dog in a pet shop, and the guardian is so surprised that the dog won't sit on cue? That is because they simply have not proofed the behavior to that point; it's probably a fast, reliable, and sharp looking sit at home. Make sure to take opportunities to reinforce occurrence of the behavior in many different places and under many different circumstances. However, you do not need to get to this level of proofing before you can begin working the other D-parameters. Get a good start on distraction, but if you choose to work another D-parameter, relax distraction until you work that other D-parameter up. Then you can start combining them. Distance will involve and require duration—therefore, it is best to work duration up before introducing distance.

Duration is run the same way as distraction. Set a specific criterion, and establish it reliably before increasing it again. You will have been reinforcing immediately upon the dog sitting until now. So, begin to expect at least two seconds on maintaining the sit position before reinforcing. Move at the dog's pace to ensure almost all of the trials meet the criterion. When the dog fails to meet the criterion duration, administer extinction or negative punishment, identify your failure in getting the behavior, and try again.

In the case of distance, you may be able to simply inch your way further from the dog through successive trials, but in many cases, you will push it a little too quickly, and the dog will approach and sit. You may need to have the dog tethered to something so that they cannot approach you. In any case, work this D-parameter up gradually as with the others, and once it is well on its way, you can begin combining D-parameters. When you combine more than one D-parameter, remember to build them up gradually again.

Set the criteria in all of these parameters to ensure success in most trials, but with a level of challenge that maintains progress. This judgment in maintaining smooth progress and minimal frustration is the trickiest set of trainer "chops" to teach trainers and the most challenging skill to acquire primarily because it requires the generalization of many related behaviors to be exhibited reliably and quickly. Attend to expanding your repertoire in this regard; the appendix on trainer exercises will help. Attend to and recognize inefficiency and ineffectiveness in your training behaviors in order to differentially reinforce your own effective training practices. At the same time that you are training others, be they the dog or a guardian, you are also training yourself.

Discrimination Training

Depending on whether you have trained this behavior first, or if you have other behaviors trained also, you should work on intercue discrimination training. Once you have two behaviors trained, you should run a series of trials cuing one or the other in a random manner, reinforcing criterion behaviors and extinguishing noncriterion ones.

This will be a good test of stimulus control, since so many things except for the cue itself will be the same in both arrangements. Remember the differential outcome effect—use distinct reinforcers for each behavior and your training will be more efficient and effective. Once you have three behaviors trained, you will find it is even more challenging as you randomly cue different behaviors. That is because with two behaviors, the strategy of simply changing position can work, assuming you don't cue a behavior the subject is already in the position for—with three behaviors, this strategy will only be effective 50% of the time (rather than 100% with two behaviors).

Introduce Release Cue

Once you are ready to begin phasing out the conditioned reinforcer, which until now has been acting as the release, you can begin using a release cue in its place. The release cue will act as a conditioned reinforcer in place of the click. Most trainers use "okay" as the release word. You can introduce the release cue as you train. Begin delivering the release cue right before treat delivery, instead of the click. If the dog does not break position when released, you can prompt it easily enough with open arms, backing up, and praising the dog, or else offering the treat at a slight distance, requiring the dog to break position to eat it.

Phase 4. Maintenance

Once you have the final form, speed, and latency criteria of the target behavior, it is on cue, and reliably proofed through the three D-parameters, you can begin working toward maintenance. There is not always necessarily a clear line between fluency and maintenance phases. You will likely want to continue to develop proficiency in new locations or with new distractors etc., but once you are well along with that, it is time to begin transitioning from the intensive training activities of the fluency development phase to less intensive maintenance of the fluency you have achieved.

Begin generalizing the reinforcers from just the treats, for instance, to praise some times, and a petting and perhaps a quick tug-of-war game, as long as these things are actually reinforcing. Remember also that the clicker is just for acquisition and training toward fluency. Start reinforcing with the unconditioned reinforcers and leave the clicker for new parameters. Begin using fewer trainer-mediated reinforcers too. Use activity reinforcers, or what is commonly referred to as the Premack principle, in order to help you maintain control over the behavior. For example, if eating is reinforcing, then take the opportunity to require a sit before allowing the dog their food. If going outside or having a leash put on acts as a reinforcer, require a sit while you open the door or prepare the leash. The same goes for sniffing fire hydrants or meeting other dogs etc. The goal in this phase is to work toward simply maintaining what you have achieved training wise with minimal contrived activity outside of the cues. If at any point any component of the training seems to be deteriorating, refresh the training by building that parameter back up.

Common Challenges

For some breeds of dog, the sitting position is seemingly uncomfortable and hence aversive. In these cases, you will be imposing a positive reinforcement contingency over an existing punitive contingency. In practice, this usually means slow awkward training. Although the sit behavior is useful, especially when you want a dog to wait without moving for more than a few seconds, or as a greeting behavior to prevent jumping up etc., it might be worth considering using a down position, or if this too is punitive, then training a good solid stand and a wait, since the dog will often already be standing. In this case, you can specifically work remaining in place for the stand as part of your proofing of this behavior.

Some dogs will tend to crane their necks and turn around, or stand, or jump up, rather than easily take a seated position to target a treat during prompting. If you are raising the treat too quickly or high over the dog's head, they will often turn or jump up instead of sitting. In that case, experiment with moving more slowly and maintaining the treat closer to the dog. For dogs that simply scuttle back, rather than crane their head to target the treat, consider training with the dogs back against a wall or corner.

Down

Phase 1. Preliminaries

Behavior Objective

S^{Ev}: Verbal "Down."

Behavior: Contact both elbows and both hocks to the ground.

Criteria: Latency—2sec.; duration—until released or cued otherwise, minimum 3min.; frequency—100% through 10 trials; distance— minimum 6 meters; distraction—various; time point—3 sessions at ~5min. each.

Again, this is a function-based definition because there can be different discrete behaviors exhibited to achieve this position. The dog could lie down from a seated or a standing position. Just as before, ensure that you train for both specific behaviors. I have provided a definition for a formal sphinx-style down, but you can adjust the definition to allow for an informal down on one hip rather than requiring both hocks be placed on the ground. When training down, I allow either option to satisfy the operant criterion. The distraction criterion is vague here as well because this is a general set of guidelines. Either ensure it is specific to your requirements, or provide a brief addendum with some kind of specific criteria to refer to.

Identify the conditioned reinforcer and unconditioned reinforcer you will use.

Phase 2. Acquisition

Utilize the same establishing operations as discussed for sit.

In the case of down, prompting is usually quick and easy. To prompt down, place a small treat between your thumb and fingers, and lure the down. Luring a down is a little trickier than sit. You may need to kneel or sit on the ground to start with. Once the dog is targeting the treat, move your hand slowly straight down to slightly forward, between the dog's front paws. Many dogs will bow their front ends rather than lower their whole body into a lying down position. Usually, if you wait a couple seconds, the rear end will also go down. If you cannot manage to generate the down position this way, you may need to sit with one leg bent, to form a triangle tunnel, and lure through the tunnel. Alternatively, if the dog is much bigger, you may need to use a table or chair. In any case, you form a tunnel with them on one side and you on the other, and lure them down and into the tunnel, so that they are forced to lie down to continue targeting the treat. You would then need to fade the obstacle as well. Generating the down position can sometimes take finesse and creativity. As soon as the dog achieves a down position, click and treat, and repeat through several trials. You should observe that evoking the behavior becomes smoother and easier.

Phase 3. Fluency

Follow the same general steps to train for fluency of down as you did for sit.

After the first few trials, begin fading the food-in-hand prompt as described under sit.

You should now be prompting without food in your hands at all. The luring motion should be taking on stimulus control of the behavior at this point. Before this becomes too well established, begin fading the prompt, transferring stimulus control from the lure motion to a hand signal. The hand signal for down is a palm down motion from a bent arm to a straight arm, while standing straight up. This resembles the lure motion, and so transferring stimulus control is a fairly easy process. Do this incrementally and gradually, and the dog should continue to exhibit the behavior reliably through each trial. If not, this means you are likely moving too quickly through this process.

Until this point, the behavior has been on CRF. You can now move to an intermittent schedule of reinforcement and begin thinning that schedule. The schedule of choice for down and similar behaviors is a variable ratio schedule.

Now that you are reinforcing some and not all of the responses, and the contingency is not on too sparse a schedule, you should take this opportunity to refine the form, latency, and speed as needed. Work through one criterion at a time, and take the schedule back to CRF, re-thinning it each time you up the criterion.

Once you have the behavior in the form, and with a latency you are comfortable with, you are free to establish the verbal cue.

You now have the target behavior under stimulus control, and it is time to begin proofing the behavior against the three D-parameters. Remember to work only one at a time while relaxing the criteria for the others that have already been conditioned, and with each newly introduced parameter, re-thin the schedule from CRF. Work distraction, distance, and duration in the same way that you did for sit.

As explained under sit, you should promote discrimination between the cues you have trained to this point. If you have only worked sit and down, you can work some pushups by cueing each in turn. Remember to include some cues for the position they are already in, so as to ensure the cue is not simply cuing change of position.

Phase 4. Maintenance

Once you have the final form and latency criteria of the target behavior, it is on cue, and reliably proofed through the three D-parameters, you can begin working toward maintenance. Continue to develop proficiency in new locations or with new distractors etc., but once you are well along with that, it is time to begin transitioning from the intensive training activities of the fluency development phase to less intensive maintenance of the fluency you have achieved.

Begin generalizing the reinforcers as you did with sit.

Common Challenges

As with sit, lying down can be uncomfortable for some dogs. In these cases, as with sit, consider proofing a good solid stand and wait position instead. However, more commonly, the down position is used for longer duration maintenance of position than would be comfortable for a stand or even sit. In that case, consider specifically training a comfortable down behavior. First, ensure what they lie down on is soft enough. This is particularly important for dogs with minimal fur and fat (such as Dobermans, Greyhounds, Boxers, and Dalmatians). Second, train them to lie down, not in a sphinx position with their midline straight on the floor, but rather leaning to a side with one of their hips on the floor and both front elbows on the floor. Find a position and solution that will work, but if you cannot, consider using some other behavior to achieve your goals when a soft thick bedding material is not available.

For some dogs, lying down seems to be a more vulnerable position, particularly when they are around other dogs, and especially if they are unknown dogs. Attend to the context in which you train and cue the down position. Consider using a sit or some other behavior that causes fewer vulnerability related behaviors in the dog (i.e., reluctance, escape, emotionality). If remedial socialization and behavior change programming is required to reduce fear, consider doing so.

Small breed dogs in particular are averse to the down position. It can be challenging to lure down and other position behaviors in some small breeds too. Consider starting the training as you sit beside the dog for the initial acquisition stage. Attend to the speed and distance from the treat to the dog that you use in luring, and adjust as necessary.

Some dogs will lower their front end to target the treat, but never lower their rear end or it takes a very long time before they do so. As mentioned above, consider sitting and creating a triangle tunnel with one bent leg to lure the dog through. Although physical manipulations are usually more disruptive, and even sometimes aversive in training, consider a very light touch to the top of the dog's back between the back hips. This is not a push or shove, but just a touch, which directs the dog's attention to the kinesthetic position of their rear quarter. If this works, it will work well and quickly, and you can fade that tactile prompt very quickly, but if it does not work quickly, it is best to abandon it. Please do not misunderstand these instructions. This is a mere touch to direct attention, rather than a pushing motion, and if it does not work right away, discontinue it. If the touch is strong enough, it will elicit the opposition reflex and fail, so it must be simply a brief touch to elicit kinesthetic awareness behaviors. In cases where this might be appropriate, it works quickly, which in turn prevents a lot of frustration. A mere touch, discontinued if it does not work quickly, should not be aversive at all and is less aversive than the frustration of ineffective training. Use any physical manipulation with great caution and avoid where possible. Another option is to gradually shape the down position.

Stand

Phase 1. Preliminaries

Behavior Objective

S^{Ev}: Verbal "Stand."

Behavior: Assume position with legs straight and all four paws on the ground with no other body parts touching the ground, at ~90 degree angle with the floor.

Criteria: Latency—2sec.; duration—until released or cued otherwise, minimum 2min.; frequency—100% through 10 trials; distance— minimum 6 meters; distraction—various; time point—3 sessions at ~5min. each.

This is another function-based definition because the dog might stand from either a seated or a down position. Training stand can be useful for applications in grooming and veterinary exams. It is also useful in that it allows a third basic position (along with sit and down) for training intercue discrimination, which can improve training of sit and down, the arguably more important of the three position behaviors. The distraction criteria is vague because this is a general example, so either ensure it is specific to your requirements, or provide an addendum with some more specific criteria.

Identify the conditioned reinforcer and unconditioned reinforcer you will use.

Phase 2. Acquisition

Utilize the same establishing operations as discussed for sit.

In the case of stand, prompting is usually quick and easy. To prompt stand when the dog is seated or lying down, place a small treat between your thumb and fingers and get the dog to target it. Once the dog is targeting the treat, move your hand slowly up a bit and straight away from the dog toward you about one dog step. They will stand to track the treat. Reinforce this the instant they are standing. Repeat through several trials until it is smooth and reliable.

Phase 3. Fluency

Follow the same general steps to train for fluency of down as you did for sit.

After the first few trials, begin fading the food-in-hand prompt as described under sit.

You should now be carrying out the prompt without food in your hands at all. The luring motion should be taking on stimulus control of the behavior at this point. Before this becomes too well established, begin fading the prompt, transferring stimulus control from the lure motion to a hand signal. The hand signal for stand is having your arm straight at your side with the palm toward the dog and moving it backward behind you (arm still straight). Use this hand signal as the S^{Ev} until the behavior is exhibited to criteria.

Now move to an intermittent schedule of reinforcement, and begin thinning that schedule.

Once you have the behavior in the form, latency, and speed you are comfortable with, you are free to establish the verbal cue with the procedure previously outlined.

Begin proofing the behavior against the three D-parameters. Remember to work only one at a time, and use the advice previously outlined.

As explained under sit, you should promote discrimination between the cues you have trained to this point. At this point you can work a three-way discrimination, which is particularly useful because the next cue given is not equivalent to a simple change in position; it may be one of at least two different positions. Remember the differential outcome effect; use distinct reinforcers for each behavior, and your training will be more efficient and effective. Once this is going well, include a test trial, cuing the behavior the dog is already in the position for to see if they remain in that position or change positions. Extinguish any changes in position and positively reinforce maintenance of position.

Phase 4. Maintenance

Once you have achieved the final form and latency criteria of the target behavior, and it is on cue and reliably proofed through the three D-parameters, you can begin working toward maintenance. Continue to develop proficiency in new locations or with new distractors etc., but once you are well along with that, it is time to begin transitioning from the intensive training activities of the fluency development phase to less intensive maintenance of the fluency you have achieved.

Begin generalizing the reinforcers as you did with sit and down.

Common Challenges

It can sometimes be challenging to maintain a stand still, because walking is done in the standing position (rather than the seated or down position). In these cases, it is simply a matter of working the duration component more gradually and using highly effective reinforcers as well as managing concurrent contingencies (i.e., distraction) more closely. Alternatively, when stopping after walking, a sit with duration behavior cued by the stopping itself is useful.

Wait

Phase 1. Preliminaries

Behavior Objective

S^{Ev}: Verbal "Wait."

Behavior: Cease moving if in motion and remain motionless otherwise.

Criteria: Latency—0.5sec.; duration—remain in place until released or cued otherwise, minimum 2min.; frequency—100% through 10 trials; distance— minimum 4 meters; distraction—various; time point—6 sessions at ~5min. each.

Wait is similar to a stay cue except that it is not used for duration maintenance for behaviors you have already cued. In those cases, simply train the behavior to be maintained until the dog is released—no secondary stay or wait cue is required. Wait can be useful at doors, when being fed, before grabbing a toy, or in any circumstance where you would like the dog to briefly halt their advance. Again, in actual cases, make distraction criteria specific in the definition, or provide an addendum with explicit and unambiguous distraction criteria.

Identify the conditioned and unconditioned reinforcer you will use.

Phase 2. Acquisition

Utilize the same establishing operations as discussed for sit.

Training wait is all about increasing duration gradually. Begin with a simple wait-appropriate arrangement. I will use waiting for a food bowl to be presented, but you can start with waiting at a doorway or other scenario. An advantage of starting with waiting for food is that it generates an intrinsic reinforcer and the continuous schedule it necessitates is more suited to the beginning of a training program. In any case, you will promote generalization to these other situations as you proceed with the training. You can ensure more trials by presenting only an eighth to sixteenth of the dog's meal on each trial. You may adjust the specific procedure to allow for any differences in how you prefer to present meals. Make sure you see the challenges section below before deciding to start with this reinforcer.

Begin by approaching the dog's bowl with kibble. Rather than requiring some specific behavior such as sit, simply present a hand in front of the dog's face, palm facing them, and quickly pour the kibble into the bowl (with a cup or some other container that allows for a quick pour). The palm hand signal is likely to attract at least a little initial attention and pause, giving you the time you need to immediately click and allow access to the food (the clicker is usually held in the cup held hand). The dog will then begin eating the food, providing positive reinforcement for the behavior. Remember that whether the dog is sitting or standing does not matter, and in fact, it can be more useful if you achieve a mix of these positions in order to achieve appropriate generalization and discrimination. Repeat this sequence through several trials until the meal has been fully presented. If the sequence is smooth and reliable at that point, you can move right to the fluency stage. Otherwise, repeat this for the next meal until the sequence is smooth and reliable with the minimal duration.

Phase 3. Fluency

Without prompts and especially prompts involving the conditioned reinforcer, fluency is a simpler process. Furthermore, because wait is used in instances where access to a reinforcer is simply delayed, there is no need to involve complex schedule thinning procedures, making the process even simpler. Although training for form, latency, and speed is not usually required, the three D-parameters are vital.

Once the sequence is smooth and reliable at this minimal duration, transfer stimulus control to a verbal cue. As before, say "wait," present the palm hand signal, and then release when the dog has ceased approaching. Repeat through several trials in order to condition the verbal cue, whereupon, you can drop the hand signal.

Once the verbal cue is established, begin gradually increasing the duration criterion. If you were requiring the dog to wait for a half of a second, begin requiring a full second for several trials, and once this is smooth and reliable, set the duration criterion to two seconds. If the dog breaks wait before being released, say "Oops," prevent access to the food in as nonconfrontational a manner as can be arranged and try again. Move through the duration steps slowly, and avoid extinction and negative punishment trials as much as possible as this will be frustrating for the dog and could lead to problem side effects. Try to begin making the duration seem random around a gradually increasing mean average. For example, one second, then two, then a half, and then two, and then two, and then one, and then three, and then one, and then two etc. Remember to adjust the criterion gradually, enough to minimize extinction and negative punishment trials, and also keep the progress smooth. Also maintain minimal distraction while you work on duration.

Start utilizing a release word. To do this, say the release word, usually "okay," right before you click. You can click as soon as the dog begins moving, but the use of a conditioned reinforcer is not usually necessary after a release.

It can be useful to begin working generalization with treats and toys, requiring a wait before accessing them when placed near the dog. This allows you to administer more frequent trials, and makes it easier to take to different places. Start close to where you feed the dog, and as usual, when instating a new D-parameter, relax the others. For example, begin with minimal duration, and work your way back up. This should go more quickly this time. Then practice in different places, each time relaxing the duration and rebuilding it. Once this is going smoothly, begin using the wait cue for other situations, such as waiting before going through a doorway or the opportunity to play with another dog etc. When you introduce a different item, reset the duration criterion and build it back up, and go back to CRF and re-thin the schedule. Try to maintain minimal distraction through these trials. Once this is going smoothly, you can work in the distraction criteria. Begin using the wait for more highly effective reinforcers, that is, things that are tougher to wait for. In each new case of distraction, reset and rebuild the duration component.

Phase 4. Maintenance

Continue to generalize to different stimuli and settings. Also, continue to generalize the reinforcers, utilizing more nontrainer-mediated activity reinforcers (aka, the Premack principle) versus more trainer-mediated extrinsic reinforcers. The task in the maintenance phase is simply to ensure that you continue to present trial opportunities to keep the training fresh. If, at any point, the training begins to deteriorate, refresh the training with more frequent sessions with initially relaxed duration and distraction, and build them back up.

Common Challenges

Some dogs will charge right for the food even before you finish pouring. If you cannot get a wait long enough to pour the food and click, try not to allow access to the food until you have released the dog from the wait but do not get into a wrestling match over it. Instead, try doing the exercise with a less reinforcing food item and doing so after the dog has eaten a full meal. You may need to start with some other reinforcer that can be controlled more easily and is not quite as effective a reinforcer to help ensure that you can get the wait long enough to build on.

The more effective the reinforcer you are cuing the dog to wait for, the slower you will have to go in terms of upping the duration criterion and the more trials you will have to put in. If you are getting too many extinction or negative punishment trials, this usually means you are moving too quickly or not putting in an adequate number of trials before upping the criterion.

Take it / Drop It

Phase 1. Preliminaries

Behavior Objective

S^{Ev}: Verbal "Take it."

Behavior: Take and hold the object being presented in the mouth.

Criteria: Latency—2sec.; duration—maintain until released or cued otherwise, minimum 10sec.; frequency— 100% through 10 trials; distance— minimum 4 meters; distraction—various.

Behavior Objective

S^{Ev}: Verbal "Drop it."

Behavior: Release from the mouth whatever is in it.

> **Criteria**: Latency—1sec.; frequency—100% through 10 trials; distance— minimum 4 meters; distraction—various; time point—6 sessions at ~5min. each.

Drop it and take it are useful because they allow you to get potentially dangerous things away from the dog quickly. It is helpful to train take it and drop it together, since exhibiting one provides a perfect opportunity to exhibit the other, and because take it is usually an effective reinforcer for drop it. This also provides a good basis for training retrieve later.

Phase 2. Acquisition

Utilize the same establishing operations as discussed for sit.

Ensure you have a list of all the dog's most effective reinforcer items. These are usually toys. Start with the least effective item, and if need be, ensure satiation. Hold the item, and encourage the dog to chew on the other end of it. Keep hold of the toy. Once they have it in their mouth, say "drop it," and then hold up a very effective treat. The dog will usually let go of the item to investigate the treat, especially if you started with a minimally effective reinforcer for them to hold onto and a relatively effective reinforcer to trade for it. As soon as they open their mouth, click, deliver the treat, and offer the toy back while you are still holding onto it. If you are pretty sure they will take the toy back, say "take it" after you present it to them, but before they do take it. Repeat the sequence several more times, and then quickly attempt a trial without the treat in your hand. Behavioral momentum will make occurrence of the behavior very likely. Repeat the sequence several more times with no treats in your fingers.

For training techniques that require three hands like this, it is usually most effective to hold the toy with one hand, and the treat and clicker in the other hand. Hold the treat between the index finger, middle finger, and thumb. Keep the clicker in the palm of the treat hand, with the button available to the small or third finger. You could hold the toy and clicker in one hand, but the clicker will then be pretty close to the dog's ear, and this might startle them.

Begin testing the effectiveness of the take it cue by waiting a couple of seconds before delivering the cue. If they mouth at the item before the cue is delivered, say "oops," and pull it away. Then repeat offering the opportunity to wait for the toy again. Once they wait for the cue, before attempting to take it, click, and provide the toy. Extinction and negative punishment are aversive, though mildly—try to minimize these trials with a graded approach. Start with a couple seconds and only build up gradually, ensuring you get very few punitive trials.

Next, run through this training protocol with the item next on the list of most effective reinforcer items. Work your way through each of the items on the list in this manner. Start to practice relinquishing constant contact with the item too, allowing the dog to simply drop the item, so that you can pick it up and offer it back to them. Occasionally, practice not offering the toy back to the dog. In that case, provide several treats that will take them a few seconds to find on the floor and eat while you place the item out of sight. It is important that the dog be conditioned such that the item sometimes won't come back. The distraction and the highly effective nature of the treats will help maintain the behavior under this condition.

Phase 3. Fluency

Once you have worked your way through most of the dog's favorite toys, begin practicing trials with other items outside of training sessions. Part of what controls the behavior is the trainer-mediated and controlled training session arrangement. Practice delivering the cue with these items at seemingly random times, as well as when the dog is already in contact with the items, without you having encouraged them to take it first.

Begin proofing the behavior against the three D-parameters. In the case of take it and drop it, all three are applicable—as always, work through one at a time and relax the other (as well as the schedule of reinforcement) when upping a parameter level. Duration is a special case in training for drop it training. Your goal is to administer the drop it cue, have the dog drop the item, and wait for an extended period of time, before they are cued to take it or are released. This allows you to administer the cue from a distance and cover that distance while the dog continues to wait without taking the toy back. Practice in close proximity first, and gradually increase the time between dropping it and reinforcing it with the opportunity to take it again. Approaching the dog and item is likely to be a distraction, so work that separately from duration training and then combine them afterward. Distance, as usual, involves administering the cue from further and further away from the dog. After duration is covered, work distance gradually and incrementally. You can work a sit into this sequence if you like. This would be a behavior chain of dropping the item and then sitting.

Phase 4. Maintenance

Continue to generalize the behavior to various items, at various times, and in various places. If, at any point, any component of the training seems to be deteriorating, refresh the training, taking a run through building that parameter back up.

Common Challenges

One particular challenge you might face with some dogs is that they do not tend to take things in their mouths, particularly when offered by someone by hand. In that case, break the process down into smaller steps. Begin with an item that the dog is more likely to take. Place it down on the ground so that you are not holding it. Begin shaping interest in the item, and then closer and closer approaches to taking it. Aim, initially, for a touch and then for taking the item in their mouth. Use highly effective reinforcers. Put a cue on this. Once this is complete, you should find it much easier to train the dog to take it from your hands. To begin, hold the same toy up close to their mouth, and reinforce tolerance and interest related behaviors through several trials. You may find that they begin to take it on their own, and if that occurs, reinforce it, and build on that. If they do not take it, touch the toy to their mouth to encourage them to take it. If none of this works, you may elect to work the drop it and take it without your actual contact with the toy. This will then likely involve shaping. Many dogs tend to retrieve with little or no trainer-mediated intervention, and if this is the case, you might be able to take advantage of that to train take it and drop it.

Here (Recall)

Phase 1. Preliminaries

Behavior Objective

S^{Ev}_1: Verbal "Here."

Behavior$_1$: Begin approaching the caller.

Criteria: Latency—2sec.; speed—at least a trotting gate; frequency—100% through 10 trials; distance— minimum 15 meters; distraction—various.

S^{Ev}_2: Arrives at person.

Behavior$_2$: Sit in front of called, facing caller.

Criteria: Latency—1sec.; duration—maintain until released or cued otherwise, minimum 2min.; frequency— 100% through 10 trials; distraction—various; time point—10 sessions at ~5min. each.

This is a behavior chain since there are two distinct behaviors exhibited in sequence, with only one cue at the beginning, and reinforcement provided by the trainer only after the last behavior. We can supplement the definition with a task analysis:

Upon being called, the dog will:

• Approach caller

• Sit in front of caller, facing caller.

Coming when called is extremely important, largely because it helps us manage where the dog is, and get them away from potential problems. Recall training is often challenging, but usually just because guardians have managed to effectively counter-train it prior to being coached to train it by a professional (and then often during and afterward too). Three common mistakes are: 1. The verbal cue is used before the behavior is reliable, and hence the cue is weakened as an S^{Ev}. 2. Guardians tend to inadvertently impose negative punishers, and in some cases, positive punishers for coming when called, particularly outside of formal training sessions. 3. Guardians expect too much, too quickly, especially with regard to distance and distraction, which degrades the effectiveness of training. Avoid these three common mistakes, so that the behavior is much easier to train.

In a way, it is preliminary to training that we ensure coming to people is always reinforcing and never punitive, or at least as close as possible to this ideal. This should be the guiding rule before, during, and after training, both in training sessions per se and out. Reinforcing does not always mean providing treats or toys when dogs come to us. It means generally being a source of all sorts of reinforcers and the source of very few aversers. It means becoming a conditioned reinforcer like a clicker. Avoid calling a dog in order to carry out tasks like nail trimming or getting into a crate, if this will be aversive, and if it is, then work on desensitizing the dog to these things and otherwise reducing the aversiveness of them. Instead, work tirelessly to ensure that being near you, and coming to you, is as reinforcing as is possible!

A common pitfall scenario for training a solid recall occurs outside of training sessions, wherein the guardian has the dog outside and calls the dog to come inside. The dog either comes, and being brought inside punishes coming to them, or else the dog does not come to the guardian, because competing contingencies prevail, thereby weakening the recall cue. Thus far, we have a lose-lose scenario.

It is best to avoid this scenario to begin with, but if the guardian determines that it is unlikely that the dog will come to them in this situation, they commonly face a choice to enforce it by going to get the dog, or to continue attempting to persuade the dog to come to them, or they give up and wait. Here again, we have a lose-lose scenario.

Guardians will frequently ask the trainer, "What do I do when I call the dog and they do not come to me?" In this case, remind clients not to cue the behavior unless they are pretty sure the dog *will* come to them. In these early stages, a light long-line leash is an option that allows the guardian to gently control the dog. Another option is to wait for the contingencies to change, making coming inside more reinforcing than not. Feeding a meal or special treats upon coming inside can help in this regard, as can having favored toys available inside only.

You can of course manipulate the contingencies yourself, rather than wait for satiation of being outdoors and deprivation of being indoors. A squeaky toy might lure the dog in. Although not ideal, it does contribute to your reinforcing effect and minimizes certain lose-lose scenarios involving waiting or coercing the behavior. In any event, avoid forcibly retrieving the dog (often called 'enforcing the command' by those inclined to use this as a basic strategy in training the recall). If you go get the dog, this commonly results in one of two outcomes: either the dog runs away and you end up getting sucked into playing the 'keep-away game,' or you do get the dog and the coercion deteriorates your relationship (i.e., making social contact with you punitive rather than reinforcing). You do not want approaching the dog to come to cue them to run away from you—this can be dangerous. Coercion is wrought with so many problems; it is best to focus on management and prevention, and if need be, even on bribing temporarily in emergencies. Occasionally in the early stages of training a recall, if I have made an error and face this situation, I have commonly had success with running around the yard to get the dog to chase me, and once the dog is really into it, I run inside, where they tend to reliably follow. Do this too much though, and they will catch onto the trick. Once inside, I treat, play, and generally make them really glad (so to speak) that they came in.

The target behavior is for the dog to quickly come to you from wherever they are. Although not required in all cases, it is a good idea to include sitting facing you when they arrive and allowing their collar to be grabbed (which could act as a conditioned reinforcer actually). This becomes a sequence of distinct behaviors exhibited one after the other with the single cue and no other trainer-provided cue interjected before the sitting behavior.

Identify the conditioned and unconditioned reinforcer you will use.

Phase 2. Acquisition

Utilize the same establishing operations as discussed for sit.

Because this behavior is frequently required in everyday life outside of training sessions, there are a few rules to adhere to. First, avoid punishing either remaining near you or coming to you. Avoid, for instance, calling the dog to you for some kind of reprimand or when you need to do something that might be aversive such as clipping nails or the like. Try to also avoid calling the dog when coming will end reinforcing activities, such as playing or interacting with another dog. Being near you and coming to you must always be reinforcing, ideally more reinforcing than any other contingency, which is a tall order so heed these rules.[34]

You can play a come-to-me game with the dog and two people. As always, start acquisition training in a very low distraction environment like a hallway or boring room. Each person should take turns calling the dog (without the here cue for now) away from the other person, clapping and encouraging in order to prompt the behavior. As soon as the dog gets to the person, the person should immediately request a sit and grab the dog's collar, followed immediately by positive reinforcement.

Once this is well under way, you can begin calling the dog without a partner. Choose these times carefully! Ensure a high degree of likelihood that the dog will come to you, away from whatever they are doing.

Once these are fairly smooth and reliable, you can move on to training for fluency.

Phase 3. Fluency

Now, begin fading the prompt, and install a temporary cue. You will still have some shaping to do in order to hone certain features of the behavior, such as the speed with which they run to you, and the latency between cue and initiation of the behavior, but it would be useful to have a verbal cue to use in the meantime. I like the phrase "come-on" but you can choose something else. Begin fading the prompts by saying

---

[34] One thing I personally do, because my dog loves in-shell peanuts, is drop one in the backyard and then, seemingly out of the blue, I call my dog and when he gets there I point to the peanut. I do this at least every couple days, and when I call him in the back yard, he comes running eagerly. This is just an example of ways to keep being near you and coming to you reinforcing. Find effective ways to keep the dog eager to run to you.

"come-on" in a happy tone, and follow that with the prompts. After a few trials, begin gradually reducing the prompts; the verbal cue, which should have taken on stimulus control, should evoke the behavior alone. If you need gentle praise while the dog is on their way to you, you can use that but fade the praise prompts through several trials as well.

Now move to an intermittent schedule of reinforcement, and begin thinning that schedule as outlined previously. Unlike most other behaviors, it is usually advisable to maintain a recall on a fairly rich schedule of reinforcement, to keep it highly reliable.

Begin refining the form, latency, and speed of the behavior. As usual, work one at a time, and each time you introduce a new feature, bring the schedule back to CRF. Remember, relax the three D-parameters and schedule of reinforcement, but do not relax form, latency, and speed; once you achieve progress in these features of the behavior, maintain them.

Begin proofing the behavior against the three D-parameters. For this application, you will focus heavily on distraction. Begin incrementally increasing distraction at a pace that still allows you to achieve success in at the very least 95% of your trials. At first, it is usually best to arrange for highly contrived and controlled environments. Begin working in more real world distractions as you proceed to proof the behavior.

You might arrange for a two-person recall game, wherein the person that the dog is near has toys or treats readily visible to the dog, giving them a "reason" to remain there. The trainer calls the dog away from a short distance. If the cue fails to evoke the behavior, the distractor does not relinquish any of the reinforcers. Try again, adjusting the level of distraction as appropriate until you achieve success. Praise enthusiastically if the dog moves toward you in order to prompt or encourage coming to you, if needed. If they turn away, stop praising. Do not cue the behavior again; deliver cues only once per trial. Once the dog does come to you, cue the sit, gently grab the collar, click and provide a hidden treat, and allow them immediate access to the distractor and their treats or toys. Repeat the procedure several times until the recall becomes reliable. Once it does, you can work on increasing the level and variety of distractions, including different locations. Cueing a recall away from a reinforcer is a big step—take it gradually.

Once you have worked through increasing levels of distraction and several different kinds of distraction as well as a variety of locations, you can begin more spontaneous real-life trials, calling the dog away from increasing levels of distraction, ensuring that the behavior is reinforced. Another good game to play at this stage is calling the dog away from a distraction of some kind only to immediately release and reinforce with the opportunity to reengage the distractor. This is useful, especially when the dog is playing with other dogs. In all of these cases, it is important to take a graded approach. Start by only expecting to call the dog away from minimally distraction, then, increase that level of distraction gradually, only after it has been mastered. Avoid too many of these in a row, as they will become frustrating and aversive.

Once you have the behavior's form and latency meeting objective criteria, and you have worked distraction and distance up to appropriate levels, you are free to establish the final verbal cue. To transfer stimulus control from the temporary cue to the permanent one, use this sequence: "here," followed by "come-on." This will evoke the behavior, which you then reinforce. Repeat through several trials, until you can drop the old temporary stimulus from the sequence.

Phase 4. Maintenance

Continue to generalize the reinforcers utilizing the Premack principle in order to help you maintain control over the behavior by providing the opportunity to exhibit other more likely behaviors. If, at any point, any component of the training seems to be deteriorating, refresh the training by taking a run through building that parameter back up.

Common Challenges

By far, the most common challenge with recall is failure to achieve sufficient mastery at one level of difficulty before moving to the next. In other words, people usually expect too much, too soon, in this training, and they fail to manage the situations adequately in order to ensure successful rehearsal. The recall faces competing contingencies almost by definition since the dog will usually be contacting some reinforcer when you call them. More than most behaviors (along with off and loose leash walking), distraction is a ubiquitous and powerful challenge. The reinforcement for approaching you must surpass the reinforcement available elsewhere.

Off

Phase 1. Preliminaries

Behavior Objective

S^{Ev}: Verbal "Off."

Behavior: Look away from whatever is being attending to but has not yet been taken in mouth.

Criteria: Latency—1 sec.; frequency—100% through 10 trials; distance— minimum 4 meters; distraction— various; time point—5 sessions at ~5min. each.

The off cue can be useful to help redirect dogs away from things that might harm them or to aid in other training endeavors. Although it is sometimes framed in 'what not to do,' off is best framed in a positive form. The target behavior off is for the dog to move their muzzle away from what they are attending to when the cue is given. The behavior objective is defined as looking away although it can be useful to include stepping away from the stimulus as well, since proximity allows the stimulus to exert stronger control over the behavior; it may become strong enough that close to exert control over the behavior again. This is a matter of defining the behavior. It can also be useful to cue a sit immediately following the off cue, or you can chain them so that the off cue evokes looking away, then sitting and waiting. Alternatively, you can specifically train the dog to both look at you and sit. Again, define the behavior for the specific requirements sought.

Off can be a double-edged sword, and caution must be exercised when considering its use. It is common for problem behaviors to be chained with off. Any time you use a cue that is administered during or immediately after a problem behavior, such as off, to "redirect" a dog

away from something, you risk training the chain of exhibiting the problem behavior, thereby making available the off cue, and hence the off behavior and reinforcer it generates. Off is best used in the moments before a problem contact behavior is exhibited when the dog is merely attending to the stimulus off which you want to call their attention. In emergencies, drop it can be used for getting the dog to let go of something they have in their mouth.

The off cue, as I will present it here, will cue looking away from whatever they are attending to, but have not yet taken in their mouth. This is a function-based definition and as such the operant can allow for various specific behaviors. It is good practice in that case to ensure that you include various specific behaviors in your training. In specific cases, it is also a good idea to provide an addendum to your definition of specific distractions. If you find that a specific behavior emerges in the training, you might also elect to adopt that as the specific response set for the cue.

Prepare a list of effective reinforcers, in rank order, that can be used for training. Start with a small treat as the first item, but ensure it is a minimally tasty treat to ensure success. This first one should be a small treat as it will be in your hands and used as the unconditioned reinforcer. The list should have as many items as can be generated because it will be the list that is worked from all the way to the maintenance stage. It should include things like garbage cans, other dogs, and fire hydrants—things that will attract your dog.

Identify the conditioned and unconditioned reinforcer you will use.

Phase 2. Acquisition

Utilize the standard training practices previously discussed regarding setting the dog and yourself up for success.

One way to train off is to shape it. Begin by holding a treat in your hand far out to your side away from you. Make sure the dog sees that there is a treat there. Hold it out of reach so that they cannot get at it—simply wait. Timing is vital here. Eventually, the dog will glance away from that hand. This is usually *very* brief the first time! The instant they glance away from the treat, even very briefly, click and release the treat from your hand. Repeat the process several more times, requiring only a glance away. You should find the dog more readily looks away from the hand. Once you find this is proceeding smoothly, you can up the ante a little bit, and set the criterion to a definite look away that lasts a full second. Repeat through several trials. Once it is smooth and reliable, set the criterion to two seconds, building it up gradually and incrementally in that manner until you have five seconds or so.

Once these are fairly smooth and reliable, you can move on to training for fluency.

Phase 3. Fluency

There are no contrived prompts to fade, making the process a little simpler at this stage. Start by putting the behavior on an intermittent schedule of reinforcement, and refining the form, latency, and speed as needed. At this point, the held out hand functions to evoke the behavior. Once you have the behavior exhibited to criteria, establish the verbal cue for the behavior. Give the off cue, present the hand and the behavior should occur. Reinforce the behavior. Repeat through several trials until the verbal cue is established.

Once you have the verbal cue established, begin generalization training. Start by putting the hand that has treats in different positions and directions. Then, once that is solid, begin applying the cue to treats that are not in your hand. Then begin applying the cue to other things and in different places. Remember to relax the three D-parameters, and return to CRF when introducing a new criterion feature such as this. Expect only the brief look away first, and you can build the duration back up gradually.

At this point, begin proofing the training against the three D-parameters. It is usually best to begin with more controlled situations with trainer-mediated reinforcers, and work more intrinsically reinforcing real-world situations in later. Start using more effective reinforcers, such as better treats or toys, and after that, begin mild deprivation to increase the rate of responding even more. It would be a good idea to plan some of your distraction items ahead of time. Disengaging from approaching or eye contact with another dog is often a high level distraction, as is approaching to sniff a fire hydrant or garbage can. Work through your list of increasingly effective reinforcers. Remember to relax duration and distance when introducing a new feature. Similarly, you might work the duration up to 15 seconds. You may not need more than this for general use. Distance would include increasing how far you are from the dog and stimulus when you deliver the cue.

Once you have worked through increasing levels of controlled and contrived distraction, including several different kinds of distraction and a variety of locations, start more spontaneous real-life trials, cuing the dog to disengage from increasing levels of distraction in the real world, ensuring that the behavior is reinforced.

Once the cue is effective in a wide variety of situations, begin thinning the schedule. It is usually a good idea to maintain a rather rich schedule of reinforcement for off.

Phase 4. Maintenance

Continue to generalize the reinforcers, utilizing the Premack principle in order to help you maintain control over the behavior by providing the opportunity to exhibit other, more preferred, behaviors. Often the most effective reinforcers will be reestablishing contact with what they were called off of. However, this will not always be acceptable, so continue to include controlled and contrived trials for stimuli you can allow them to contact, and have highly effective extrinsic reinforcers ready for times when you cannot allow continued contact with the stimulus in question. If at any point any component of the training seems to be deteriorating, refresh the training by taking a run through building that parameter back up.

Common Challenges

Some dogs, particular active breeds, will jump up at the hand during the initial stages of your shaping program. You can try training at times when jumping up will be less likely such as after exercising. You can also use negative punishment or extinction trials for jumping up, if necessary. The best option may be to lower yourself so the dog does not need to jump up to access your hand. You have to ensure you have a good grip on the treat and that you do not release it until you have clicked for a criterion response. They will mouth and nibble, but you will simply wait for the glance away. Typically, at first, the looks away are glances at you as if to say "Hey, what's up? Let go my Eggo."

Another common challenge is the potential for a behavior chain to develop. In some cases, attending to the object may become reinforced by the opportunity to respond appropriately to the off cue. In other words, the dog looks at the problem stimulus because that leads to the off cue and then a reinforcer. If moving toward and attending to something makes available the opportunity to move away from it in order to contact treats, then you can expect the rate of contacting the problem stimulus to increase. Carefully observe for increased interest in problem stimuli after off training has started. It is best to manage the environment so that dogs cannot access problem stimuli and to use off only for situations where you did not anticipate contact with it. If a problem chain is conditioned, try to manage access to the stimulus as part of an antecedent control strategy instead of continuing to strengthen a behavior chain. Another tip would be to use the off cue for a wide variety of items in training but not for any one item extensively. If you find that you are using the off cue for one item quite a bit, you should find a way to preemptively manage access to that item to prevent use of the off cue.

Let's go (Walking on Loose Leash)

Phase 1. Preliminaries

Behavior Objective

S^{Ev}: Leash on.

Behavior: Walking adjustment behaviors such that the shoulders stay within 5 feet of the handler (Leash tightens at 6 feet indicating a noncriterion behavior).

Criteria: Frequency—100% through 10 trials; distance— maintain minimum 3 standard city blocks (approximately 411 meters or 1350 feet); distraction—various; time point—14 sessions at ~5min. each.

Walking with a slack leash rather than a tight leash is important and challenging to train. Some might say it is a "natural" behavior, but of course all behavior is natural. What this likely means is that the general strategy of quickly approaching something reinforcing tends to be prepotent over approaching more slowly or walking away from it, for instance. Furthermore, most dogs move at a quicker pace than most people. The opposition reflex can often encourage dogs to pull against a tight leash as well. What's worse is that most dogs—even puppies—who pull on leash have a strong history of reinforcement for that behavior. It can be challenging to avoid the problem behavior while you establish a preferable one.

While some trainers tend to frame this behavior in a negative form, stating what behavior we want to avoid, rather than the behavior we want to achieve, the operant behavior for walking on loose leash can be stated positively as walking close to the handler, a function of proximity and the required operants to achieve that as part of a function-based definition. One may specify a side to walk on as part of their criteria. One may also specify a very close proximity to, for example the left leg of the handler, and train a formal heel. We do often frame loose leash walking in negative terms for a useful reason—a tightening leash is an indication that a mutually exclusive noncriterion behavior is occurring, assuming we define walking close to the handler such that it approximates the leash length (usually a standard 1.8 meter / 6 foot leash, held close to the handler's hip).

There are several ways to train loose leash walking. I will elaborate a straightforward method. Before beginning, prevent pulling on leash as much as possible in nontraining session times. Every instance of pulling on leash will make progress through the training process more challenging, because you will have to countercondition it. I also recommend that you use a standard body harness rather than a neck collar, as this will reduce the opposition reflex that challenges your training. There are likely times when the dog will be less likely to pull. Try to identify these times and begin training then. For instance, many dogs will pull less when they are walking inside rather than outside, or walking toward or away from home rather than the opposite, or after a good bout of exercise. Most dogs pull less in novel environments/neighborhoods. Try to begin training at the times and places where pulling will be least likely, and work your way through a ranked list of these situations. This will help set both of you up for success.

Identify the conditioned and unconditioned reinforcer you will use.

Phase 2. Acquisition

A graded approach works well for training loose leash walking. Rather than providing the dog the straight opportunity to either pull or not, and reacting differentially to each with reinforcement and punishment, set yourselves up for success by setting the criteria low, and working the criteria up gradually and incrementally to keep the progress smooth and efficient, with a very high rate of success. Begin holding the leash with your dog seated or standing still beside you facing the same direction. Press the hand that is clasping the leash handle up against your belt line. This will ensure that the distance to the end of the leash is a stable 1.8 meters / 6 feet at all times, and so that you will not be modifying distance with your reach.

Although being on leash will set the occasion for keeping close to you, a cue such as "let's go" can be useful since the dog may interact with the environment on walks, and you will want a cue to proceed with walking. When initiating your movement, cue let's go, take a step forward, and as the dog begins to walk click and treat after that first step. Repeat through several trials. Once that is smooth and reliable, set the criterion to two steps. If the dog bolts forward at any point and the leash goes tight, say "Oops," stop, and do not move or engage the dog for a few seconds. Evaluate whether you are moving too quickly through the task increments, and lower them if need be to ensure that you minimize the number of negative punishment trials. Proceed after the negative punishment interval once the dog is not pulling on leash. Work your way up in this manner, ping-ponging the criterion, until you can get several steps walking on loose leash with very few noncriterion behaviors.

Use direction changes to help get more steps per trial and avoid negative punishment trials. Walking on loose leash is really made up of a long series of evocative stimuli and modifications to walking behavior; the dog attends to your trajectory and speed, and these cues evoke the changes in their trajectory and speed. When you change directions, you encourage the dog to attend more closely to your location, and it puts you further ahead of them, which allows for a greater number of steps before they pull on leash. It also increases interest. Once you have taken several steps and are getting to your current limit, try changing directions at a 45 to 90 degree angle for instance. Consider using a greater angle relative to how close the dog is to the end of the leash. For example, if the dog is still walking close to you, a slight change in direction can spice up the walk a bit, but if the dog is getting close to the end of the leash and it is about to go tight, use a wider angle, maybe even 90 degrees or more. Avoid jerking the leash though; the leash should only be gently tightened to evoke the dog's change in direction. A tight leash will come to evoke attending to you for direction cues.

Novice trainers often use the leash during training to generate the behavior, rather than focusing on the training. Maintain the leash length consistently. Again, to keep the leash at a constant predictable length (not adding your arm length to it) and prevent inadvertent prompting with it, you can hold the leash with your hand pinned to your hip. You can place your thumb into the waistband—this acts as a quick release so that you don't get pulled over if the dog bolts for some reason; your thumb will come out of your waistband, and you'll have a brief interval in which to prepare to maintain your hold on the leash and prevent a sudden jerk on the leash.

Phase 3. Fluency

Continue to work toward more steps between reinforcers, thinning the schedule as you proceed.

Next, begin proofing against the three D-parameters. You can use reinforcers found in the uncontrived environment as distractors. For example, if the dog indicates an interest in sniffing a hydrant or meeting another dog, make access to these things contingent on walking close to you until you arrive at the thing. This exercise is best reserved for when you are far enough along in the training to be confident that you will succeed. You can include a release word here, however it is not usually necessary. The "let's go" cue can be used to get back on track.

Duration would be how long you walk before reinforcing. Work the duration gradually, and as usual, relax other D-parameters when you increase the duration.

Distance is not applicable to walking on loose leash since it is an up close behavior only.

Phase 4. Maintenance

Continue to generalize the reinforcers utilizing the Premack principle in order to help maintain control over the behavior with the opportunity to exhibit other more preferred behaviors. If at any point any component of the training seems to be deteriorating, refresh the training by building that parameter back up.

Common Challenges

Rehearsal of Pulling

By far, the most common challenge in training walking on loose leash is that guardians allow too many reinforced occurrences of pulling behavior. If training is to be effective, the dog must not be allowed opportunities to rehearse the problem behavior, even though this is indeed an inconvenience. If walking on loose leash is ever to be successful, pulling must be extinguished! Help clients brainstorm ways to prevent and manage situations where the dog might pull on leash. Where necessary, use a distinct and salient restraint device when the dog will pull, to help protect the training associated with the usual harness (via discrimination training).

Diehard Puller

A strong history of reinforcement for pulling can be a major obstacle to training. In these cases, the same procedure discussed above can be used, but the progress will be much slower, and the training will be much longer, because pulling will need to be extinguished. In some cases, an anti-pull harness might be considered.

Trailing Behind

Some dogs seem to hunker down like a "stubborn donkey" and refuse to move forward. They may or may not pull forward on leash at other times, but when a dog refuses to move forward, attempting to pull or otherwise force them forward, usually results in a longer battle. First, identify whether the dog may have medical problems, perhaps with arthritis or dysplasia in their joints, or if the dog is heat intolerant. Identify if the dog seems fearful of something specific, and if so, avoid that situation while trying to train loose leash walking. This reaction should be addressed with a proper behavior change program. If the dog trails behind in specific situations, then perhaps a previous experience with this situation was overwhelming or otherwise aversive. This too requires desensitization. If this does not seem to be the case, then be patient. Wait a few moments with a slack leash, and perhaps then gently verbally coax the dog forward. If the dog does not respond to this, discontinue coaxing, and begin a shaping program for moving forward. The benefit here is derived from not only achieving reinforcement opportunities, but also that the positive reinforcers will respondently countercondition any problem emotional arousal occurring in that situation. Start by perhaps cueing a couple of other behaviors, such as down and sit or look, just to get into the habit of taking direction. Be patient and have fun, especially at these times! Find a location that is least likely to evoke reluctance. Now, observe for the slightest relaxation in stance or lean forward, and click and treat that, shaping forward motion. Repeat several times, and then adjust the criteria, requiring slightly more of a lean or movement forward. In this way, shape the let's go behavior. Work your way up to places that more readily evoke reticence.

Dog is Too Strong or Big Compared to Guardian

When the dog is exceptionally strong or large compared to the guardian, this makes good training practices even more important. Rather than manhandling the dog, identify and instate effective reinforcement. Carry out the training as described, but put particular attention into ensuring successful trials, particularly with raising distraction levels. That said, this situation could be particularly challenging because if the dog does barge forward toward a reinforcer, the guardian may not be able to effectively ensure extinction. Consider using an anti-pull harness for these dogs for such situations. Avoid relying on anti-pull devices to make pulling aversive. Focus on controlling the dog's behavior with positive reinforcers and extinction where necessary. However, for times when the guardian simply cannot effectively control the dog, the anti-pull harness may improve controllability. If the situation is extreme, then the guardian should consider hiring a capable dog walker.

Dog is "Crazy"

Although we do not frame it quite that way as professionals concerned with clarity, we are quite familiar with the complaint that walking on leash is impossible, because the dog is "crazy." Determine specifically what actual behaviors are being exhibited and what stimuli are controlling them. This encompasses various scenarios such as a dog that expends extensive energy engaging in many behaviors rapidly (e.g., bolting in different directions, chewing at the leash, bouncing or jumping). The key element is that the dog engages in various noncriterion behaviors rapidly. This is common with some puppies and dogs new to leashes, or dogs with bodies in an activity deprived state. It can also be common with dogs that are fearful or generally risk averse. These noncriterion behaviors function to self-distract or escape something.

If the dog is new to leashes, introduce the leash slowly, and shape tolerance related behaviors with increasing contact with the collar and leash. If the dog is generally risk averse or fearful, instate a behavior change program to change this, and come back to loose leash walking when you can, or else find a time and place where you are able to bypass these behaviors. If it turns out that the problem is associated with excess stimulation, find a minimally arousing environment for the initial stages of walking on loose leash. Work increasingly arousing environments as part of proofing for distraction practices. Carry out the training after an extensive exercise or play session, or identify times for the dog when the problem is less likely. Exercise is commonly very helpful in these situations. In any case, make arrangements to set the dog up for success as much as possible and maintain the basic strategies of training. Make the behavior you want more likely and other behaviors less likely, set the criteria low, and gradually and incrementally work your way through the levels of difficulty with a graded approach.

Go to "bed"

Phase 1. Preliminaries

Behavior Objective

S^{Ev}_1: Verbal "Go to bed."

Behavior$_1$: Proceed to a designated mat.

    Criteria: Latency—2sec.; speed—average walking gate; frequency—100% through 10 trials; distance—minimum 6 meters; distraction—various.

S^{Ev}_2: Arrives at mat.

Behavior$_2$: Lie down on the mat.

    Criteria: Latency—1sec.; duration—maintain until released or cued otherwise, minimum 6min.; frequency—100% through 10 trials; distraction—various; time point—4 sessions at ~5min. each.

This is a behavior chain since there are two distinct behaviors exhibited in sequence, with just one cue at the beginning and reinforcement provided by the trainer only after the last behavior. In that case, we can supplement the behavior objective with a task analysis:

Upon being cued to "go to bed," the dog will:

- Proceed to the designated mat

- Lie down on the mat.

This cue can be used to direct the dog to go to specific places. What actual cue you select is based on what location you want the dog to go to. It is often used to train a dog to go to a crate or bed, and that is the context in which I will outline the training, but it can be used to direct the dog to other locations, or to find and go to specific people. Usually, trainers condition a behavior chain that involves going to the location and then sitting or lying down once they get there. The operant associated with this cue is for the dog to immediately proceed to a specific place when cued and remain there until released. I will outline the training below with the cue "go to bed" to cue a dog to go to their mat or bed.

Phase 2. Acquisition

Utilize the same establishing operations as discussed for other behaviors.

The most effective and efficient way to train this behavior is with the use of a remote treat dispenser such as the Manners Minder® by Premier (premier.com) since it helps with administering treats from a distance. However, I will outline the training without such a device. Remember to begin in a minimally distracting environment.

Forward chaining is suitable for a simple chain of behaviors such as this. I will assume the dog already exhibits lying down on cue, but if this is not the case, train that behavior on its own. Next, train the dog to go to the mat on cue. Start by standing only a meter (a little over three feet) from the bed with the dog beside you. Deliver the temporary cue of pointing to the mat, and immediately lure the dog with a treat to the bed. As soon as the dog is standing on the mat, click and release the treat. Repeat through a few trials. Begin fading the food-in-hand prompt to an empty handed prompt.

Both behaviors that compose the chain should be acquired at this point, though minimally, and not yet linked together.

Phase 3. Fluency

Begin the fluency stage by chaining the behavior together. Point to the mat to cue the behavior of going to the mat, and for now, still from close by. Once at the mat, cue down right away. As soon as the dog lies down, click and treat. Repeat through several trials. Test the effectiveness of the pointing cue by waiting a couple seconds once the dog gets to the mat to determine if the dog will also lie down. If the dog does lie down right away, click and treat and repeat through several trials. If the dog does not lie down right away, cue lying down and practice several more trials before testing again and until the dog does lie down once they get to the mat. Review the section on behavior chaining for more detailed elaboration of chaining procedures.

Put the reinforcement on an intermittent schedule, and gradually thin it in a ping-pong fashion.

Next, begin proofing against the three D-parameters. If you begin with duration, remember to keep distance and distraction minimal, and to briefly reinstate a CRF schedule. Instead of clicking immediately upon the dog getting to the mat or lying on it, wait an extra second or two and then click and treat. Gradually work the duration up to a couple of minutes, and begin thinning an intermittent schedule of reinforcement again.

Once you have a reliable duration, begin working distance. Go back to CRF and relax the duration feature as you start from gradually increasing distance from the mat when you cue the behavior. Ensure that you include the special feature of cuing the behavior when the mat is not directly in the dog's sight. Again, once you have the distance criterion reliable, put the behavior back on a thinning intermittent schedule.

Finally, you can proof the behavior against distraction. Start with minimally distracting stimuli present while relaxing the schedule of reinforcement, duration, and distance criteria. Begin introducing incrementally more distracting stimuli into the environment, until the dog exhibits the behavior reliably even under moderately to very distracting stimulation. Put the behavior back on a thinning schedule of reinforcement, and then begin working the features together.

Some dogs will run smoothly through this process, while others will require remedial work at certain stages. Be prepared to observe the progress of the training, and adjust as needed to ensure success. You should now be able to cue the behaviors from a greater distance, under distracting circumstances, and the dog will reliably go to the mat, lie down, and remain there until released. At this stage, replace the click with a release word.

Once the behavior chain is more or less where you want it, criteria wise, transfer stimulus control from the temporary cue of pointing, to a permanent verbal cue. Say "go to bed," and then point to the mat, at which point the dog will exhibit the behavior and you will reinforce the behavior. Repeat through several trials until you can drop the old temporary cue from the sequence.

Phase 4. Maintenance

Continue to introduce new distractions as they become apparent, thin the schedule of reinforcement, and keep up regular practice to ensure the training is maintained. If at any point any component of the training seems to be deteriorating, refresh the training by building that parameter back up.

Common Challenges

One of the major challenges in training a dog to go to and lie down on a mat is to maintain the effectiveness of the reinforcer. Usually, lying on a mat, even with a treat coming their way after some period of time, cannot compete with concurrent contingencies. That is, the dog lies down, but then gets bored and gets up to do other things instead. One trick is to ensure that you work the duration up gradually, and manage distraction so that it is incrementally increased very gradually (so the rest of the room is boring, at least initially). Also, use highly effective reinforcers. Another trick to addressing this is to consider providing some ongoing reinforcer at the mat location. You could tie a rope to a Kong, and attach that to the crate or an eyehook screwed into the baseboard near the mat. You could have treats in the Kong or peanut butter inside of it. This will keep the dog interested and make being at the mat reinforcing, since this is the only place they can access that particular reinforcer. You can also get remotely released treat dispensers that you can keep near the mat.

CHAPTER 8. TRAINING CHALLENGES AND SPECIAL CASES

Behavioral Objectives

The objective of this chapter is to measurably expand the reader's repertoire of behaviors in relation to describing and relating the principles of behavior. Upon successfully integrating the concepts outlined in this chapter, the reader, where under contingencies to do so, will accurately:

- Describe common challenges in training dogs and general strategies for overcoming these challenges.

Multi-Dog Training

Karen London and Patricia McConnell wrote a terrific book called *Feeling Outnumbered? How to Manage and Enjoy Your Multi-Dog Household*, in which they outline a basic strategy for working with dogs who reside together. Being among the first to abandon the outdated practice of "supporting the hierarchy," London and McConnell (2001) outlined an operant conditioning approach that has proven very successful for many trainers, myself included, over the years. This general approach is outlined below.

Train Each Dog Individually

Guardians should arrange to have time alone with each dog for training. This can be incorporated into walks and play sessions, or exercise sessions as well as training. With multiple dogs providing a significant distraction for each other, it can be challenging to compete with, and soon, cues lose their evocative capacity. The guardian must train each dog individually to start with. Whereas it might be omitted when training an individual dog in many cases, ensure that the dog's name precedes all cues. This will be a cue for attention and a S^{FA} for exhibition of the behavior to be cued.

Train in Pairs

Once you are at a reliable point in individual training, you may start training the dogs in pairs, even if you have several dogs. Ensure you precede cues with the dog's name. Carry out much the same training as you did with the dogs individually, but review it with the other dogs present to ensure appropriate discrimination training so that each dog exhibits the behavior they are cued to exhibit and other dogs do not.

You can also work on group cues, using a group name such as "everyone," followed by the cue. Only those dogs who exhibit the behavior are given treats. This group cue will come in handy when the client wants all the dogs to respond to a cue. For instance, it can be useful to be able to cue everyone to sit.

Train in Groups

Once you have worked your way through training each pair combination to a reliable level of distraction, you can start combinations of three dogs. The training will proceed in much the same way as with pairs. Once significant progress has been made in these small groups, in each possible combination of three, you can start adding in any other dogs within the household, until you have your whole group working together. Clients should be encouraged to maintain the training by continuing to work with the dogs individually and as a group, and applying the training to everyday life when possible.

Training Toy Breeds

Toy breed dogs are frequently fearful, especially when close to people walking around, because they are at significant risk of injury from being stepped on. Consider at least administering the acquisition stage of training while you are seated on the ground next to the dog, both to prevent emotional arousal from moving around near them, but also to get closer to the dog in order to achieve the maneuvers appropriately. This will need to be faded.

Another challenge, with training toy breed dogs, is not really a challenge with the dog him or herself, but rather with guardians. Because toy breeds can be physically manipulated so easily, and the ratio of size between dog and guardian, people frequently do not train their toy breed dogs. Sometimes they simply fail to recognize a reason to do so, and/or sometimes they simply find it challenging because of the dog's size. Lack of training is likely the major reason for the stereotype of the "snappy and yappy" toy breed dog. People fail to take these and other problem behaviors or lack of training as a serious problem. It is important to recognize the need for basic training and to emphasize this to guardians. A well-trained dog of any size is at less risk.

Social Contact not an Effective Reinforcer

For some individuals, social contact is not an effective reinforcer, and this can affect training quite dramatically—people become quite used to utilizing social reinforcement. We often tend to identify a treat as the reinforcer for a behavior we are training, but reinforcement is frequently a package of stimuli including the social contact that comes with exhibiting social behaviors (such as during training) and receiving the reinforcer. Even if praise or touch are not used during the training, and verbal and visual prompts are not used, which they frequently are, the social contact that otherwise accompanies training contributes to generating and reinforcing behaviors. With this major source of motivation reduced or eliminated, training can be more challenging.

As with any motivation related problem, we look to problem conditioning that influences the motivation, and establishing and abolishing operations (deprivation and satiation respectively) that affect it. Is there an aversive history between the trainer and dog, or with some aspect of the training environment, contributing to influence motivation? Perhaps the dog has a history of aversive conditioning that, through generalization, affects social motivation? Perhaps the dog lacks adequate socialization? Identifying this history can suggest ways to change these contingencies. It can suggest specific stimuli to which the dog needs to be desensitized. Generally, social motivation can be affected with reinforcement rich social interaction. Identify and resolve (either by desensitization or simply eliminating) problem aversive contingencies. Reduce aversive stimulation that is associated with both the dog and trainer. Is there excess and overwhelming, or otherwise stressful contact between the dog and trainer?

Satiation, with regards to contact with the person, can reduce the reinforcing effect of contact with the person, and normalizing the amount and intensity of contact with the person can reduce the satiation effect and increase motivation. This is not to promote social isolation and strong deprivation states! We are talking about fixing problem situations where too much social contact is causing a satiated body. Next, increase the magnitude and rate of contact with reinforcing contingencies associated with the dog and trainer. Hand feeding of favored treats and food can help. Participate in games and other reinforcing activities. End sessions on a positive note before the dog becomes excessively satiated with the contact. Try to become a source of more reinforcement for the dog in general without overdoing it. As social motivation increases, training should become more fun and productive.

Food not an Effective Reinforcer

For many dogs, food is simply not very effective as a reinforcer. In many cases, you can find better treats and deprive the dog of this most effective reinforcement so as to maximize its effectiveness. Where this does not increase motivation, consider other reinforcers such as contact with a favored toy, perhaps involving a quick game of tug-of-war with the trainer. For some dogs, praise and certain specific kinds of physical contact can be an effective reinforcer. The trainer may need to experiment with different kinds of social contact to determine what is reinforcing. Usually, gentle to moderate contact on a shoulder works well. Observe what the dog expends significant energy behaving to contact on a daily basis for reinforcers, including activity reinforcers. Once you have a list of effective reinforcers, consider *mild* deprivation to increase their effectiveness.

Hyperactivity

Some dogs are so hyperactive that it becomes a significant disruption to training. This is common with certain breeds and with puppies/adolescents. The most common solution for this problem is exercise and then manipulation of excess stimulation during training. Exercise sessions should be carefully designed, ideally with the help of at least a veterinarian, if not a canine fitness consultant with specialized skills in working through aerobic exercise programs, and ideally implemented under supervision. But in many cases, guardians alone can increase exercise, as long as they operate within the medical and biological condition of the dog, and work up gradually. The sessions should be scheduled regularly and ideally involve games to make it fun. Ensure warm ups and cool downs, and observe carefully for indications of fatigue. Some benefits of moderate to intense appropriately implemented exercise programs can be observed after only a few sessions but most require several weeks before they are realized. The trainer should also choose times of day that are more conducive to training.

On top of large muscle mass related physical conditioning, behavioral conditioning can also help. Training games that emphasize patience and focus, as well as creativity and persistence, can improve focus in general (see O'Heare, 2011).

Sensitivity and Risk Averse in General

Dogs who are generally sensitive and risk-averse, need a careful approach. Trainers need to attend to and recognize escape contingencies and sensitivities so they can avoid these forms of stimulation while working through their training. In some cases, these dogs are sensitive to social pressure and cower when they are towered over or approached. In these cases, train while sitting beside the dog, perhaps right on the ground. Face slightly away and avoid staring at the dog. Avoid sudden movements and be calm, but gently praising. Train in an environment that you are sure you can control. Take extra care to avoid aversive stimulation, such as techniques involving extinction or negative punishment trials. Ensure success by moving at an appropriate pace. Utilize a very careful graded approach, and begin introducing simple shaping exercises with minimal prompts. Generally, free-shaping can reinforce creativity and persistence in general (O'Heare, 2011). Desensitization work might be necessary in severe cases of risk aversion.

Easily Frustrated and Impulsive

Frustration refers most narrowly to the blocked access to reinforcers. It can be defined more broadly to involve the emotional arousal elicited by extinction. *Impulsivity* refers to the tendency for a dog to seek out immediate smaller reinforcers when faced with concurrent contingencies with delayed access to a much greater source of reinforcement—they go for the quick fix, rather than putting in slightly more time and effort for a much greater gratification. Dogs that are impulsive and easily frustrated must be handled carefully. They can be conditioned to delay gratification and experience less frustration if the contingencies are arranged so. The trick here is to take a graded approach, specifically with regard to response effort and duration features of training. Gradually train behaviors that require duration but move at a pace that allows the dog to succeed with contacting highly effective reinforcers that require a bit more effort and time. Similarly, use shaping exercises with minimal prompting to condition creativity and persistence that will allow them to easily work around frustrations. By emphasizing success generated by creativity and persistence, the dog comes to respond to frustration, not with strange noncriterion behaviors, but rather with other novel productive behaviors and strategies that will access the reinforcer (O'Heare, 2011).

APPENDIX 1. TRAINER EXERCISES AND SKILLS DEVELOPMENT

Behavioral Objectives

The objective of this appendix is to measurably expand the reader's repertoire of behaviors in relation to describing and relating the principles of behavior. Upon successfully integrating the concepts outlined in this appendix, the reader, where under contingencies to do so, will accurately:

- Analyze their training behaviors for effectiveness and efficiency, providing data by which trainers may reinforce effective behaviors, extinguish ineffective behaviors and shape their training chops.

This appendix is composed of a series of exercises that trainers may engage in to help expand their repertoire of effective training behaviors. They are designed to build on one another—early exercises providing repertoire expansion necessary for later exercises. Trainers should work through the exercises sequentially from beginning to end, to benefit most from the exercises.

Video-record all of your exercise sessions. A big part of the conditioning experience will come from observing and scrutinizing the video, rather than carrying out the training exercises alone. In many cases, it is a good idea to repeat the exercises after observing the video and noting deficiencies to be improved. Continue to carry out the exercises, observe the video, and repeat this sequence until you are demonstratively proficient with the exercise. The suggestion for a pat on the back is not a joke—literally mark your success with a reinforcing activity. This will improve your conditioning.

Exercise #1. The Bouncing Ball Exercise

This exercise will help you improve these behaviors or features of behaviors:

- Timing

- Concentration

- Clicker accuracy/dexterity

- Quantitative tracking behaviors (basic).

We will begin with the basic bouncing ball exercise, and move to the more advanced tossed ball exercise following demonstrated proficiency here. You will need an assistant, a bouncing ball, a clicker, and video-recording equipment. Video-record all sessions. Have your assistant bounce a ball with a variable interval (with a range of around one to ten seconds) between bounces. They should bounce the ball ten times in the first set, take a 30 second break, bounce the ball ten more times for the second set, take another 30 second break, and then bounce the ball ten more times for the third set. Your objective will be to click the clicker at the exact moment the ball bounces on the ground each time. Carry out this exercise with your favored hand, and repeat the exercise with your other hand. Confirm your accuracy by observing the video. The click should occur precisely at the moment the ball contacts the floor. Use checks and X's to help you record criterion behaviors (perfect timing) and noncriterion behaviors (off timing). For any off timing behaviors, is there a trend in terms of whether you click after or before the bounce? If so, this can be used to help you improve your timing for the next round. Repeat the exercise until you have achieved 29 out of 30 precisely timed clicks with each hand. Once you have completed this exercise, pat yourself on the back, and follow up with treating yourself in some way that is reinforcing (literally)!

Exercise #2. The Tossed Ball Exercise

This exercise will help you improve these behaviors or features of behaviors:

- Timing

- Concentration

- Clicker accuracy/dexterity

- Quantitative tracking behaviors (basic).

For the tossed ball exercise, you will carry out the sequences exactly the same as in the Bouncing Ball Exercise except that the ball will be tossed between one and four feet into the air instead of bounced on the ground. This exercise is more advanced because the bouncing is approximately a fixed distance, whereas the tossed ball will have a much more variable distance, as well as a lack of auditory feedback as the ball contacts the surface when the click is supposed to occur. Click the clicker at the precise instant the ball reaches the apex of its arc. Once you have completed this exercise with a success rate of 29 out of 30 with each hand, pat yourself on the back, and follow up with treating yourself in some way that is reinforcing (literally)!

Exercise #3. The Ball and Treat Exercise

This exercise will help you improve these behaviors or features of behaviors:

- Timing

- Concentration

- Clicker accuracy/dexterity

- Quantitative tracking behaviors (basic)

- Accurate treat delivery to stationary target.

This exercise builds on the ball exercises and introduces another behavior set. Training requires that a number of behaviors be exhibited, either consecutively or sequentially, in a short period of time, and this exercise will help increase the number and level of difficulty of behaviors you can exhibit before becoming task saturated.

You will need an assistant, bouncing ball, clicker, standard drinking glass, treat pouch, dog-training treats, and video-recording equipment. Video-record all sessions. Carry out this exercise exactly as in the basic

Bouncing Ball Exercise previously described, except this time, you will be incorporating treat delivery as well. Instruct your assistant to allow you a maximum of one full second ("one alligator") to deliver your treat before they begin counting silently toward their inter-trial interval. Carry out the exercises right beside a table at about waist height. Have the drinking glass placed on its side on the table propped with erasers, or something similar, so that the glass does not roll away. Your objective will be to click precisely at the instant the ball bounces, and within one second, retrieve a treat from the pouch and place it into the glass without knocking the glass out of position. Run through the series of three 10-trial sessions, using your favored hand for clicking and your other hand for treat delivery. Repeat the process, switching hands.

When observing and quantifying your accuracy, you will track for click timing and treat delivery accuracy. Track the number of times you clicked precisely when the ball bounced, and track the number of treats administered into the glass within one second of your click. Missing the glass and/or delivering the treat outside of the one-second interval are noncriterion behaviors.

Repeat the exercise until you have achieved 29 out of 30 precisely timed clicks, and 29 out of 30 accurate treat deliveries. Once you have completed this exercise, pat yourself on the back, and follow up with treating yourself in some way that is reinforcing (literally)!

Exercise #4. Planning List of Behavior Approximations for Shaping

This exercise will help you improve these behaviors or features of behaviors:

- Judging appropriate behavior approximation size based on how difficult different components will be

- Breaking approximations into smaller sub-approximations

- Planning for acceptable operant approximations.

Planning a shaping project requires a repertoire of various behaviors, and one of them is planning your list of behavior approximations. Although one must remain flexible in training to quickly accommodate unexpected events, prevent frustration, reduced rate of responding, or to take advantage of sudden leaps in progress, one can only really be truly flexible if one prepares a plan that allows for such contingencies. In this exercise, you will practice planning a list of behavior approximations for a training project, including allowing for acceptable deviations.

Choose a behavior to shape. This should be a behavior that is more or less unlikely to occur frequently in its final form, and that is not readily prompted in its final form. Examples of relatively simple behaviors can be rolling over, spinning in a circle, or crawling under a bar set to the dog's chest height.

First, prepare a list of behavior approximations for the behavior. The approximations should be large enough so that the dog is not rapidly skipping multiple steps at a time, but small enough that progress remains smooth and efficient. Ensure that each approximation describes specific body part movements—that they are operational. Second, for each approximation, break it down into three small sub-approximations, in case you need to quickly utilize them to prevent frustration. Third, look at each approximation. For the particular behavior identified, is there an acceptable alternative response set that still progresses toward the terminal behavior? In other words, prepare yourself now for any step along the way where you might not immediately get the specific approximation you listed, but you might get another variation or type of behavior that is still a suitable approximation toward the terminal behavior. This may not be possible for all terminal behaviors and is usually more applicable to more complex terminal behaviors. If you need to continue a new branch of approximations from there to your terminal behavior, do so. Otherwise, note where it connects back to your initial list of approximations.

Once you have completed your list, you should be well prepared for deviations and challenges, such as the dog progressing more quickly than anticipated, or becoming frustrated due to too large a step, or bored by too small a step. Making these judgments in the training situation requires another set of skills, but the repertoire of behaviors practiced in this exercise will help ensure you are prepared for it, and sets you and the dog up for success—it establishes a stronger foundation and demonstrates the benefits of planning ahead.

Consider doing this exercise with the other two simple behaviors and then perhaps for a more sophisticated behavior to challenge yourself.

Once you have completed this exercise, pat yourself on the back, and follow up with treating yourself in some way that is reinforcing (literally)!

Exercise #5. Shaping a Friend

This exercise will help you improve these behaviors or features of behaviors:

- Timing

- Concentration

- Clicker accuracy/dexterity

- Relying less on trainer-mediated prompting

- Planning behavior approximations for a shaping procedure

- Identifying target behavior suitable for trainer proficiency

- Maintaining high rate of reinforcement to avoid reduced rate of responding and frustration (on the fly judgment related behaviors)

- Treat handling.

Planning Stage (You as Trainer)

You will need a clicker and at least two people for the exercise (although it is more fun with three or more). You will also need a piece of paper and writing instrument for your planning stage.

This exercise is an excellent way to practice shaping without subjecting a dog to the often-inevitable frustration and confusion associated with novice trainers carrying out an advanced training procedure. It is based largely on an excellent game (the Training Game) found in *Don't Shoot the Dog* by Karen Pryor, with the addition of a concerted shaping plan before the game, and an exercise analysis stage at the end—a kind of debriefing. As always, video-record your training exercises.

There will be two projects in this exercise, one in which you are the trainer and the other in which you are the subject. In the first project, your assistant is assigned to be the subject and you will be the trainer. The subject leaves the room for the planning stage. Identify an operationalized behavior to train the subject to exhibit. Write down your target behavior and prepare a plan of approximations just as you would if you were planning a dog training project.

Training Stage (You as Trainer)

Once you have a plan, the subject may come back into the room and training begins. No speaking or contrived prompting is allowed; this includes subtle head nods and noises or other facial expressions. Prompts can sometimes be justified in this exercise in order to work through a particularly frustrating series of trials, but these are not usually the first choice in preventing or working through these situations, so use them if you absolutely need to, but focus on preventing the need for them—working through these challenges with adjustments to approximation size and pace.

Click for successive approximations of the target behavior in accordance with your training plan, but be prepared to adjust your tactics where appropriate. Maintain a high rate of reinforcement to ensure smooth training and minimal frustration or confusion. In place of the unconditioned reinforcer, use nickels for this exercise. Hand them to the subject—they may put the nickel in their pocket. This helps simulate treat delivery. When the subject finally exhibits the terminal behavior, the game is over.

Exercise Analysis (You as Trainer)

Once the terminal behavior has been achieved, observe the video several times, each time looking for specific things.

First, observe for clicker accuracy. Did you click at precisely the correct time? How many clicks out of the total number would you judge to be precisely accurate?

Second, observe again for pace management. Did you set the approximations at suitably sized steps to maintain smooth progress and prevent frustration? Where you did not, had you planned appropriately ahead of time for these occurrences? In the training session, did you remain flexible, and adapt quickly and appropriately to adjust the approximation size and reinforcement rate to manage the frustration? Did any superstitious behaviors occur, and if so, did you work through them or use extinction to prevent them from becoming too disruptive?

Third, observe again, now looking for prompts. Did you rely solely on reinforcing from among variations exhibited without contrived trainer-mediated prompts, or did you prompt? Although this exercise features avoidance of prompts in order to focus on other skills, prompts can be used sparingly in shaping programs and should be used where it will prevent frustration. Did the prompts you used function to move past a particularly troubling series of extinction trials or were they unjustified? Ask yourself whether you could have avoided any of the prompts and still staved off frustration? How could you have done so?

Next, ask your assistant for their observations on the experience. Ask them if they were confused or frustrated at any point, and if so, why they believe they became confused and/or frustrated. Ask them open-ended questions about their general evaluation of your skills as a trainer and what they believe might have been improved. Ask any other participating observers this as well.

Finally, identify at least three distinct skills that you believe were least proficiently demonstrated in your training, and for each, identify specific ways they can be improved. This might mean what you could have done differently, but it also means how you will change your training practices to adjust for this and refine these particular skills.

Planning Stage (You as Subject)

Carry out the exercise again, this time with your assistant carrying out the training and you acting as the subject. Have your assistant plan a shaping project for you to engage in as the subject. Coach them how to go about doing this. You may want to video your coaching so that you may analyze that afterward as well.

Training Stage (You as Subject)

Your assistant may or may not be a proficient trainer. If they are not, take this opportunity to coach them on the basics of choosing a suitable behavior and suitable behavior approximations, as well as on timing and the rules to reinforce while avoiding prompts. This can be a repertoire expanding conditioning experience. If your assistant is already a proficient trainer, ensure they know what is expected from the exercise and proceed. Ensure you video record this session as well.

Exercise Analysis (You as Subject)

Once you have exhibited the terminal behavior, you have the opportunity to evaluate many of the same skills, but this time for someone other than yourself. This change in perspective can be an exceptional conditioning experience.

First, take note of your feelings. Feelings are your experience or awareness related behaviors in response to emotional arousal (which itself is the physiological processes going on inside you). Do you feel exhilarated and excited or bored? Do you feel frustrated? Attempt to identify likely causes for these feelings. What exactly about the experience elicited these feelings? Translate these into accurate descriptions of training proficiencies and deficiencies. Once you have a list of training deficiencies, for each one identify what actions ought to have been exhibited instead, and also separately, how a trainer ought to have handled the situation as soon as it became clear that frustration or confusion did occur.

Next, observe the video for the same type of things you observed in your own training video. Look for timing and management of pace etc., and make notes on each.

Once you have completed this exercise, pat yourself on the back, and follow up with treating yourself in some way that is reinforcing (literally)!

Exercise #6. Targeting

This exercise will help you improve these behaviors or features of behaviors:

- Timing

- Concentration

- Clicker accuracy/dexterity

- Location of treat delivery

- Handling multiple items at once.

For this exercise, you will need a targeting stick (or suitable stand-in such as a pencil), treats, treat pouch, clicker, and a dog. This simple exercise is a good place to start expanding your skills in dog training, because, while it is fairly simple, it also involves several key skills in training. One new skill this exercise presents is choosing a location to deliver the treat, which will impact how the behavior comes to be exhibited—this will be discussed below. Another new skill that this exercise introduces is handling multiple pieces of equipment at the same time. In this case, you will be handling the clicker, the target stick, and treats at the same time, requiring you to use at least one hand for more than one piece of equipment.

Part of the conditioning experience for this exercise will be a practice session without the dog present, so that you can find the handling solution that works best for you; better to identify this with the dog absent, rather than expose them to changes in technique and possible fumbling. Some trainers hold the targeting stick and clicker in the same hand, using their free hand to retrieve and deliver treats, while others hold the clicker in one hand and the target stick in the other, and of these people, some transfer the target stick to their other hand or under their arm quickly before retrieving and delivering the treat with that hand, or else they simple retrieve and deliver the treat while still holding the target stick in that hand. I prefer the first method described, but many trainers have mastered these latter techniques, so run a few trials alone practicing each method with an assistant standing in as the subject. They can touch the end of the target stick with their finger, and that allows you to try placing the target stick, clicking, and delivering a treat to their same hand that they used to touch the stick. Take note of whether you are more likely to fumble with one method or another and which one allows you to deliver the treat most quickly and accurately. Notice whether holding the target stick interferes with pulling a treat from the pouch. One thing that you might notice only when working with a dog is that if you deliver the treat with the hand that holds the target stick, the dog may attempt to touch the stick rather than take the treat, because this is the behavior the stick evokes. However, moving the stick to your other arm can take a second or so away from treat retrieval. These are fantastic experiments to conduct first hand so practice each method.

Planning Stage

Once you have found the method that you believe will work most efficiently for you, you are ready to begin target training a dog. As with any training project, prepare a plan ahead of time. In this case, you will likely be able to achieve the final form of the behavior, so you do not need to shape this behavior. You might shape a little bit to tighten up the spot touched or the latency, but we can leave this aside for now and treat this as a simple differential reinforcement procedure. Write down your target behavior in operational terms. You can plan to measure the frequency of the behavior since it is most informative to measure how many times the dog exhibits the behavior out of how many opportunities they are provided to exhibit it. You can track that when watching the video of your sessions. Gather and place all of your equipment.

Present the targeting stick to the dog within a few inches of his or her nose. The dog will likely sniff it, since dogs are biologically disposed to sniff novel items. If they do not contact the tip of the targeting stick within a few seconds, pull it away, turn away for a few seconds and then present it again. If this is not working, you should increase the salience of the stimulus by rubbing treats on the tip of the stick (although this is rarely necessary). The instant the dog touches the tip of the stick, click, retrieve, and deliver the treat to the dog's mouth at their head height. Where you deliver a treat matters. You could just click and drop a treat to the ground, but this will impact the behavior you are training. If you deliver treats on the ground after the targeting behavior, you will likely notice that the dog responds to presentation of the stick with touching it and then quickly lowering their head down to the ground. This might not be a problem in some circumstances, but this exercise will allow you the opportunity to practice delivering treats at a specific spot in order to promote a nice clean targeting behavior without subsequent byproduct behaviors.

Repeat through a few more trials, and you should see it becoming smoother and more reliable. Begin presenting the stick about five or six inches away from the dog's nose, and once that is reliable, present it far enough away that it requires a couple steps for the dog to get to it. Once you have this trained reliably, begin presenting the stick on either side of you randomly. You should very quickly have this behavior exhibited at a frequency of 100%. Once you have achieved ten in a row, touched within a couple seconds of presentation while you change the location it is presented, you can consider the project a success.

Exercise Analysis

Now observe the video. Take note of your timing. Was it precise each time? Were you able to deliver the treat within one second every time? Did you click any times accidentally when the behavior was not exhibited? Were there any extinction or negative punishment trials? If so, why? Did you increase the difficulty level too quickly? How did you work through this on the next trial? Finally, find something that you could improve upon. Write that down, as well as exactly what you can do to improve that aspect of training.

Once you have completed this exercise, pat yourself on the back, and follow up with treating yourself in some way that is reinforcing (literally)!

Exercise #7. Simple Shaping Project

This exercise will help you improve these behaviors or features of behaviors:

- Timing

- Concentration

- Clicker accuracy/dexterity

- Relying less on trainer-mediated prompting

- Planning behavior approximations for a shaping procedure

- Identifying target behavior suitable for trainer proficiency

- Maintaining suitable energy/enthusiasm level

- Maintaining high rate of reinforcement to avoid reduced rate of responding and frustration (on the fly judgment related behaviors)

- Setting criteria for next behavior approximation to avoid excess extinction but still reliably responding at the next approximation.

You will need a clicker, treats, treat pouch, paper, pen, and a reinforcer-deprived dog for which a clicker acts effectively as a conditioned reinforcer and video equipment.

Building on your work shaping a human behavior, we proceed now to transfer these skills to working with dogs. In this exercise, you will shape a simple behavior with your dog. This will build on the exercises you have already completed and introduce the challenge of shaping with a dog. Choose a behavior that suits your situation; for this exercise, it will be something related to a cardboard box. If the box is large and low enough, in relation to your dog, you might shape stepping into the box with all four legs. If the box is small enough, you might train the dog to pick the box up in their mouth or to push the box with their nose for half of a meter. You may choose another behavior, but ensure whatever you choose is a single discrete behavior and not a sequence of behaviors.

Planning Stage

Begin by defining your target terminal behavior operationally, as well as the behavior approximations you will use to achieve it. Remember to plan for acceptable variant operants and the necessity to break a step down into smaller steps.

Training Stage

Begin training, utilizing the skills you have been practicing up until this point, including precise timing of the click, treat delivery within one second, and accurate placement of the treat to avoid post-reinforcement behaviors that might disrupt training. Maintain a high rate of reinforcement to avoid reduced rate of responding and frustration.

Once you have achieved a behavior approximation to where the behavior is stable, move to the next approximation. Take care at this point, as this is a skill we will be evaluating in this exercise. If you wait too long after achieving reliable responding at one approximation step before setting the next approximation, the behavior will have become well conditioned or entrenched, and this will require more extensive extinction when you reset the criteria for the next step. If on the other hand, you reset the criteria for the next step too quickly before the behavior is stable, the dog may fail to exhibit the next approximation at all. You are aiming for level of reliability such that when you instate extinction, there will be sufficient behavioral variability to achieve your next approximation, but not so much that the dog gets too rigid in exhibiting only that one behavior. This judgment call relates to the size of the approximation too, since behavior is only so variable, and you need that step to be small enough that a little variability in responding will lead to the next approximation being exhibited. It is a constant balancing act of criteria size and criteria change timing that represents a major difference between the chops of a professional and those of a novice. Emphasize this on-the-fly judgment in this exercise by attending closely to the rate of responding and reinforcement, and any disruptions to smooth continuous conditioning. Also ensure you use an appropriate level of animation or energy/enthusiasm to keep the process fun and smooth.

Continue training until the dog exhibits the criterion terminal behavior five times in a row when the box is presented. You should keep sessions generally short and stop while the training is still fun for all concerned. You will likely be able to complete this training in a single session, but if you need to take two sessions, do so. In that case, remember to end a session on a positive note, and when you start a new session, review earlier steps before proceeding further into the list.

Exercise Analysis

Observe the video several times, looking for specific things each time. Take note of all the things that we previously practiced, such as the precise timing of your click, whether you retrieved and delivered the click within one second, whether you delivered the treat precisely, whether you missed any opportunities to click, and how many times you clicked for an error. It should become habit for you to evaluate these same things every time you evaluate your own training skills. Note how well you planned your approximations. Were all the approximation steps a suitable size, or did you need to adjust them, and if you did, how might you plan more effectively next time?

This time, we are also evaluating energy level; that is, how you use tone of encouragement, tone of voice, and how animated you move in order to maintain the dog's rate of responding at an appropriate level. Were you animated enough or perhaps too much? Take special care to look for your proficiency with the last two behavioral objectives identified for this exercise.

Observe at least one time through for maintaining a high rate of reinforcement and ensuring that by adjusting approximation size correctly. Did the dog become frustrated or bored at any point? If so, why? What can you do to avoid this? If it occurs, what can you do quickly to get back on track?

Observe at least one time through for timing, regarding instating the extinction criterion for the present approximation step and instating the reinforcement criterion for the next step. Were the first few responses at the new step confusing for the dog? Did the dog continue to exhibit the previous approximation behavior more than a couple times, or did behavioral variability occur, but the next approximation step was not exhibited quickly? These are disruptions to the smoothness and efficiency of training. Ask yourself how you could have planned more effectively to avoid that or how, when you changed from one approximation to the next, that might have impacted upon this disruption. Specifically, what could you do to avoid, and also to respond to, these disruptions. Write your questions and answers down on paper. If this exercise did not go perfectly smoothly, try again, this time with a different behavior.

Once you have completed this exercise, pat yourself on the back, and follow up with treating yourself in some way that is reinforcing (literally)!

Exercise #8. Task Analysis for Chaining

This exercise will help you improve these behaviors or features of behaviors:

- Identifying discrete behaviors in a behavioral situation involving a series of behaviors exhibited one after the other.

You will need paper and a pen for this exercise.

Even many simple behavior situations that we seek to train involve more than one discrete behavior. For example, if you train a dog to go to a mat, you usually want the dog to go to the mat, and then once there, to lie down on the mat. These are two discrete behaviors, and you do not want to have to cue the down separately. Likewise, if you want to train a dog to bring something to you, they have to go to the item, pick it up, and then bring it to you, involving three discrete behaviors. Some training will involve some very complex behavior chains, such as those used in training dogs for TV or movie scenes.

A requisite skill set associated with chaining involves planning the sequence of behaviors. To plan a sequence of behaviors in a chaining project, you conduct a task analysis. In most cases, you will observe dogs exhibiting the behavior you plan to train, and from that, identify the discrete behaviors that make it up. In other cases, you may be able to simply visualize the occurrence.

Part of the skill in carrying out a task analysis and planning a chaining project involves determining what the discrete behaviors are. Any behavior can be broken down into multiple finer motor actions and so part of the judgment regarding what is a discrete behavior is context related and depends on the scale of appropriateness to the task at hand. For example, taking a sip of water from a glass that you are already grasping might seem to be a single behavior but it might better be analyzed to be two behaviors: raising the glass and then taking a sip. You might even break it down into several discrete behaviors involving finer motor actions involving the lifting of the glass, opening the mouth, generating a firm seal with the glass with the mouth, moving the tongue to allow water into the mouth, closing the mouth, removing the glass away from your face, and finally swallowing the water. But it can get unproductive for the context of your purpose at a certain point. Determining appropriate discrete behavior demarcation points, for training the specific chain you plan to train, requires balancing the scale of specificity.

In this exercise, you analyze a complex behavioral event, breaking it down into appropriately sized discrete behaviors. First, identify a complex behavioral episode on which you can carry out a task analysis. If you cannot think of a behavior episode yourself, use the behavioral episode of having a dog go get you a Pepsi from the fridge. Start by observing a dog exhibit the behavior chain, or visualizing it. What are the discrete behaviors in this chain? When shall you rightly end the chain? Shall you end once they get to you, or do you plan them to drop it for you, or sit with it in their mouth without dropping it, or will there be a cue delivered once they arrive that ends the chain itself? These are the kind of considerations that are part of establishing a behavior objective, consequently determining what you analyze specifically.

Decide on the specific operational details of the general prescription above for this exercise.

Second, observe dogs actually exhibiting this sequence of behaviors. Is it useful to consider each step (assuming there are steps) as a discrete behavior, or is simply walking adequate? The answer to this question tends to be somewhat obvious, but why? What variables determine your answer? Does it have to do with what will tend to occur normally as dictated by natural selection of a body so structured to generate such behavior prepotently (like lapping up water, and actually swallowing it, or taking one step, and tending to take more if the target they are approaching is further away)? Carry out your analysis until you are satisfied that it contains sufficient but not excessive individual links.

Once you have completed this exercise, pat yourself on the back, and follow up with treating yourself in some way that is reinforcing (literally)!

Exercise #9. Simple Chaining Exercise.

This exercise will help you improve these behaviors or features of behaviors:

- Discriminating between suitability of different chaining procedures

- Determining whether shaping or simple differential reinforcement is most suitable to a task

- Transferring stimulus control to attach links in the chain.

Planning Stage

You will need a clicker, treats, treat pouch, your task analysis from exercise #8, reinforcer-deprived dog for which a clicker acts effectively as a conditioned reinforcer, and video equipment.

In this exercise, you will build on the task analysis you developed in exercise #8 and actually carry out the training required to achieve this chain. The exercises are becoming more challenging and advanced, requiring many more skill sets combined in one project. You already have a task analysis completed, so this will be the basis for your chain. One of your next goals will be to decide which particular chaining strategy will be most suitable to your project; will you utilize forward or backward chaining? Consider your project, and write down your choice of strategy and the reasons why this strategy is more appropriate to your project than the others.

Now that you have your basic strategy decided, you will need to consider how you will train each behavior. For each discrete behavior, write out how you plan to train it. This should only take a few words per behavior, since you are more or less deciding whether to shape it or just differentially reinforce it, and whether to prompt it or not, and if so, how. Next, plan specifically how you will fade prompts where appropriate and transfer stimulus control of each behavior to completion of the behavior before it. Write this down as well. Now you should have a basic plan of action.

Training Stage

Your next task is to carry out the training. Handle it systematically, training each behavior or segment as required and appropriate to your plan. Treat each behavior (or set of behaviors) as a discrete training project until it is time to chain them. Once the dog exhibits the entire sequence of behaviors, without any prompts or cues after the very first one, five times in a row, perfectly to criteria, you are finished this exercise.

Exercise Analysis

Review your video several times. As before, review for the usual set of accuracies described for previous training exercises. After this, consider any difficulties or disruptions that may have occurred. What were they and what caused them? What changes to your plan or your reaction to the disruptions would generate more effective and efficient training? The skills we are evaluating are broader than in the initial simpler exercises and so our questions are generally broader as well. Your goal will be to evaluate your planning and execution of the training project, and identify the strengths and weaknesses. Recognize particular excellences and also the behaviors you could improve. The trick to making them a conditioning experience that will result in an expansion of your repertoire of effective and efficient training behaviors is to identify these deficiencies, explain explicitly what caused them to be deficiencies, and explicitly identify what can be done to make them more efficient. This will be your task in the exercise analysis for this exercise.

Once you have completed this exercise, pat yourself on the back, and follow up with treating yourself in some way that is reinforcing (literally)! This was a big project and your pride deserves some pride reinforcement.

Exercise #10. Discrimination and Generalization Training

This exercise will help you improve these behaviors or features of behaviors:

- Planning for an appropriate level of discrimination and stimulus generalization

- Carrying out discrimination and stimulus generalization training.

You will need a clicker, treats, treat pouch, reinforcer-deprived dog for which a clicker acts effectively as a conditioned reinforcer, and video equipment.

Most of our exercises thus far have focused on the planning and acquisition stages of training. In this, our final exercise, we will focus on some behaviors associated more with the fluency and maintenance stages of training. Recall that in discrimination training we oppose the general tendency toward stimulus generalization by narrowing the range of stimuli that will evoke the behavior of concern. We decide the specific stimulus to control the behavior and rule out similar stimuli. How narrow or tight you make this depends on your objectives for the behavior. For example, you may want the word "sit" to evoke sitting behavior and not similar stimuli such as "sip," but you likely want "sit" verbalized by other people as well as verbalized by you to evoke sitting. This is an instance of allowing a certain amount of stimulus generalization. Too narrow or too broad and the cue becomes less useful.

Training Stage

Start by choosing a behavior that has not undergone any discrimination and generalization training yet. You might have a behavior you have been working on that is just not at that stage yet, or you may need to train a behavior from scratch. In that case, choose a simple behavior such as spinning in a circle, rolling over, or high five. The simplicity of the behavior does not matter for this exercise, so choose something that can quickly and easily be trained to this level. Once the behavior is reliable, and under stimulus control, begin discrimination training, ruling out similar stimuli. Reinforce for the target stimulus and not for other similar stimuli. Take it to a level that is appropriate for the behavior in question. This includes trials allowing for appropriate stimulus generalization (such as having other people deliver the cue, or you cuing it while facing away from the dog or lying down, rather than standing). The trick in this exercise is to rule *in* all applicable stimulus conditions and rule *out* all inapplicable stimulus conditions. Once the behavior is reliably evoked by appropriate stimuli, and yet is not evoked by several similar stimulus conditions, you are finished the training component of the exercise and can move to the exercise analysis stage.

Exercise Analysis

Observe the video of the training several times. As usual, observe for the common mechanical and judgment skills evaluated in previous exercises. Then, observe how effectively and efficiently you conducted your discrimination and stimulus generalization training. Did it run smoothly, or did anything cause frustration or otherwise disrupt training? What exactly were they? What exactly could have been done to prevent these disruptions? What can you do next time in response to these disruptions that would minimize them and get back on track? Write these things down. Consider this exercise as a whole, and identify any behaviors that might improve your efficiency in carrying this kind of training out.

Once you have completed this exercise, pat yourself on the back, and follow up with treating yourself in some way that is reinforcing (literally)!

REFERENCES

Alexander, S. (2003). The Quicker Clicker Kit!

American Heritage Dictionary of the English Language. (Ed.) (n.d.). *Mind*.

American Psychological Association. (2014). How does the APA define "psychology"? Retrieved February 19, 2014, from http://www.apa.org/support/about/apa/psychology.aspx#answer

Association of Animal Behavior Professionals (2008). Professional Practice Guidelines Retrieved November 11, 2008, from associationofanimalbehaviorprofessionals.com/guidelines.html

Azrin, N. H. (1956). Some effects of two intermittent schedules of immediate and non-immediate punishment. *Journal of Psychology, 42*, 3–21.

Behavior Analyst Certification Board (2010). Guidelines for Responsible Conduct for Behavior Analysts. Retrieved from http://www.bacb.com/index.php?page=85

Bailey, J. S., & Burch, M. R. (2005). *Ethics for behavior analysts: A practical guide to the Behavior Analyst Certification Board guidelines for responsible conduct*. Mahwah: Lawrence Erlbaum Associates.

Balaban, M. T., Rhodes, D. L., & Neuringer, A. (1990). Orienting and defense responses to punishment: Effects on learning. *Biological Psychology, 30*, 203–217.

Bond, C. (2007). The effect of jackpots on response. Unpublished Research project for Diploma of Canine Behavioral Sciences. *Companion Animal Sciences Institute*.

Catania, A. C. (1998). *Learning* (4th ed.). Upper Saddle River: Prentice Hall.

Chance, P. (2009). *Learning and behavior* (6th ed.). Belmont: Thomson Wadsworth.

Cooper, J. O., Heron, T. E., & Heward, W. L. (2007). *Applied behavior analysis* (2nd ed.). Upper Saddle River: Merril Prentice Hall.

Delta Society (2001). Professional Standards for Dog Trainers: Effective, Humane Principles. Naches AVE SW: Delta Society.

Donaldson, J. (2005). *The culture clash* (2nd. ed.). Oakville, Ontario: James and Kenneth.

Estes, W. K. (1944). An experimental study of punishment. *Psychological Monographs, 57*(3), 1–40.

Fraley (2008). *General Behaviorology: The natural science of human behavior*. Canton: ABCs.

Fraley, L. E., & Ledoux, S. F. (2002). Origins, status, and mission of behaviorology. In S. F. Ledoux (Ed.), *Origins and components of behaviorology* (Second ed., pp. 33–169). Canton: ABCs.

Hiby, E. F., Rooney, N. J., & Bradshaw, J. W. S. (2004). Dog training methods: their use, effectiveness and interactions with behaviour and welfare. *Animal Welfare, 13*, 63–69.

Laraway, S., Snycerski, S., Michael, J., & Poling, A. (2003). Motivating operations and terms to describe them: Some further refinements. *Journal of Applied Behavior Analysis, 36*(3), 407–414.

Ledoux, S. F. (2014). *Running out of time: Introducing behaviorology to help solve global problems*. Ottawa, Ontario.

Ledoux, S. F. (2002a). An introduction to the origins, status, and mission of behaviorology: An established science with developed applications and a new name. In S. F. Ledoux (Ed.), *Origins and components of behaviorology* (Second ed., pp. 3–24). Canton: ABCs.

Ledoux, S. F. (2002b). Increasing tact control and student comprehension through such new postcedent terms as added and subtracted reinforcers and punishers. In S.

F. Ledoux (Ed.), *Origins and components of behaviorology* (Second ed., pp. 199–204). Canton: ABCs.

Lerman, D. C., & Vorndran, C. M. (2002). On the status of knowledge for using punishment: implications for treating behavior disorders. *Journal of Applied Behavior Analysis, 35*, 431–464.

London, K. B., & McConnell, P. B. (2001). *Feeling outnumbered? How to manage and enjoy your multi-dog household.* Black Earth: Dog's best Friend, Ltd.

Miltenberger, R. G. (2008). *Behavior modification: Principles and procedures* (4th ed.). Belmont: Thomson Wadsworth.

Nation, J. R., & Woods, D. J. (1980). Persistence: The role of partial reinforcement in psychotherapy. *Journal of Experimental Psychology: General, 109*(2), 175–207.

O'Heare, J. (2011). *Empowerment training: Training for creativity, persistence, industriousness, resilience & behavioral well-being.* Ottawa: BehaveTech Publishing.

O'Heare, J. (2013). *The least intrusive effective behavior intervention (LIEBI) algorithm and levels of intrusiveness table: A proposed best-practices model Version 5.0.* associationofanimalbehaviorprofessionals.com/liebi50.pdf.

O'Heare, J. (2007). *Aggressive behavior in dogs.* Ottawa: DogPsych Publishing.

Pierce, W. D., & Cheney, C. D. (2008). *Behavior analysis and learning* (4th ed.). Mahwah: Psychology Press.

Pierce, W. D., & Cheney, C. D. (2013). *Behavior analysis and learning* (5th ed.). New York: Psychology Press.

Pryor, K. (1999). *Don't shoot the dog! The new art of teaching and training.* New York: Bantom Books.

Schlinger, H. D., & Blakely, E. (1994). The effects of delayed reinforcement and a response-produced auditory stimulus on the acquisition of operant behavior in rats. *The Psychological Record, 44*, 391–409.

Schlinger, H. D., & Blakely, E. (1987). Function-altering effects of contingency-specifying stimuli. *The Behavior Analyst, 10(1)*, 41–45.

Sidman, M. (2001). *Coercion and its fallout* (Revised ed.). Boston: Author's Cooperative, Inc. Publishers.

Vargas, J. S. (2009). *Behavior analysis for effective teaching.* New York: Routledge.

Vargas, J. S. (2013). *Behavior analysis for effective teaching* (2nd ed.). New York: Routledge.

Weatherly, J. N., McSweeney, F. K., & Swindell, S. (2004). Within-session rates of responding when reinforcer magnitude is changed within the session. *Journal of General Psychology, 131*(1), 5–16.

INDEX